Escaping Stalag Luft III

FROM THE WOODEN HORSE to THE GREAT ESCAPE

Escaping Stalag Luft III

FROM THE WOODEN HORSE to THE GREAT ESCAPE

STEPHEN WYNN

Pen & Sword
MILITARY

AN IMPRINT OF PEN & SWORD BOOKS LTD.
YORKSHIRE - PHILADELPHIA

First published in Great Britain in 2025 by
Pen & Sword Military
An imprint of
Pen & Sword Books Ltd
Yorkshire - Philadelphia

ISBN 978 1 39900 018 5

Typeset in INDIA by IMPEC eSolutions
Printed and bound in England by CPI Group (UK) Ltd, Croydon, CRO 4YY

The Publisher's authorised representative in the EU for product safety is
Authorised Rep Compliance Ltd., Ground Floor, 71 Lower Baggot Street,
Dublin D02 P593, Ireland.
www.arccompliance.com

For a complete list of Pen & Sword titles please contact:

PEN & SWORD BOOKS LIMITED
George House, Units 12 & 13, Beevor Street, Off Pontefract Road,
Barnsley, S71 1HN, UK
E-mail: enquiries@pen-and-sword.co.uk
Website: www.pen-and-sword.co.uk

or

PEN AND SWORD BOOKS
1950 Lawrence Rd, Havertown, PA 19083, USA
E-mail: Uspen-and-sword@casematepublishers.com
Website: www.penandswordbooks.com

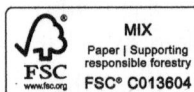

MIX
Paper | Supporting
responsible forestry
FSC
www.fsc.org
FSC® C013604

Mark Christopher Pettigrew (Grew)

2 April 1958 – 26 January 2021

Beloved husband to Pam, father to 3 daughters and 2 sons

'Simply the best'

In our hearts forever

Contents

Introduction		ix
Chapter One	A Brief History of Stalag Luft III	1
Chapter Two	Stalag Luft III Camp Newspapers	9
Chapter Three	Visits by the International Red Cross	13
Chapter Four	The Great Escape by Flight Lieutenant Bennett Ley Kenyon, DFC	25
Chapter Five	Marcel Eric Zillessen RAF	33
Chapter Six	Alan Bryett RAF	36
Chapter Seven	Statement by Anthony Eden to the House of Commons	40
Chapter Eight	Letters from W/O George Dormer Anderson	44
Chapter Nine	The Trojan Horse Escape	51
Chapter Ten	Roger Joyce Bushell	61
Chapter Eleven	The Tunnels – Tom, Dick and Harry	67
Chapter Twelve	*Oberst* Friedrich Wilhelm von Lindeiner-Wildau, Commandant of Stalag Luft III	73
Chapter Thirteen	Howard Goolding Cundall and the Radio Transmitter	78
Chapter Fourteen	The Escape Committee and Workers	80
Chapter Fifteen	The Fifty Murdered Escapees	83
Chapter Sixteen	The Escapees Who Survived	146
Chapter Seventeen	Wilfred Bowes and Frank McKenna	187
Chapter Eighteen	Those Responsible for the Murders	192
Chapter Nineteen	Paul Brickhill	207
Epilogue		210
Sources		212
Author Biography		214
Index		216

Introduction

❖

Prior to becoming a writer, this author served for thirty years as a police officer. Back in 1984, in the early months of his service, he was deployed several times on the Miners' Strike. On one of those deployments, he and several of his colleagues paid a visit to one of the still-operating mines and went underground to the coalface; an experience that he had no desire to ever repeat.

This is his memory of that occasion:

Back in 1984 I was 26 years of age, a stoic character by nature, but nothing could have prepared me for going down that mine. To be honest, I am not even sure why I went, because it certainly was not mandatory. The offer was made for us to make the visit, and I was one of those who put his hand up to go.

To begin with everything went nice and smoothly. We got changed into fluorescent orange overalls and a hard hat. We then went deeper underground, although I am not sure how far down we travelled. When the cage finally came to a halt, it opened up on to an enormous, cavernous space, and I remember thinking to myself, 'This is OK, what's all the fuss about?' My attitude soon changed, however, when we were taken into an opening no bigger in size than the gap between the legs of the back of a chair. Just for 'safety reasons', after we had all entered this miniscule tunnel, they turned the lights out so that we could experience what it would be like in an emergency. I tend to believe they did it just to frighten us, but either way, it was not a nice experience.

How long the tunnel went on for, and how long I was in it for, I could not tell you. All I remember thinking was not to scream out and potentially embarrass myself in front of my colleagues, and more importantly, the miners. It remains to this day the scariest thing that I have ever experienced. Every sinew in my body wanted to shout out

'Get me out of here', but you could only go as fast as the man in front of you, who you could not even see because of the utter darkness. The man at the front of the queue was a miner, and he certainly was not moving that fast at all. For anybody who suffers with claustrophobia, going down hundreds of feet into a mine and crawling along a coalface is definitely something I would not recommend.

During the Second World War, escaping from a prisoner of war camp was the dream of every prisoner. They saw it as their duty to return to England and once again fight against the evil tyranny of Nazi Germany. Stalag Luft III, located in German-occupied Poland, some 100 miles southeast of Berlin, was one such camp.

On the evening of 29 October 1943, in the first of one of the more audacious escapes, three men tunnelled out of the camp in what was to become known as the Trojan Horse Escape. The men used a gymnastic vaulting horse to hide inside and dig their tunnel, whilst several of their fellow POWs spent hours, every day for several weeks, vaulting backwards and forwards over the horse.

The second major escape from the camp – and one of the most audacious and daring escapes of the whole Second World War – took place on 24 March 1944. More than 600 men had been involved in the digging of tunnels, making civilian clothes, maps, compasses, as well as forging much-needed documentation for the escaping POWs. The original plan was for 200 men to escape, although in the end only seventy-six made it out, with all but three of them being recaptured.

What the brave men of Stalag Luft III experienced during their escape, and those who were still left in the tunnel, can only be guessed at, but if it was half as bad as what I experienced going down that coal mine in 1984, it would have been horrible.

Waiting for me when I got back to the surface was a warm shower and a nice mug of tea. For the men coming out of the tunnel at Stalag Luft III, it was a whole different world.

CHAPTER ONE

A Brief History of Stalag Luft III

❖

Throughout the Second World War, Germany had its own unique way of dealing with the detention of prisoners of war. In essence, each branch of Nazi Germany's war machine was responsible for the Allied equivalent, meaning that all enemy aviators and air crews were the responsibility of the *Luftwaffe*.

Stammlager Luft, which translates as 'Main Camp Air', was abbreviated to *Stalag Luft*. The German prisoner of war camp known as Stalag Luft III was located near the town of Sagan, Lower Silesia, in what was then Nazi Germany, but is now Żagań, Poland. Opened in the spring of 1942, it covered an area of some 60 acres in size and was surrounded by 5 miles of perimeter fencing. One of the main reasons for the camp's location was that the ground it was built on had a very sandy subsoil, which the Germans felt would make it extremely difficult, even nigh on impossible, for those held there to even consider attempting to tunnel their way out of. This was not just because of its softer and naturally collapsible consistency, but because the surface soil was, by contrast, a dark grey in colour. This meant that any subsoil brought to the surface to be disposed of from tunnelling exploits would be easily and quickly noticed by the camp guards. To further deter prisoners from the thought of tunnelling, each of the accommodation huts was raised 2 feet off the ground to enable guards to be able to clearly look underneath them. As is well known, the British and other Allied POWs proved these assumptions to be incorrect on two occasions.

The camp actually consisted of a number of different compounds. What was known as the East Compound was completed on 21 March 1942, with its first inhabitants being British and Commonwealth officers who arrived in the early days of April 1942. But at that time, the camp was not in a particularly good condition. This was mainly due to the lack of support and funding needed to build the camp, which was not forthcoming from *Luftgau Kommando III*, located in Berlin, and which had overall responsibility for the geographical area Stalag Luft III was located in. It was answerable to the German Air Ministry on such matters as administration, camp maintenance, all building materials required to build a POW camp, as well as air defence for the camp located in a particular *Luftgau* (Air District). Fortunately, the *Luftgau* acquired the assistance of a Major Jakob, a member of the Army Reserve, and who by trade was a master craftsman from the nearby town of Sagan. What helped the situation further was the discovery by Major Jakob that amongst the camp guards was a man who had been an architect before the war, and two others who had worked in the construction industry. The main workforce allocated by the German authorities to help build the camp had been Jewish slave labourers, although this group of men was soon replaced by Yugoslav and Russian POWs.

The Centre Compound opened on 11 April 1942 for British and Commonwealth non-commissioned officers (NCOs). The North Compound, for British airmen, which is where the 'Great Escape' would later take place from, opened on 29 March 1943, whilst the South Compound, which was set aside for American aviators, opened in September 1943. Finally, the West Compound, for American officers, was opened in July 1944. The camp's prisoners chose to refer to themselves as *Kriegies*. This was an abbreviation of the German for prisoner of war, *Kriegsgefangene*.

Each of the camp's five separate compounds housed fifteen single-story, pitched-roofed huts for living quarters, each of which were 10x12 feet in length, and housed a total of fifteen men sleeping in five triple-deck bunk beds. At its peak, the camp was home to approximately 11,000 men, of which 7,500 were from the United States Army Air Force, 2,500 were from the British RAF, with just under 1,000 officers from other Allied countries, including Australia, Canada, New Zealand, South Africa, Poland and Czechoslovakia.

For all POWs there were three main aspects of being incarcerated that made camp life difficult. In no particular order these were: the lack of food, boredom and missing their loved ones. However, there was a routine to life as a POW at Stalag Luft III, which for many was a big help as it allowed them to keep their focus. This was an important aspect of camp life, which was made even more difficult because nobody knew when their captivity would come to an end.

The day began relatively late, with the morning roll call not being until 10:00, meaning most men did not get up until about 09:45, giving them fifteen minutes to wash, dress, have a quick drink of tea or coffee, and eat a slice of bread with jam, on their way to the camp's parade square. Because of the prolonged reduction of food intake, very few men had the need of a morning bowel movement, which helped reduce the time needed between them waking up and being on the parade square by the allotted time. Some of the more active POWs even went for early morning runs around the camp, prepared fires and filled up the water pots that provided the morning's tea and coffee.

After the morning's roll call parade had finished, the Germans turned on the hot water so the men could shower, but this did not include everybody. Only 120 men, in groups of 24, were allowed to shower each day. It was after this time that the monotony of the daily routine of camp life began in earnest. In no time at all men started to head in a myriad of different directions, criss-crossing each other in what appeared to be total chaos, but was far from it. For some, their task for the day was to clear away the morning's breakfast cutlery, plates and pans, whilst those who were rostered for cooking duties made their way to the camp kitchen. Others went on their way to a particular class, or to the library to read a book or camp newspaper, or study for a forthcoming exam. Four of the camp's huts were used as daytime classrooms and helped provide a total of thirty-seven day classes on different topics, all of which were provided and supported by the camp's very own education department, more regularly referred to as *Kriegie Kollege*. Available courses covered such diverse topics as differential calculus, accounting for the small business, and body building. The Young Men's Christian Association (YMCA) in Geneva assisted with the men's educational courses by providing textbooks. There were also lectures and discussion groups for the men to take part in. One of the lectures that was delivered was entitled, 'Married Happiness'; not something that would have been high on the list of most of the prisoners at such a time in their lives. Instead, learning a foreign language was high on the list of courses the men wanted to take. Maybe with escape in mind, the most popular of the languages selected by the POWs was German, with Spanish and French close behind.

Prisoners detained at Stalag Luft III were, of course, fed, but as with life amongst the civilian population, and the need by the German authorities to feed their own military forces, food was not in a plentiful supply. It is not as though food could simply be purchased in bulk from a supermarket whenever there was a need to do so. Food was rationed, it was hard to come by, and the distribution of it was a logistical nightmare with a war going on.

What helped supplement the meagre rations provided by the German authorities were food parcels sent to prisoners by their families back home, in addition to Red Cross parcels. The problem was that with food being so scarce, not all parcels reached the camps and their intended recipients, with some being pilfered long before they reached the camps.

The other avenue that was open to the POWs to supplement their paltry food rations was to grow their own vegetables in little gardens established around the camp. There was even a bartering system in place amongst the POWs, known as 'Foodacco', which allowed the transfer of surplus items for points, which could then be used by the recipient to obtain other items, such as powdered milk, butter, jam and oatmeal. In relation to food, some items were intentionally hoarded for special occasions such as Christmas. This ensured that there was plenty of food to go around for everybody on the big day. Birthdays were more difficult, because with so many men in the camp, there were a lot more of them to cater for, but they did their best. Amongst the weekly Red Cross food deliveries, each POW was provided with a number of items, two of which were a bar of chocolate and fifty cigarettes, which quickly became the most popular form of legal tender in the camp. Each of these items was eagerly sought throughout the camp, but not so readily available, and so provided whoever had the most with a great bargaining power.

When it came to mealtimes, men usually ate with their fellow hut mates, but this was not a practice that was carved in stone.

Life in general usually determines that 'necessity is the mother of all invention', and Stalag Luft III proved this. Pans used for cooking were made from discarded tin cans, broom heads came from string salvaged from the wrappings on parcels, and chairs were made from wooden Red Cross boxes. Even winter had its advantages when handmade freezers were used to make ice cream for the camp mates.

Parcels sent by loved ones back home, along with Red Cross parcels, were usually delivered on Tuesdays and Thursdays. However, these were not kept by the individual they were intended for, but instead were all put together and their combined contents, whether it was food or personal items, were shared out equally. Sometimes these parcels would have been rifled through, or stolen completely, before they arrived at the camp. After all, this was wartime, and food in particular was in short supply, no matter who you were. Civilians, German soldiers, camp guards, and POWs all survived on very meagre rations.

As the food provided by the Germans was roughly half the number of daily calories the POWs required, it is easy to see just how important the Red Cross parcels and packages from home were to the men's very survival.

Another interesting aspect of camp life was the fact that captured officers received 'pay', despite the fact there was no requirement for them to actually carry out any kind of work. Non-commissioned officers, meanwhile, were expected to work but did not receive any such payment. Payment to officers was not made in German currency but in what was known as *Lagergeld*, or paper money, which was used in the camp by POWs to purchase certain items such as food, sports equipment, or books. But the officers were not greedy and instead pooled and shared their camp money with their less fortunate NCO colleagues. POWs were not permitted to possess German currency in camp, and doing so was a punishable offence as it was deemed to be an important aspect of any potential escape attempt.

Next to reading, the receiving and writing of letters to family and friends was the next biggest pastime for POWs. It helped keep them connected to their families and homes, which for many of them were literally thousands of miles away. The anticipation of receiving a letter from home was palpable, but the actual receiving of it was so much nicer. A man could receive as many letters as were written to him, but he was restricted on how many he could send himself. The limit was four postcards and three letters every calendar month, which usually meant writing to just one person, such as a wife or mother, and then asking them to pass messages on to other family members or friends. How much could be written depended on how small and neat a man could write. On top of this, censorship, not just by the Germans but also by the country of receipt, meant the men had to be mindful of what they wrote if they did not want everything to be blacked out. Another aspect of the sending and receiving of mail was how many weeks it took to arrive in camp. Letters posted in America usually took five weeks to arrive, from Canada it was three, and from the UK it was four. However, with ships crossing the Atlantic being targeted by German submarines, mail did not always reach its intended recipients.

All Stalag Luft III's POWs, regardless of their country of origin, had to wear military uniform at all times, with civilian clothing forbidden. This was the aspect of escaping which made it extremely dangerous for those determined enough to attempt it. Being captured in civilian clothing could result in a man being shot. Somewhat ironically, the one item that would have been extremely important for a man to have on his person during an escape attempt would have been the POW identity disc given to them by the German camp authorities. This would have proved the true identity of the person wearing it, no doubt saving the man's life in the process. Under the terms of the Geneva Convention, it was stipulated that servicemen, captured or otherwise, should always be attired in their military uniform, or run the risk of being shot as a spy.

Being an Allied POW had its problems, not just with the German camp authorities, but initially with fellow Allied POWs, especially if no one else in the camp knew who they were. The concern was that the Germans would put one of their own men in the camp, masquerading as an Allied POW. If such an attempt was successful, it could totally undermine any escape attempts being planned. There was a process in place to try to prevent this from happening at Stalag Luft III, which in essence meant that any new man who came into the camp had to be vouched for by two men who were already there. If this was not possible, they had to undergo questioning by the camp's senior ranked POWs. Even if all the questions were answered correctly, and to the senior officer's full satisfaction, the man in question had to be escorted around the camp, night and day, until the senior officers were convinced that he was a genuine POW.

The Allied airmen who found themselves incarcerated as POWs at Stalag Luft III were, in the main, treated well by their German guards, who generally stuck to the spirit of the aims and intentions of the Geneva Convention. Although there were moments of loneliness and hunger, for both food and the companionship of a loved one from back home, overall the men were in good spirits and found plenty to laugh about. They even had their own form of camp language, mostly so that even if the Germans overheard a particular conversation, they would not fully understand the true meaning of what was being discussed. This was not something that was unique to Stalag Luft III and occurred in all similar POW camps, although there may have been the odd variation here and there. Here are just a few such examples of camp vocabulary:

Cooler – The camp's prison block.
Ferret – A German guard tasked with detecting Allied escape tunnels.
Goon – A German guard.
Goon Tower – A German sentry box.
Lagergeld – A paper military currency used inside the camp for transactions and officers' pay.
Penguin – A POW disposing of tunnel soil in the camp's gardens.
Stooge – A POW engaged in watching the German guards.

Stroller – A German guard on patrol inside the camp.
Weasel – A German guard, often seen in company with a
    Ferret.

Stalag Luft III remained in operation as a POW camp until January 1945, when the camp and its remaining occupants, mainly those who had been too sick to walk, were liberated by Soviet forces.

The following is taken from the website of the USAAF 303rd Bombing Group and describes what happened to the prisoners following the camp's liberation:

Russian troops were approaching Sagan, Poland. At 11:00 PM on 27 January 1945, the Germans marched the POWs out of Stalag 3 with Spremberg as their destination. The exodus was harrowing to POWs of all compounds, especially to those of the South Compound who made the 55 km from Sagan to Muskau in 27 hours with only 4 hours of sleep. At Muskau they were given a 30-hour break for recuperation and then marched another 25 km to Spremberg. On 31 January the South Compound men, plus 200 men from the West Compound, went to Stalag 7A at Moosburg by rail; 'forty-and eight' boxcars packed 50 men and one guard in each boxcar. The trip took two days and two nights. On 7 February the men from the Centre Compound joined them. The North Compound fell in with the West Compound at Spremberg and on 2 February entrained for Stalag 13D at Nurnberg, which they reached after a two-day trip.

On 13 April 1945, after an approximate three-month stay, the Americans were told that they must evacuate Stalag 13D and march to Stalag 7A at Moosburg. The main body reached Stalag 7A on 20 April 1945. Many POWs dropped out of the march en route to Moosburg and the German guards made no serious attempt to stop them. The POWs were liberated by General Patton's 14th Armored Division on 29 April.

CHAPTER TWO

Stalag Luft III Camp Newspapers

Like several POW camps on both sides, Stalag Luft III published a number of different newspapers during the years it held Allied prisoners. Whether a camp had such a publication was purely down to those who were held there. They did not appear because the senior British officer of the camp dictated that there would be such a publication, but because an individual, or a small group of individuals, decided to publish one. When men are incarcerated for an unknown period of time, one of the main factors they have to deal with is boredom, but because time was in plentiful supply, the men needed things to focus on to help them cope with the prolonged periods of boredom. Writing, producing and publishing a newspaper, news sheet, or magazine, was one such thing.

As well as being a big help for the POWs, they also provide historians with a real insight into camp life and a better understanding of how men survived the mental aspect of their prolonged incarceration.

One of the newspapers published at Stalag Luft III was an American paper called *The Kriegie Times*. The edition dated 8 February 1944 contains a number of articles by some of the camp's very own 'roving reporters', including one written by 2nd Lieutenant Sidney Shore of the USAAF, which looks at the general day-to-day life for men in the camp and certainly dispelled any misplaced rumours about how glamorous life was for them.

Day begins at 9:45 with 1st call for apell. Some intrepid souls rise at 8 to jog round the camp, build fires and carry water for morning brew, but this is not the norm. The average Kriegie gets up just in time to make 10 o'clock roll-call. Long practice has eliminated waste morning motions and 15 minutes is ample time to dress, wash and gulp down coffee. Bread and jam is consumed on the way out to parade.

When weather permits, ranks are opened for calisthenics. A snowball fight, rain a prelude to dispirited huddles. At the adjutant's dismissal command the shower sprinters are off. Authorities allow men to take hot showers in groups of 24, at a daily average of five such groups. Fastest man is also the cleanest. As one apologist puts it, however, if a guy doesn't race, he doesn't need a shower so often.

Dismissal begins the daily routine of camp. Classes, library, cooking schedules and belated breakfasts clear the field. Necessity has developed latent mechanical abilities. Pans are fabricated out of tin cans, brooms of string, chairs from wooden Red Cross boxes. The handy man is the hero of camp.

The Circuit newspaper was printed and published by men in the camp's South Compound, where Americans from the USAAF began arriving in October 1943. In a copy of the newspaper dated Monday, 10 April 1944, just two weeks after the Great Escape (also Easter Monday), one of the articles was entitled, 'Other Camp Publications Have Short Durations'.

The CIRCUIT had not been long in publication when the American spirit of competition prompted the appearance of two other news sheets, 'The Shaft' and 'The New Yorker' the latter fashioned on the US publication of the same title. Their run was brief but brilliant.

The Shaft was printed by hand and appeared weekly. The cartoons and prose of Joseph Boyle and Ten Eyck, assisted by Norman Retchin

Barrington III, provided more humour than the conservative news coverage of *The Circuit.*

Additionally, a paper in English published by the Germans for American POWs included summaries of foreign news, plus sports items and local news from the States.

Another paper called *The Daily Recco* was published by men from the Centre Compound. On 15 February 1943, the Allied POWs were bored, if not slightly restless. Alan Mackay, an RAF bomber pilot and a trainee journalist before the war, attempted to raise morale amongst his fellow camp mates and so created *The Daily Recco.* Each day he would pin a copy of what he had put together on the camp's notice board for others to read. The paper consisted of a number of interviews with other camp mates, up-to-date gossip and any relevant news received from the UK.

Another paper, *Scangriff,* was first published sometime in 1944. The man behind *Scangriff* was Flight Lieutenant Mark S. Winston, who had been shot down over Rostock, Germany on 20 April 1943. Winston was helped with his newspaper by Flight Lieutenant Paul Brickhill and Flight Lieutenant Ley Kenyon.

In 1946, Brickhill published a book entitled *The Great Escape,* which was his personal account of his time spent at Stalag Luft III, including the part he played in the actual escape. Kenyon, meanwhile, was an extremely good artist who provided a number of drawings of the construction of the tunnel 'Harry', some of which appeared in Brickhill's book. Originally, Kenyon's drawings were hidden in the closed down 'Tom', but were retrieved after the camp was liberated and given back to Kenyon when they were returned to England after the war.

The name *Scangriff* was supposedly derived from mixing the word 'scandal' with the title of a German newspaper of the day, *Der Angriff.* In his 'Australians at War' film archive interview, conducted after the war, Flight Lieutenant Horace Fordyce of the Royal Australian Air Force, who served with No. 458 Squadron and was shot down in June 1942, provided a different explanation as to the origins of *Scangriff's* name. (Fordyce would later be the last man to enter the tunnel during the Great Escape but turned back when he heard shooting coming from the exit):

We had a magazine called *Scangriff*. Now in the air force you scan a map, you get the good 'griff', that's the good information, so we called the magazine, *Scangriff*. And of course, angriff is a German word meaning attack. So, it was a very good name, and the magazine was called *Scangriff*, and if you read it, you will see that it had all sorts of things. Some of which were true, and some were just funny, but there was always enough truth and we pinned these on the notice board. One man would type them, and I would do the headings in coloured paint and perhaps do a little sketch, and we would pin them on the notice board.

A final newspaper entitled the *Gefangenen Gazette* was an American offering published by the American Red Cross. Although predominantly for an American audience, prisoners from any English-speaking nation were glad of the opportunity to read something. The newspaper included up to nine pages of articles, drawings and cartoons.

Newspapers performed an important role within POW camp life. Besides providing a stream of humorous anecdotes and extended information, they also provided the men with a purpose, an element of control, and a feeling of ownership.

CHAPTER THREE

Visits by the International Red Cross

❖

Sunday, 13 September 1942 saw the first visit to Stalag Luft III by Mr J.E. Friedrich, a representative of the International Red Cross. At the time of the visit, the camp consisted of just the East and Centre compounds. Each time such a visit took place, an in-depth report was completed by the visiting Red Cross representative, but for some reason the report, or any of the subsequent Red Cross reports, never included the name of the camp's commandant, despite the fact that from spring 1942 until the end of the war, the German officer in charge of Stalag Luft III was *Oberst* (Colonel) Friedrich Wilhelm von Lindeiner-Wildau.

Every time a visit by the Red Cross was made, its representative would be escorted around the camp by the senior British officer and the person referred to as the *homme de confiance* (Man of Confidence). The man who held the position of senior British officer at the time was Group Captain Herbert Martin Massey, who was also the man who ultimately authorised the Great Escape and gave it the go ahead. Massey had been serving with No. 7 Squadron during the second of the thousand-bomber raids that took place on the night of 1/2 June 1942, when his Short Stirling bomber was shot down over the Dutch coast. He survived the crash and following capture by the Germans, was sent to Stalag Luft III.

Massey's Man of Confidence on the day of the Red Cross visit was Flight Sergeant Day, who essentially provided the link between the camp's senior Allied officers and the men.

Mr Friedrich's subsequent report from his visit to the camp showed the Germans had a total of 2,557 officers and men held in captivity. These men came from eleven different nations, with the largest proportion of prisoners hailing from the UK.

Of the non-commissioned officers, sixteen were physically unfit for service because their wounds were so severe (loss of a limb, fingers or sight) that they were deemed suitable to be repatriated back home, as they were clearly never again going to be fighting soldiers. It was noted that the number of POWs in the camp at any given time was fluid. On the day of Friedrich's visit, forty-six officers had left Stalag Luft III for Oflag XXI-B, with a further 100 being due to join them in a matter of days.

Friedrich's report was broken down into a number of different headings, covering all relevant aspects of camp life for the POWs.

Location and Accommodation

The camp was established about six months ago. For this purpose, an area of about 300 by 200 metres has been cleared in a pine forest near a small town, and the prisoners are still busy uprooting trunks near the barracks. These are made of wood, are new, spacious, and well built, and provide enough room for between four and twelve officers. Those of the non-commissioned officers were separated into two large rooms, about eighty prisoners in each. The wooden bunks are on several floors. Light and electric lighting are sufficient.

Each prisoner has at least two blankets. The benches are filled with wood wool. Non-commissioned officers have no wardrobes or suitcases to hold their belongings. They lack space and fresh air in their rooms which have tables, but only some of the bunk beds have stepladders. On the other hand, there is no shortage of space around the barracks, and the prisoners have managed to grow flowers, a few tomatoes and other vegetables in the sand. Finally, the field has been turned into a sports plaza in several places, a football pitch is especially large.

The camp is divided into four distinct but adjacent sectors. The barracks and cottages of the German staff; a hut containing the infirmary, a barracks for food and one for clothing and showers. The enclosure containing the barracks for non-commissioned officers is separated from the officers' barracks by a high palisade. These two categories of prisoners are thus found to have practically no contact with each other, except between the heads of department, when donations from the Red Cross arrive, the need to use the infirmary, or monthly sports meetings.

Food

The men of confidence control the usual rations. See attached menu. The contribution of the cultures undertaken by the prisoners is insignificant. One kitchen is reserved for officers and two for non-commissioned officers.

They were well set up and the meals were prepared by the prisoners under the direction of German personnel, and according to the menus established by them.

In each hut there are one or two wood burning stoves allowed for the prisoners to cook their private food, but these would only meet the needs of a small number of the prisoners.

The surface area of the heating plates is to be enlarged in the near future. The non-commissioned officers had a wood burner for an average of eighty prisoners. As there is no refectory, the prisoners eat their meals in their dormitories.

Clothing

Each prisoner has at least one uniform in good condition and a good pair of shoes. There are stocks of uniforms and other items of clothing which are received via Red Cross deliveries.

The prisoners wash their clothes themselves in special wash-houses with planks inclined on either side of the long terracotta basins, with running water. This category of prisoner is particularly demanding from the point of view of clothing, food, comfort, etc. compared to those of other arms and other nations.

In the case of Red Cross shipments, it must be taken into account that it appears that the Luftlager III appears to be intended to become the central supply camp for members of the Air Force.

Canteen

The canteen is practically non-existent, due to the difficulty of obtaining items of common use. There are no drinks or food.

Hygiene

The infirmary is run by a German non-commissioned officer, assisted by a major and a captain of the British army. It is very well located and includes a dental officer, or a German military dentist, who treats about thirty prisoners a day.

A workshop for the manufacture of dental prostheses is to be annexed to it in the near future. Patients with gastric ailments receive a special diet thanks to the British Red Cross convalescent packets. Of the thirty-six wooden beds, thirty-three are currently occupied.

Prisoners in the camp may take at least one hot shower per week; but cold water is abundant. There is a shortage of toiletries such as toothbrushes, razor blades, toothpaste, combs and clippers. The water drainage is not done well, but it would be possible to remedy this situation promptly in preparation for the winter. The pipes are lacking and the many septic tanks that have been dug are proving to be ineffective, the sand, which is almost fine, quickly becomes impermeable by the soapy greasy waters. The dump tanks are just enough to maintain the level under the latrines, which are placed without small separate buildings. These buildings are being transformed under the direction of, and according to the plans of a prisoner, Lieutenant-Colonel Clarke, 27, of the American Air Force.

The health of these prisoners is excellent. The climate is very healthy, and this category of prisoner obviously represents an elite from a physical point of view.

Leisure, Intellectual and Spiritual Needs

At first, there was no worship for want of chaplains and priests, but at present there is a captain Robinson (Church of England) and civilian intern priest, Abbé Goudrey, regular president of religious services.

Intellectual activity is very advanced (theatre, cinema, orchestra, various courses). This activity is encouraged by the camp authorities, who make certain items (drawing instruments among others) available to the prisoners.

Several qualified teachers who are conducting these courses, urgently require 3,000 sheets of writing paper, six boxes of compasses and six T-sets and squares. For the orchestra, it would be light music and strings for instruments.

In the case of shipments, it must be borne in mind that the camps of officers and non-commissioned officers are practically completed separate, with no possibility of communication.

Sports

The Luftlager III is a real sports training camp, where all sports, boxing, fencing, athletics, unpacked games, etc. are engaged in.

It is important to send as many sporting goods of all kinds, as possible to these prisoners, especially rugby balls, table tennis and boxing gloves.

Discipline

All camp personnel, commanders and sentries are part of the Luftwaffe. The prisoners' relations with them are very good and even cordial.

The surveillance measures are obviously very strict in view of the extremely numerous escape attempts. The rooms and prisoners are searched frequently, and the camp Commander has a varied and well-stocked escape museum.

Correspondence

Since September mail has not been sent in accordance with the order of the Wehrmacht command of 17 July 1942. The mail arrives with some slowness; this is due to the lack of censors who understand the very different languages in which some prisoners correspond (the officer of surveillance is responsible for censoring Polish mail, which he alone possesses among the staff. Polish officers complain that they have never received books in their own language).

Collective Shipments

In this regard, everything is in order. Trusted men would like to have a larger stock of standard parcels to be able to cope with the possibility of new arrivals. It should also be remembered that from autumn onwards, Luftlager III will be considered a distribution centre for Luftlager I and III annex, a former barracks on the other side of the city, which is currently being converted for some 1,000 non-commissioned officers.

The men of confidence controlled these shipments but with some restrictions from the Abwehr (limitation of the distribution of food, clothing, and blankets to avoid the constitution of clandestine stocks, for the manufacture of escape clothing).

Conclusion

If the camp is good, this is largely due to the quality of both staff and the prisoners. The issue of sewerage and heating of barracks in the winter needs to be reviewed.

Not mentioned in the report was the fact that the camp's senior British officer, the camp's Man of Confidence and members of the visiting International Red Cross, had a private meeting away from the potential prying eyes and ears of any German guards. Their discussion covered various points, not all of which were complaints, with a number simply looking at ways of improving procedures already in place within the camp.

Delegations from the International Red Cross paid further visits to Stalag Luft III throughout the course of the war. The contents of these reports were laid out in a similar way and under the same headings. Two of these visits took place before the Great Escape on the night of 24/25 March 1944.

The next visit was on Monday, 22 February 1943, with the International Red Cross representatives being Mr Friedrich and a Dr Bubb. By now the Americans had arrived at Stalag Luft III and the report contained the details of both senior American and British officers, along with their individual Men of Confidence. For the British this was still Group Captain Massey, but Flight Sergeant Day had been replaced by Flight Sergeant James Deanes. The Americans were represented by Lieutenant Colonel Clark Jr. and Flight Sergeant G.A. Dillard. In addition to the previous nationalities represented at the camp, the list now included airmen from Ireland, South Africa, America, Lithuania and Palestine.

The latest report showed just how organised the camp was becoming. As from 1 December 1942, a finance policy had been put in place by the British with the main finance committee consisting of the senior British officer, which at the time was Group Captain Massey, along with each of the block commanders. There was also a sub-committee, which was also known as the Standing Finance Committee, which consisted of Group Captain Kellett, the committee's chairman; Flight Lieutenant Stark, the camp accountant officer; and Flight Lieutenant Gillies, the assistant camp account officer.

The report highlights the different types of educational courses available in the camp. Nearly all the courses were held in the camp's library between 12:30 and 21:00 and consisted of law, navigation, building work, electrics, German, motor mechanics, shorthand, engineering, bookkeeping, accountancy, agriculture, window dressing, music, bookkeeping, art, and Spanish. It was also possible to apply to take exams in nearly all of the courses.

The next visit took place on Monday, 26 July 1943, with the International Red Cross representative being a Doctor Lehner. The senior British officer in charge of the British and Commonwealth prisoners was now Group Captain Kellett, with the Man of Confidence shown as being Wing Commander H.M.A. Day. The senior American officer was Colonel C.C. Goodrich.

The report began with the following remark, explaining the absence of Group Captain Massey: 'Group Captain Massey is currently in the Lazaretto in Obermaasfeld to completely finish the healing of his fracture. He will take over management of the camp in 4 to 5 weeks.'

On the day of the visit to Stalag Luft III, the report noted that in the East and Centre compounds there was a combined total of

663 officers, along with 86 non-commissioned officers and privates. Of the officers, 622 were from the RAF, 36 from the Royal Navy, as well as 5 from the British Army. Of the NCOs and privates, seventeen were from the RAF, two were from the Royal Navy and sixty-seven were from the British Army. By comparison, in the North Compound there were 1,133 officers and 184 NCOs and privates from Britain, America, Canada, Australia, New Zealand and South Africa.

The following is typical of the type of information Red Cross visit reports included. Besides the numbers and nationalities of the prisoners who were held there, it also provided a description of the conditions the men lived in, the type and quantity of food they were provided with, where they ate their meals, the state of their clothing, the overall hygiene of the camp, the medical facilities, educational provisions such as books, writing materials, available courses, the men's religious needs, mail, work details, discipline, and any worries, concerns or complaints that the prisoners made to the visiting delegate.

The report also includes a detailed description of the camp, as well as the different compounds contained within it. It also provides the number of huts in each of the compounds and how many men were housed in each.

The report states that the entire camp was divided into three compounds: East, Centre and North. The South Compound was still under construction at the time of the visit and not yet completed. The North Compound, meanwhile, had only been completed a few weeks beforehand and was where the entire contingent of American prisoners was detained.

The East and Centre compounds represented what had initially been the main camp. The South Compound, which was still unoccupied, was specially designed for occupation by American forces. The report outlines that when the building work within the camp is eventually completed, there was talk of separating the prisoners according to their nationalities, and although nothing had been finalised, Captain Donald had already been identified as a potential Man of Confidence.

The report goes on to say that the North Compound included eleven large huts that could each hold eighty men. These huts were divided into smaller rooms which could accommodate between six and eight American officers, and that all the rooms were well ventilated and lit. The rooms included a number of cupboards that were used for storing the men's personal belongings, or as food pantries. With the numbers of men in the camp it was far from being overcrowded.

In the centre of each of the huts was a long wash basin which had between twelve and sixteen taps. To keep the huts warm, especially during the winter months, there were small wood burning stoves in each of the rooms. One of the huts was for use as an administration block, another as a theatre and a third as a kitchen.

The report also included a piece about conditions in the camp and potentially how quick and easily disease could spread if not taken seriously and treated expediently.

> There are reports of fleas in some barracks. In addition, people in this camp complain about the abundance of mosquitoes. The Men of Confidence have asked the German administration for mosquito nets for the windows. Until now, it has only been possible to install them in the infirmary and in very few barracks, and it seems possible that more mosquito nets can be provided to prisoners. It is for this reason, the camp occupants would be grateful to the British and the American Red Cross for providing them with mosquito nets, in the form of gauze.

As was commonplace with such reports, they always finished with an overall conclusion. This is what Dr Lehner had to say about his visit to Stalag Luft III: 'This camp as far as sanitary facilities, recreation, intellectual and spiritual needs are concerned, seems good. Relations between the Men of Confidence, their helpers and the German authorities have not however been so easy since the recent events.'

Unfortunately, there is no further explanation as to what the 'recent events' referred to might have been.

After the Great Escape and the mass murder of fifty of those who escaped from the camp, two more Red Cross visits took place, one on 22 May 1944, just two months after the mass escape, and the final visit taking place over two days from 24-25 November 1944.

The visit on 22 May 1944 was carried out by two members of the International Red Cross: Dr Rossel and Monsieur Paul Wyss. Following the mass escape on 24/25 March 1944, the camp commandant *Oberst* Friedrich Wilhelm von Lindeiner-Wildau had been removed from his position and replaced on 6 April by the Wehrmacht officer *Oberst* Werner Braune.

The report began in a slightly confusing way because it did not include the details of either the American or British senior officers in charge. Instead, it listed the names of seven men who were shown as the Men of Confidence. This would appear to be a mistake, as the four Americans listed all held the rank of colonel, while the three British all held the rank of group captain. The three Americans were Colonel D.T. Spivey, who in essence would appear to have been the senior American officer of the Centre Compound; Colonel C.G. Soodrich, who held the same position in the South Compound; Colonel Darr Hayes Alkire, who was in command of the West Compound; and Colonel Wilbur Aring, who appears to have been an assistant to the others.

The subsequent report detailing the Red Cross' visit to the camp began with an introductory note, which included comments about the Great Escape.

The Kriegsgerfangenen-Lager No. 3 of the Luftwaffe, actually comprises six district camps, including three British and three American. Since the attempted escape of the seventy-six British officers, the Men of Confidence have only been able to correspond with each other by letter. The German military administration, the Red Cross stores and the lazaretto, were the only ones centralised. For the rest, the separation of the different camps is as complete as possible. The delegates were only allowed to speak to the most senior officers in rank (a Man of Confidence) one after the other, as the Abwehr would not authorise a meeting. It will therefore be necessary to specify throughout the report the part of the camp in question.

Under the heading of 'Discipline' on pages 5 and 6 of the report, is the following reference to the escapees who had been recaptured and murdered by the Germans:

On the night of March 24-25, 1944, seventy-six prisoners escaped from the North Camp. Shortly afterwards, the camp commandant informed the senior British officer that forty-one of these prisoners had been shot during the escape. Nine more names were later added to this list, giving a total of fifty dead out of the seventy-six who escaped. The officers in charge immediately took steps to inform the International Committee of the Red Cross and the Protecting Power.

The whole file of this case is at this very moment in the hands of the Protective Power and is under investigation.

Every effort has been made by the camp officers to store the personnel belongings of the deceased officers to be passed on to their next of kin as soon as possible.

Discipline in the camp became very severe after this escape. The state of mind is, of course, extremely bad because of the deaths of the fifty officers. For example, the German authorities have taken a painful measure for the prisoners, the confiscation of all the dried fruits of the collective shipments. These fruits are delivered directly to the kitchen and prepared collectively under control. The prisoners had set up a still out of tin cans and their clandestine distillery worked so well that it produced sufficient liquors.

During the search, German authorities seized a supply of fifty vials. The German authorities said that this traffic was becoming far too dangerous not to interrupt, as some prisoners drunk, could have left their barracks at night without heeding the warnings of the barbed wire and risking being shot.

What is not made clear in the report is whether the timing of the Red Cross' visit was simply coincidental, and their representatives were only informed of the killings on their arrival at the camp, or whether their visit came about as a direct result of the killings of the escaped prisoners.

It is believed that in the days after the escape, with the news of the deaths having been received at the camp, the prisoners at Stalag Luft III began collating the names of the escapees who they believed were subsequently not accounted for. The list contained forty-seven names. It is thought that during the Red Cross visit, the new senior British officer, Group Captain Douglas Wilson, managed to hand over a list of these names to Dr Rossel and Monsieur Wyss, although neither man made any mention of this in their subsequent report.

The last visit to the camp by the International Red Cross took place over two days from 24-25 November 1944 and was conducted by Dr Rossel and Dr Lutz Thudichum. There were noticeable differences between this visit and the previous Red Cross visits to the camp. Firstly, this one took place over two days, and the two delegates also interviewed the camp's commandant and his assistants. Such meetings were not included in any of the reports from previous Red Cross visits, suggesting that they never took place. One of the questions asked was why the officer in charge of the Red Cross was not allowed to walk freely around the camps.

The reply from the German camp authorities was as follows: 'The Commander cannot authorise him to do so. Exchanges between camps should be limited. This restriction only dates back to the mass escape of March 25.'

On 24 and 25 November 1944, Dr Rossel and Dr Thudichum paid a two-day visit to Stalag Luft III. This was the final Red Cross visit made to the camp during the war and came just two months before the camp was liberated by Soviet forces in January 1945.

The visits made by members of the International Committee of the Red Cross were invaluable interventions and ensured to a large extent that the provisions of the Geneva Convention were being adhered to and maintained. For those being held in the camps, the visits were also a reminder that they had not been forgotten and that they still had a voice.

CHAPTER FOUR

The Great Escape by Flight Lieutenant Bennett Ley Kenyon, DFC

❖

Flight Lieutenant Bennett Ley Kenyon, DFC, was a member of the Royal Air Force Volunteer Reserve (RAFVR). Born on 28 May 1913 above the family-owned undertaking business in Kensington, he was educated at Marylebone Grammar School. He loved the underwater life, swimming, snorkelling, photography, and painting in watercolours, later attending art schools in London and Paris, where he specialised in watercolours, and even taught his favourite subject, watercolour design and shading. He was very mild mannered and while he fully understood his many talents, to others he appeared as being somewhat on the shy side.

With the outbreak of war in September 1939, Kenyon volunteered for service in the Royal Navy, specifically in submarines. When he was called up in early 1940, it was not to the Royal Navy but rather the Royal Air Force, where he found himself allocated as a lorry driver. He re-mustered to air gunner in March 1941 and graduated with a commission of pilot officer in the October.

On 5 March 1942, Pilot Officer Kenyon reported to No. 419 (Moose) Squadron RCAF, at RAF Mildenhall, Suffolk. In late April 1942 he flew his first operation, as a rear gunner for Flight Sergeant Fawcett, in Wellington Z1053.

The RCAF soon discovered that his artistic talents made Kenyon an exceptionally good rear-gunner, who was able to recognise enemy aircraft in a split second. In August 1942 he was promoted to gunnery leader and began teaching aircraft recognition, gunnery instruction, and evasive tactics for escape from Germany if aircrews were shot down. Before going on combat operational missions, training aircrews flew various exercises designed to prepare them for the realities of actual operational flying. These operations were referred to as 'Bulls-eye' and took place over a number of British cities, where the crews learned how to avoid searchlights and night fighters. Having mastered these skills, the crews were then required to find a target over France, and sometimes Germany, where they would drop leaflets. Some of the crews, whilst still in their training phase, took part in minor raids designed to take the German night fighters away from the main bombers force. These flights were just as dangerous, sometimes even more dangerous than actual operations, as training crews had no combat flying experience. Kenyon survived fourteen of these training sorties, which were not counted as combat operations.

On the evening of 16 September 1943, Kenyon took off on his forty-fourth wartime mission from his home base at RAF Middleton St George in County Durham (the squadron having moved from RAF Mildenhall on 10 November 1942), in his Halifax II LW240 bomber. The aircraft never made it back to England after it was attacked by two enemy aircraft when homeward bound after having carried out an attack on the French town of Sainte-Mondane. Kenyon and his seven crew mates all managed to parachute from the stricken aircraft into the darkness of the night and remained at large for ten days before he was captured on 27 September near Dax, as he made his way to the neutral country of Spain. The pilot of the aircraft, Flight Lieutenant A.N. Quaile, was captured and ended up as a prisoner of war at Stalag Luft III. Pilot Officer Lawrence E. Aspinall, who was the navigator, was also captured and ended up in Stalag Luft I. Sergeant E.E. Bowden, the second pilot, also became a POW and spent time in both Stalag Luft IV and VI. The four remaining crew members, Flying Officer George Thomas Graham, the flight's bomb aimer; Flight Sergeant Thomas J. Bright, the wireless operator; Pilot Officer Leonard Francis Martin, the flight engineer; and Flying

Officer Henry Frederick Ernest Smith, all managed to evade capture, and eventually made their way back to England.

Once at Stalag Luft III, Kenyon joined a number of other talented artists and was instructed by Group Captain Massey to record the work carried out by the tunnel diggers, which meant he had to go down into the tunnels himself. His part in the escape was as one of the camp's forgers, which required him to carry out the all-important role of forging the essential papers and documentation that were needed by those involved in the escape from the camp in March 1944. The intricate details required to make each of the forged documents acceptable took its toll on Kenyon's eyesight, to such a degree that he was unable to take part in the actual escape.

Some years after the war, Kenyon wrote about the escape and the almost frenetic pace that it took on once the word 'Break' had been given just after dusk on Friday, 24 March 1944. This was the signal for those at the exit of the tunnel to dig out the final few feet so that the escape could begin in earnest.

Once out of the tunnel, the first part of the plan was put into action. The first three men each dragged a rope to the edge of the woods and then remained at the end of it so that they could confirm to each escapee which direction each rope represented in terms of where each man was headed. Those making their way to Czechoslovakia and neighbouring countries followed the rope pointing south, those on their way to Sweden and northern seaports took the north-pointing rope, and those who were going to the local railway station took the rope running west.

To ensure there was not too much commotion and unnecessary noise, each escapee exited the tunnel at two-minute intervals. A big concern when planning the escape was the German guards who patrolled outside the camp's fence during the hours of darkness, some of whom had guard dogs with them. Thankfully, the guards stayed close to the perimeter fence and with the exit of the escape tunnel being some 20 yards away, close to the treeline of the woods, none of them discovered the exit point of the tunnel.

The escape had been underway for more than six hours before it was discovered. What is not widely known is the fact that at least another thirty men would have been able to escape if it had not been for a collapse in the tunnel during the actual escape. Some of the wood shorings gave way and for a period of time the tunnel was blocked with sand, so those already in the tunnel had to come back up into Hut 104 whilst the sand was cleared out of the way and the tunnel was once again made safe. If that was not bad enough, for the first time in about a week, the RAF carried out an air raid on Germany's capital city, Berlin, about 80 miles away from the camp, at a loss to the RAF of more than seventy aircraft.

This resulted in the Germans turning off all electricity in the camp for the guards' benefit as well as the prisoners'. The positive to come out of the air raid was that it certainly gained the guards' attention in the process. It was also a very inclement evening weather wise. The bombing was so intense that it shook the ground in and around the camp, causing those in the tunnel to wonder if they would get out alive. This also caused a further delay and reduced the number of men who managed to escape.

The air raid caused a further problem for the escapees as it was common practice when such raids took place for the Germans to double the guards patrolling on the exterior of the perimeter fence.

The escape continued throughout the night with the Germans none the wiser at what was taking place. All that changed at just before 05:00 the following morning, when suddenly a shot rang out. Those still in the tunnel and others waiting above ground in Hut 104 instinctively knew that the escape had been rumbled and that for them, there would be no break for freedom. The gunshot had taken place when one of the German guards had seen movement amongst the trees and had opened fire. He had no idea what or who he was firing at as he did not know that an escape was taking place. It was only when he started to make his way across to the treeline that he saw the exit to the tunnel, and with that the escape was over.

Flight Lieutenant Mick Shand, who was the last escapee to make it out of tunnel, and his New Zealand compatriot, Squadron Leader Leonard H. Trent, both members of the Royal New Zealand Air Force, had made it out of the tunnel and gave themselves up after the sentry had fired at them. The next man to stick his head out of the tunnel exit was Squadron Leader Robert Frederick 'Bob' McBride, a Canadian who had been a POW since 7 November 1942, and was a member of

No. 415 (Coastal) Squadron RCAF. He was stuck in his tracks, and with a rifle pointing at his face held by a very nervous German guard, he put his hands in the air and wedged his feet firmly on the rungs of the ladder to ensure that he did not fall back into the tunnel and potentially encourage the guard to open fire on him. Immediately below McBride, waiting for their turn to exit the tunnel, were Wing Commander Ken Rees and Squadron Leader Clive King Saxelby, DFC, AFC and bar. Waiting behind them in the tunnel was Flying Officer Jack Moul and Squadron Leader Denys Maw. When all four men realised the potential danger they were in, and in an effort to warn their colleagues of what had happened, they turned round and made their way back along the tunnel to Hut 104 as fast as they could.

Luck and good fortune fell upon those who had been patiently waiting for their turn to enter the tunnel from Hut 104. What was on the side of the POWs was uncertainty. Although the Germans knew that an escape was taking place, what they did not know was from which hut the escape tunnel was connected to. Hut 104 was one of the last the Germans decided to search simply because they had searched it so many times before. The protracted period of time allowed the POWs in Hut 104 to destroy all their documentation, get rid of their escape clothes and also eat the food rations that they were to take with them. The hut the escape tunnel was connected to was only discovered when prison guard Charles Pilz decided to enter the tunnel's exit and crawl all the way back to its entrance in Hut 104.

In no time at all the camp was swarming with German guards. For a few moments nobody had a clue what was going on. It was a combination of chaos and mayhem. The Germans did not enter any of the huts but instead boarded up the windows and locked all the doors. Those in each of the huts, whether they were in their own one or not, were not going anywhere.

Once the Germans had worked out which hut the escape tunnel began from, they searched it from top to bottom to find as much information about the escape as they could. Those in Hut 104 waiting for their turn to escape were taken outside in the cold and snow, counted and name checked numerous times, and stripped of most of their clothing as the Germans attempted to discover what documents and paperwork each of the men had in their possession.

A sight to behold, especially for the POWs, was the camp Commandant Colonel Friedrich Wilhelm von Wildau, who had been woken by his junior officer to inform him of what had happened and, in his haste, had not even dressed in his uniform. Although wearing his coat and hat, it was clear for all to see that underneath he was still in his pyjamas. Although a gentle and relatively quiet man by nature, von Wildau, possibly aware of the response that would be coming his way from higher German authorities once he had informed them of the breakout, was clearly not a happy man.

It was late afternoon before the Germans finished their search of the camp and counted the POWs time and time again, more as a punishment to keep them out in the winter cold than anything else.

In the days that followed the escape, the ones who had not been murdered were returned to the camp in dribs and drabs. Most had been held at a Gestapo prison at Görlitz and were quick to tell how the German guards would call out the names of men who would be removed from their cells, never to be seen again.

In the aftermath of the escape, Germany enacted a new way of dealing with escaped prisoners of war who were informed that 'all unauthorised trespassers would be immediately shot on sight'. The details of this somewhat different approach by the Germans were detailed to the POWs in the form of leaflets which were pinned up at different locations around the camp during the hours of darkness, when everybody was tucked up in bed. It is unclear why the Germans waited until nighttime to put up the leaflets, rather than walk through the camp during the day handing the leaflets out to the POWs. Perhaps the guards were concerned that the POWs would simply turn round, glance at them, screw them up, and then simply throw them on the ground with gay abandonment.

The heading of the leaflet said:

To all Prisoners of War!
The escape from prison camps is no longer a sport

Germany has always kept to the Hague Convention and only punished re-captured prisoners of war with minor disciplinary punishment.

Germany will still maintain these principles of international law, but England has, besides fighting at the front in an honest manner, initiated an illegal warfare in non-combat zones in the form of gangster commandos, terror bandits and sabotage troops even up to the frontiers of Germany.

They say in a captured secret and confidential English military pamphlet.

THE HANDBOOK OF MODERN IRREGULAR WAREFARE

'The days when we could practice the rules of sportsmanship are over. For the time being every soldier must be a potential gangster and must be prepared to adapt their methods whenever necessary.

The sphere of operations should always include the enemy's own country, any occupied territory, and in certain circumstances, such neutral countries as he is using as a source of supply.'

England has with these instructions opened up a non-military form of gangster war!

Germany is determined to safeguard her homeland, and especially her war industry and provisional centres for the fighting fronts. Therefore, it has become necessary to create strict forbidden zones, called death zones, in which all unauthorised trespassers will be immediately shot on sight.

Escaping prisoners of war, entering such death zones, will certainly lose their lives. They are therefore in constant danger of being mistaken for enemy agents or sabotage groups.

Urgent warning is given against making future escapes!

In plain English: Stay in the camp where you will be safe!

Breaking out of it is now a damned dangerous act.

The chances of preserving your life are almost nil!

All police and military guards have been given the strictest orders to shoot on sight all suspected persons.

Escaping from prison camps has ceased to be a sport.

The document referred to in the leaflet, *The Handbook of Modern Irregular Warfare*, was a British military pamphlet which also included the following information: 'The confidential military pamphlet must not fall into German hands. The information given in this document is not to be communicated, either directly or indirectly to the Press or to any person not holding an official position in His Majesty's Service.'

Kenyon had been asked by the camp's escape committee to complete some drawings depicting the tunnel and the escape, so that a record of what had been achieved at Stalag Luft III could be recorded for posterity. This was a task which he happily agreed to take on, and which he completed in the weeks leading up to the escape itself. The drawings were hidden in another tunnel, 'George', which was started after the commotion had died down after the mass breakout and life in the camp returned to some kind of normality. When the remaining prisoners in the camp were told they had to leave at short notice in January 1945 because Russian forces were just 30 miles away, there was no time to retrieve the drawings from where they had been stored.

Not all the prisoners in the camp were fit enough to undertake the enforced march, however, with a number of them having to remain behind in the camp hospital, mainly due to sickness. After these men were eventually liberated, one of them retrieved the drawings from the partly dug 'George', and later brought back to England, along with a mixture of other artefacts from the camp, so that what took place there would never be forgotten by future generations.

CHAPTER FIVE

Marcel Eric Zillessen RAF

❖

Marcel Eric Zillessen was born in Northampton on 14 January 1917 to a German father, Erich, and an Irish mother, Rosetta. His father was a successful businessman in the wool and textile industry, and when he left school, Marcel was employed as a sales director in the family business. Whilst in his late teens, his father decided he would benefit from being sent to live in Germany and so he become a student at the prestigious University of Berlin. A combination of having the ability to speak German due to it being his father's 'mother tongue' and living in the nation's capital whilst furthering his education, meant that by the time he left, Zillessen could read, write and speak German with complete fluency. He had also seen the rise of Hitler and the Nazi Party during his time in Berlin, as National Socialism spread across the country.

With the outbreak of the Second World War quickly becoming a case of 'when' rather than 'if', British military intelligence tried to recruit Zillessen to work as a spy because of his fluency in German and his knowledge of the country and culture. He turned the offer down, not out of disrespect, but because he wanted to be involved in the actual fighting. To that end, he joined the RAF because, if possible, he wanted to become a fighter pilot and be in the thick of the action.

He successfully completed his flying training and after becoming a flying officer, he found himself deployed to take part in the North African campaign flying Hurricanes with No.6 Squadron. He was a brave and courageous pilot, but because of his almost fearless attitude, he was shot down on more than one occasion as he took part in attacking Rommel's *Afrika Korps*. His luck finally ran out on 6 April 1943, when he was shot down near Tunis in Libya and captured. Initially, he was sent to Italy but eventually ended up as a POW at Stalag Luft III.

The following telegram, dated 1 May 1943, was received by Zillessen's father.

IMMEDIATE: E M T ZILLESSEN ESQ, C/O GERARDSON LTD, SUNBRIDGE MILLS, 129-131 SUNBRIDGE ROAD, BRADFORD, YORKS.

IMMEDIATE FROM AIR MINISTRY KINGSWAY P 6688, 1/5/43, THE NAME OF YOUR SON F/O MARCEL ERIC ZILLESEN 119089 WAS INCLUDED IN A GERMAN BROADCAST ON 28/4/43 AS A PRISONER OF WAR, STOP. YOU ARE ADVISED TO TREAT THIS INFORMATION WITH RESERVE PENDING OFFICIAL CONFIRMATION, STOP.

Once he arrived at Stalag Luft III, Zillessen's fluency in all things German quickly became apparent to his camp mates, especially the senior officers who were involved in organising and planning the forthcoming mass escape. He was brought on board to carry out a specific job the escape committee needed covering; to get to know and keep a close eye on the German 'ferrets', whose job it was to walk round the camp whilst prodding a pole into the ground to see if they could locate any escape tunnels.

One of his other useful characteristics was that he was a bit of a charmer who had the 'gift of the gab'. This was put to excellent use when it came to befriending camp guards in an attempt to glean useful snippets of information, without them realising they were actually giving anything away.

In the camp, Zillessen's other particular area of expertise that was put to good use in relation to the escape was that of forging documents the escapees would need if they were to have any kind of chance once they had succeeded in their task. A good example of this was when he agreed to write letters for some of the German guards to their girlfriends, fiancées and wives. This was a simple and easy way to obtain both writing paper and ink, both of which he needed in abundance.

It was Zillessen who was the one who came up with the way to redistribute the soil that was removed from the escape tunnels. He suggested several POWs have, essentially, sandbags on the inside of their trousers, which were activated by pulling on cords they could reach through their pockets and then blend the soil in with the soil of the numerous vegetable gardens that were situated at different locations around the camp. The POWs who did this acquired the nickname of 'penguins' thanks to the way they looked as they constantly shuffled round with their hands in their pockets from one garden patch to another, releasing the soil and blending it in.

When the Great Escape took place on the night of 24/25 March 1944, Zillessen was the last in the queue of the 200 men waiting their turn. Once the Germans had discovered the escape was underway, he had sufficient time to get back to his own hut before being discovered by the Germans in a hut that was not his.

In some respects, he could be classed as being fortunate not to have made it out of the tunnel. If he had and was subsequently re-captured, he may well have been one of those who was subsequently executed, especially because of his German connections.

When the Soviets arrived in January 1945, Zillessen avoided the deadly Long March by running off into the surrounding woods and hiding. After finally been liberated at the end of the war, he returned home to the northeast of England, where he returned to work in the family run wool and textile business. After marrying Eveline Hudson, he settled down in Bradford, although in later life the family moved to the picturesque area of Robin Hood's Bay on the Yorkshire coast, where he and Eveline ran a guest house.

It was only after the war that he discovered his younger brother, Walter, had been killed. Initially he had been reported as missing in action, but it later transpired he had been killed on 17 July 1941 whilst serving with No. 86 Squadron. Walter was buried at the Sage War Cemetery, Oldenburg, Germany, and his headstone includes the following words. 'Love lives on, a power to bless, when they who loved are hidden in the grave.' He was 23.

Marcel Eric Zillessen died on 8 January 1999, aged 81.

CHAPTER SIX

Alan Bryett RAF

❖

Alan Bryett was born in Deptford, southeast London on 18 July 1922, the only child of a lower middle-class family. Bryett's father died suddenly when he was only 11, meaning the young boy had to finish his education at St. Dunstan's College when he was 16 in order to bring some much-needed money into the family. Bryett found work as a clerk for Barclay's Bank on Brompton Road near Harrods, and although he had no particular hobbies and interests, he was an avid stamp collector.

When war was declared, Bryett was too young for the Territorial Army, unlike ten of his bank colleagues who were called up, leaving him with more work to do. Bryett volunteered for the RAF in April 1941 but was not called up until February 1942.

During the Second World War, Pilot Officer Bryett served as a bomb aimer with No. 158 Squadron, part of Bomber Command, who flew Handley Page Halifax bomber aircraft out of RAF Lissett, in Bridlington, Yorkshire. Although he got on well with all his crew, he had a particular friendship with Australian Harold Kevin Hornibrook, who during periods of leave stayed with him at his home in Bromley. Hornibrook had the rank of flight lieutenant and was the crew's main pilot.

At 20:26 on the evening of 23 August 1943, Bryett and his colleagues took off from RAF Lissett as part of a massive bombing raid on Berlin. A total of 719 Allied aircraft took part in the raid, and sixty-two of them, including Bryett's, never made it back to England.

The distance between Bridlington and Berlin was 600 miles and by the time Bryett's aircraft arrived, he could see Berlin was already on fire. It was heavily defended on its eastern side because it was the obvious route that RAF and American bombers would take to carry out their attacks on Berlin, so Hornibrook carried out his attack from the western side instead, which was not so heavily defended.

Having dropped their bombs, Bryett's aircraft was attacked by a German fighter aircraft, which caused fire to break out on one of the wings and the underneath of the main fuselage. Flight Sergeant Graham Albert George McLeod, the rear gunner, was killed by machine gun fire in the German fighter's first attack. Sergeant Lawrence George Chesson, who was the air gunner, was also killed in another burst of machine gun fire that hit the stricken Halifax, leaving Bryett; Joseph Batty, the wireless operator; Robert William Chaston, the navigator; and the pilot, Hornibrook, still alive. As the Halifax started plummeting to the ground, Hornibrook's attempts at controlling the aircraft were greatly hindered because he was blinded by the glare of several German searchlights.

There was a sudden urgency to bail out. Batty and Chaston donned their parachutes and quickly jumped clear of the aircraft, but when the aircraft's emergency escape hatch became stuck, Bryett and Hornibrook struggled to open it. After a couple of minutes, they succeeded and Hornibrook wasted no time in pushing Bryett free of the aircraft, who then had just enough time to engage his parachute before he found himself stuck some 80 feet up in a fir tree. At almost the same time, the stricken Halifax bomber exploded no more than a couple of hundred yards ahead of him at Oranienburg, about 15 miles north of Berlin. Unfortunately, Hornibrook did not make it out of the aircraft, having more than likely sacrificed his own life so that Bryett might live.

Bryett had been at large for a couple of hours, by which time it was starting to get light, so he decided to dig a shallow hole and cover himself with leaves where he would wait until dark before continuing his escape. He was captured not long afterwards, having been discovered by an Alsatian that was being used to hunt for him by a group of German Home Guard soldiers. He was then taken to the Luftwaffe headquarters in Berlin, where there were several other captured Allied airmen. From there he was taken to Frankfurt and interrogated a number of times over a period of about two weeks, before being suddenly taken out of the camp, placed in the back of a truck and taken to the local railway station. Along with a group of about thirty other Allied airmen, Bryett finally arrived at Stalag Luft III late one October afternoon in 1943, feeling completed physically and mentally exhausted. The first thing he noticed was the barbed wire that surrounded the top of camp's fences and the armed lookout towers. No sooner had he entered the camp but a senior British officer was asking the other POWs if anybody knew him. This was normal procedure to try to ensure that there were no 'spies' being planted into the camp by the Germans. Thankfully for Bryett, five men stepped forward to say that they could vouch for him.

Not long after being allocated a top bunk in one of the ten rooms in Hut 122, another airman appeared and handed him some spare clothing, razor blades, food and even a bar of chocolate. It turned out that the man in question was Wing Commander Robert Stamford Tuck, a well-known British pilot who had gained his fame from his actions during the Battle of Britain, but who had also been a fellow student at St. Dunstan's College in London.

Bryett quickly became engrossed in camp life as he adjusted to his new life as a POW. At the time he was the youngster prisoner in the camp, having not long passed his twenty-first birthday.

It was sometime in October 1943 that there was the first talk of 'something big' due to take place early the following year, but there was no clarification of what that might be.

Bryett's part in the subsequent mass breakout from the camp was as one of the 'penguins' who distributed the excavated soil from the tunnels to different locations around the compound. He was also tasked with keeping close observations on the sump in the washroom of Hut 122, checking it every hour to ensure that the level did not fall to nothing. If this happened, and one of the German guards discovered it, there was every chance that they would quickly work out it was because it was soaking away into a tunnel. He was also nominated as Little S (Security) for Hut 122.

Come the night of the mass escape, Bryett had acquired himself one of the coveted 200 nominated places who, once the signal was given, would carefully make their way along the escape tunnel to an uncertain future on the outside, but before he could get anywhere near entering the tunnel, its exit point was discovered by the guards. Whilst waiting in Hut 104 for his turn to escape, Bryett heard the sentry's gun fire and immediately realised it was the end of the escape. He quickly lit a small fire on the floor of the hut and burnt his forged passport, German money and associated documents.

The plan was for the escape to begin at 22:00 and for all the escapees to have made their way out of the camp by 05:30 the following morning. The camp's escape committee knew that not all the escapees would get that far, especially those who were at the back of the queue. But to get everybody to a neutral or safe country was never the intention of the escape. Anybody who it was felt actually had a real chance of 'making it back home' were amongst the earliest of the escapees to leave. With the following morning's parade not being held until 08:00, those leaving the camp the earliest from just after 22:00 the night before clearly had more chance of already being in neighbouring countries before the Germans realised there had actually been a mass escape. For those who were not due to leave the camp until after about 03:00, they were simply told to hide up somewhere to help with the overall disruption. There was never any real belief or intention for them to get that far from the camp, and certainly not to make it home. The fact that just by being outside the camp would mean large numbers of German soldiers were tied up for hours, if not days, was seen as a success.

Bryett later said of the escape: 'My initial disappointment at not being among the seventy-six men to get out was transformed into a grim relief when news filtered back to the camp that fifty of the re-captured men had been shot, on Hitler's orders. They were so young. Even our guards were shocked. They let us build a memorial to our friends.'

Because of the devastating outcome of the escape, and the negative impact it had on those still in the camp, all future escape attempts were forbidden by the camp's senior British officers. For them, any future attempts were just too much of a risk to take.

Alan Bryett died in January 2022 at the age of 99, making him the last surviving Stalag Luft III POW who had been involved in the Great Escape.

CHAPTER SEVEN

Statement by Anthony Eden
to the House of Commons

❖

In May 1944, Mr Anthony Eden made a statement in the House of Commons concerning the murder of forty-seven Allied airmen by German forces following their escape from Stalag Luft III and subsequent re-capture.

According to information given to a representative of the protecting power by the German authorities, in the course of a routine visit to the camp on 17 April 1944, a total of seventy-six officers had escaped from Stalag Luft III on 22 March. Of these seventy-six, fifteen had been recaptured, fourteen were still at large, whilst the remaining forty-seven had been shot, some while resisting arrest and some who were in the course of trying to escape being recaptured. The British government were understandably both surprised and somewhat shocked at these revelations, and immediately requested the protecting power to demand from the German government a full and immediate report of the circumstance in which these men had met their deaths, and an explanation of its failures to immediately report the facts of what had happened, to the protecting family.

The names of the officers who had been shot had been provided to the protecting power when they visited the camp on 17 April. Accordingly, the next of kin of the murdered officers had been informed.

Out of the those officers reported as having been killed, twenty-five were members of the RAF, six were from the Royal Canadian Air Force, three from the Royal Australian Air Force, two from the Royal New Zealand Air Force, three from the South African Air Force, four Polish officers, two Norwegians, one Frenchman from the Fighting French Air Force, and one member of the Royal Hellenic Air Force, or the Greek Air Force.

The following is an exchange which took place in the House of Commons on 19 May 1944 between the Conservative MP for Warwick & Leamington, who at the time was also the Foreign Secretary and the Leader of the House of Commons, Mr Anthony Eden, and members of the House. He began with the following introduction.

I deeply regret to have to tell the House that His Majesty's Government have received information from the Protecting Power that forty-seven officers of the Royal Air Force, and Dominion and Allied Air Forces, have been shot by the Germans after a mass escape from Stalag Luft III.

The House will wish me to express its deepest sympathy with the relatives and to pay tribute to the courage and high sense of military duty shown by all these gallant officers.

Sir Percy Alfred Harris, the Liberal MP for the constituency of Bethnal Green Southwest, and also the Deputy Leader of the Liberal Parliamentary Party, asked the following question of Mr Eden.
'Will the right hon. gentleman make it clear that the German government themselves are responsible for all breaches of international law?'

Mr Eden responded: 'That certainly is the position. As I have said, I have sent this telegram, it went actually some clays ago, to the Protecting Power, asking for this full investigation, and I would rather, I think, say no more until I get their reply.'

Mr Edgar Granville, the Liberal MP for the constituency of Eye in Suffolk, also asked a question of Mr Eden:

I am sure the House will feel a sense of shock at the fate of these brave men. May I ask the right hon. gentleman if he can say when the Foreign Office first heard this information, and when he made his representations to the Protecting Power? May I also ask the right hon. gentleman if he will make the names known in the Press, and to this House, as soon as possible, in view of the great anxiety which may be caused to the relatives of many Royal Air Force officers who are in that camp at Breslau?

Mr Eden replied:

As regards the question of anxiety, as I have said, the next-of-kin have all been informed already, so that anybody who has not been informed, need not feel anxiety. I would like to ensure that there shall be no unnecessary anxiety, and we will certainly consider the publication of the names. As regards the time when the information was received, if my memory serves me right, I think we received it four days ago, and the very next day we telegraphed the Protecting Power. We did not make an announcement then and there, because we wished the relatives to be informed first, and because we wished, if possible, to get the information for which I have asked the Protecting Power.

Major Sir Jocelyn Lucas, the Conservative MP for the constituency of Portsmouth South, asked Mr Eden if he would try to find out the name of the commandant of the camp, and anybody responsible.

Mr Eden replied that he would, but that he would 'Ask the House to let the matter rest where it is until I get the reply from the Protecting Power.'

Mr Montague, the Labour MP for the constituency of Islington West, told Mr Eden that he would 'like to identify the party to which I belong, with the expression of sympathy with the relatives which the Foreign Secretary has given to the House and to express the view that we are quite satisfied with the action he has taken.'

Mr William Thorne, the 86-year-old Labour MP for the constituency of Westham Plaistow, asked Mr Eden if he would convey the report's contents to the House.

Mr Eden agreed, but Mr Granville continued to press the matter, saying:

> Most of us have constituents who have relatives and friends in this camp, and who have been very anxious about this. When the list was first published the number was five; now the right hon. gentleman says there are forty-seven. The point I am trying to make is that the relatives of all Royal Air Force officers in this camp are wondering whether that is the complete list, or whether we are still to expect further names?

In answer to this, Mr Eden explained that: 'No list of five, or any other number, was published at all. The first published statement is the statement I have just made. So far as I am aware, it contains all the facts. That list contains all the facts in the possession of His Majesty's Government.'

It was clear from the questions asked, and the number of MPs involved in the conversation, that there was great interest and utter shock at the announcement Mr Eden made to the House. This was the first time in the war that a mass murder of British and Commonwealth forces had been reported. It was doubtless more shocking because at the time of their deaths, the men were unarmed, non-combatants and prisoners of war.

CHAPTER EIGHT

Letters from W/O George Dormer Anderson

❖

One aspect of being a prisoner of war that is often overlooked was that of receiving and sending mail to and from a loved one. The connection with home that such personal correspondence provided was invaluable and helped men who were incarcerated for an unknown period of time to keep a sense of reality. By receiving news from home about the well-being of their parents, family, other loved ones and friends, life somehow did not seem so bad. Being incarcerated in a foreign and sometimes alien environment meant there was not much for them to write about, other than how they were doing, or what the weather was like. Life in the camp was fundamentally boring. The men did not know what life had in store for them or how long they would be prisoners for. Some of the men had left behind young children, while some had not even seen their children if they had been born after they had left to go to war. Being able to receive detailed news from home helped keep men sane. It gave them something to look forward to, not only when they would receive their next letter, but in the context of what they had waiting for them when they were eventually able to return home.

George Dormer Anderson was a pilot in the RAF. The following is a letter he wrote to his parents, Mr and Mrs G.B. Anderson, who at the time were living at 66 Brooklands Park, Blackheath, London,

SE8. The letter is dated 24 September 1942, and states it was sent from Stalag Luft III. A check of the British Prisoners of War 1939-1945 listings shows that Anderson was a POW at Stalag Luft VI, which was located in Heydekrug, Lithuania. The distance between the two camps is some 330 miles. It therefore makes absolutely no sense that letters sent from Stalag Luft VI would first be directed to Stalag Luft III. The *Kriegsgefangenenpost* (POW Mail) Anderson sent to his parents is clearly marked as having been sent from Stalag Luft III.

Despite the uncertainty of which camp the letter was sent from, it is a good example of the kind of letters written by imprisoned British military personnel. They were careful about what they wrote, knowing full well that their letters would be read by German censors, and the last thing they wanted to do was to leave their friends and family feeling worried and concerned about them.

My Darling Mother & Daddy

Once more I sit down at our bare table and gather my thoughts and accumulated general togetherness, so that I can give you some idea as to my present health and daily routine. To the former I might add, I'm in the best possible health and spirits, and hope that this finds you similarly placed. No longer do we have scorching days, wherein to bask our slender bodies; but cooler days with moderate sunshine, and I'm pleased to add that this weather suites my studying capacity, to the good of my general well-being.

Until recently your mail has been coming in regularly, but the Jerries are now mucking about, so don't get alarmed if my post gets less frequent. However, I have hope! I have received your seventeenth letter. No breaks. Wisso, 'What!'

Seeing that Joan is now an established daughter, I send her my love and thank her for seven letters. I've had my letters from Michael and Mrs Parker, the office, and Eve, so please convey my love and thanks to them all. Keep 'em at it.

Now for questions and answers. Got all the gen from Mike. Who is Don T marrying? Is the bike still in running order? If so, let M use it whenever he's home.

Sing up, Daddy! Have not received parcel yet. Do not expect until November at earliest. Thank you for paying my premium, don't forget if you have any use for my allotment, use it please! At any rate I shall expect you to buy yourselves something for Noel from me.

We've got over 100 tomatoes formed and bags of lettuce and radish.

Your numbered letters get through ok. Don't believe all you read. Ha! Item of news. I've had all my curly hair cut off. What a sight! Real tough guy! Could you send a hairbrush next time? Don't bother to send a lot of useless stuff, we are adequately provided for. A small suitcase with little else is all I need. Another request. Could you get in touch with John Chadwell and let me know how he and the others are getting on, please? As to books, I have no particular choice. I will just wait and see.

Well, must close now. Love to Froggie and Mary and all and sundry. I always remember you in my prayers.

All my love & kisses
Dormer.

The letter is interesting as it shows a balance of humour and seriousness, questions and answers. It was no doubt useful for both Anderson and his parents, helping them all to navigate through what was, after all, an extremely stressful and difficult situation.

The second letter from Anderson is dated 23 February 1943 and is once again addressed to his parents.

My Darling Mother & Daddy,

A Happy Easter and the very best wishes to you both, Mike and all the family, and to all our friends, family.

For these, my last few letters, I'm changing my style, and so hope to give you a more complete picture of our life and surroundings in this dump. Feature No.1, a description of my fellow sufferers in my section of fifteen men. Ernie McConchie, father and leader of Section, New Zealander from Wellington, in the shipping trade. Almost a dwarf but a fine gymnast and swimmer. Full of fun and games but keeps us in order.

Jim Short, Carpenter from Grimsby, the life and soul of the party. Official duster-upper and bread butter-upper.

Arthur Savage, the line-shooter from Orpington. No fixed occupation, but 'a know all', and is forever arguing. These three are our elders in time served.

Feature No. 2, a description of our surroundings branding any false impressions in R + Magazine. The weather's perfect. In the middle of a forest, true, shut off from the outside world, with no sign of life at all. If a girl happens to wander in our view, well, you can guess, eyes all agoggle [sic] at this apparition.

Ground, a desert of dusty sand. We live, sleep and nibble in large wooden huts and wooden bunks. Two bare tables and aren't our seats just hard with wooden benches. The laughs on you this time, Dad. Chrystine Woodhouse is my Skipper's wife, and not a secret flash of mine. J Chadwell was my 2nd Dickie, before I came here.

Don't worry I'm keeping myself fit and healthy as possible. The Padre is giving us a series of useful addresses on moral conduct, sex relations and married life. Officers play, 'Night Must Fall', was very gripping acting. Symphony concert was wizzo, with our new US piano concert player. The best I've ever seen.

Bibles, dictionaries and excellent books arrived. Received letter from granny in Teesdale. She is strong in health but weak in mind. Father Moore is away doing chaplain duties elsewhere.

Following up them of last letter, though I'm not feeling so glum, I feel so helpless in planning my future, and in spite of your words written on my 21st, I'm asking for your help after being cooped [sic] up for a year, an office desk for the rest of my life is out of the question, that's all the C.S. offers me. So would you make enquiries, Dad, of firms as to possible prospects? I'm for about anything, so long as it entails travelling about a bit, with ever changing surroundings, especially in Europe. I can guarantee a conversational knowledge of French, German, and possibly others, plus shorthand and a general knowledge of commercial business. I shall look out for progress in your post, in this matter. Firms asked and results etc.

Our camp paper, 'Daily Recco' has just started giving us all camp news and items of interest in Kriegies letters. This is the start of my New Campaign [sic]. Bigger and brighter letters. Mail coming in slowly, have had yours of 3rd January.

Hope you are all well and cheery, I am! You are all cemented in my prayers. Lots of love as always.

Yours Dormer.

At the beginning of this chapter, doubt was shown about whether Anderson had ever actually been a POW at Stalag Luft III, so it is interesting to see Anderson mention the camp newspaper the *Daily Recco*, which was one of those produced at Stalag Luft III. By its very nature, war brings with it confusion and uncertainty, but Anderson's mention of the *Daily Recco* strongly suggests that he was in fact a POW at Stalag Luft III.

Although this letter is dated 23 February 1943, it did not arrive at his parents' home until 1 May 1944, and on the back of it he has written the words 'easter greetings & best wishes' in green, blue and orange.

Anderson had been serving with No. 149 (East India) Squadron at the time he was captured. He and his six comrades took off from Lakenheath air base in Suffolk on board their Short Stirling heavy bomber aircraft, serial number R9320, at 23:57 on the evening of 17 May 1942, on a mission to drop mines in the southern entrance to the Sound near to the Danish island of Lolland in the Baltic Sea. In the early hours of the following morning, at 01:57, the aircraft was hit by flak batteries at Wache Rødby, Kappel, and South Hafen Rødby and forced to crash land in the sea, south of the island.

Two of the crew either went down with the aircraft or were thrown from it on impact as it struck the surface of the sea. Their bodies were never recovered and have no known graves, although their names are commemorated on the Runnymede Memorial in Surrey. Those who survived the crash along with Anderson, who was the aircraft's co-pilot, were Sergeant's Gerald Grant, gunner; Ronald Jack Nason, the observer; Ronald Herbert Peek White, weapons operator; and the pilot, Flight Sergeant Graham Howard Roy Woodhouse. The crew were picked up by a local fishing boat after having climbed into their dingy and fired flares into the night sky. At 08:00 the fishing vessel, with the dingy in tow, was spotted from Rødby by Danish naval officer, Sea Lieutenant Thorklid Munch-Nielsen, who then sailed out and took the airmen on board his motor launch. Three of the crew were wounded, one severely, and all were given immediate first aid.

Munch-Nielsen's motor launch arrived back at Rødby at 08:55, where he found German Wehrmacht soldiers waiting for him, who then took the airmen into custody. It is believed that it was Anderson who was the most severely wounded airman as he was seen by a doctor, Dinesen, before being transferred to the nearby hospital in Nakskov, just 17 miles away.

Meanwhile, the other four members of the crew were driven to the German military airfield at Avnø, where they were joined later that day by Anderson. From there they were taken to Oberursel for interrogation and once that was completed, Woodhouse, Nason, White, and Grant were initially sent to Stalag Luft III, then on to Stalag Luft VI, before eventually ending up at Stalag 357 in Thorn, Poland. It was more than likely because of the severity of his wounds that Anderson was dealt with separately to his colleagues.

CHAPTER NINE

The Trojan Horse Escape

❖

Although better known for what has historically become referred to as the Great Escape, mainly due to the 1963 film of the same name, Stalag Luft III was also the location of another daring escape that took place on the evening of 19 October 1943.

The camp was heavily guarded because many of those who were held there were either prolific escapees or had made numerous attempts to escape from other camps in the past and so had been sent to Stalag Luft III because the Germans saw it as an 'escape proof' camp.

On the whole the relationship between the camp guards and the POWs was not too bad, but although a working relationship existed between the two sides, the Germans were more than happy, when there had been an infringement of prison rules, or when it suited them to do so, to administer various punishments which were often arbitrary. This usually came in the form of holding back the prisoners' mail or Red Cross parcels, as well as making them stand in the rain for long periods of time whilst on roll call, placing individuals in solitary confinement, or not allowing the prisoners to have warm water for the showers. Such tactics, however, only increased the men's resolve to escape.

The topic of escape was never far from the men's minds, but for a number of them, that is where it stayed. Never quite becoming a reality.

The successful escape attempt in October 1943 only involved three prisoners, but an escape of any size was never deemed to be a positive experience for the camp's commanding officer or the guards. The three men who escaped were army officer Lieutenant Michael Codner of the Royal Artillery, Flight Lieutenant Eric Williams, and Flight Lieutenant Oliver Philpot, both from the RAF. Theirs was a truly ingenious plan, whilst at the same time being extremely simple and straight forward.

Before any work could be started on digging a tunnel, permission was needed from the compound's escape committee. The idea was not initially met with the expected enthusiasm that Codner and Williams had hoped for, but after much deliberation, raised voices, and in-depth discussions, approval was finally given for the escape bid to go ahead, although what the escape committee thought about the chances of it being successful is not recorded.

Having settled into their new life at Stalag Luft III, Williams and Codner, along with their newfound friend, Philpot, came up with the idea to escape by using a wooden gymnastics-style vaulting horse. It was based on the Ancient Greek story that told of how Greek soldiers had finally entered the walled city of Troy during the decade-long siege, whilst hidden inside a wooden horse. The 'horse' in this instance was made from plywood utilised from Red Cross parcels and packages delivered to the camp for the POWs. With the help of other prisoners, who spent long periods of time vaulting over it, the three escapees were secretly digging away underneath it. Every day for nearly four months, four POWs would bring out the wooden vaulting horse from one of the huts and place it on the exact same spot close to the perimeter fence. Unbeknown to the German guards, inside the horse were at least two of the escapees at any one time, waiting to begin their work.

Any escape bid by means of tunnelling was at an immediate disadvantage, as the camp had been specifically designed to be escape resistant, especially for those who chose tunnelling to set themselves free. In building the camp, the Germans had put quite a bit of thought into it. The perimeter fence was intentionally placed some distance from the prisoners' huts, and the surrounding treeline was deliberately cleared to a distance way beyond the fence. This was the Germans' attempt at deterring tunnelling as a preferred means of escape, believing that the distance that would have to be tunnelled would simply be too great. The use of the vaulting horse by Codner, Williams and Philpot greatly helped in reducing the length of their escape tunnel.

All the camp's huts were raised a few feet off the ground so as to make it easier for the German guards to be able to spot the entrance to any tunnel being built by the prisoners. The Germans also employed the use of seismographs which were used to monitor ground vibrations, a natural byproduct of POWs digging a tunnel. To counter this, a large number of other prisoners would spend hours vaulting over the 'horse' each day and land as heavily as they could on the ground. How their actions failed to draw the attention from the camp guards is amazing, as this went on for months whilst the tunnel was being dug.

The vaulting horse was built slightly bigger to help accommodate the POWs, as well as their digging tools and containers for the soil. Just before dusk each day, the digging would stop, the men would cover the entrance to their tunnel with a wooden board, place compound soil around it, climb back inside the horse, and along with their digging tools, and the soil they had dug through, they were taken back to the hut where the vault was left overnight whilst they went for a well-earned shower and a nice hot mug of tea. The following morning saw a repeat of the previous day. The German guards found the POWs taking it in turns to repeatedly jump over the wooden horse, which must have looked quite amusing. Little did they know what was really going on underneath. The digging and subterfuge went on for nearly four months, beginning on 8 July right up to when the escape took place on 29 October, when the three men were finally ready to go. It was a deadline which had to be met because one of the items they had to help them with their escape was a local train timetable, which would go out of date on 1 November.

Their tunnel was started in the East Compound, some 100 feet from the camp's metal fence, but once they had dug that far, they still needed to dig at least another 100 feet so as to reach the safety of the nearby treeline. Unlike the tunnel used for the Great Escape, the three men had not supported the tunnel, meaning that at any time whilst they were digging away, they ran the risk of the roof or the sides of it caving in on them. They managed to get an air supply whilst they were digging by using metal rods to break through to the surface above them.

The closer it got to the actual escape, the more anxious and stressed the men became, but through all of this they managed to remain calm and focused on what they were about to do.

On the morning of 29 October, the wooden horse was carried out into the camp as usual by the POWs, who would then spend the following few hours vaulting over it. Hidden on the inside of the horse were Codner and Philpot, each with a different but equally important task to carry out. On entering the tunnel, both men carried on digging, with Philpot focusing on filling up the final few bags with soil. At around 16:30, the exercising came to an end and the wooden horse was taken back inside its allotted hut, but only Philpot was inside as Codner had remained inside the tunnel to continue the digging. The men then all had their dinner, after which the evening roll call was taken, with a fellow POW answering when Codner's name was called. The wooden horse was taken out for what would be the last time, but on this occasion, it had three men hidden inside it: Philpot and Williams, who along with Codner would be taking part in the escape, along with another man by the name of McKay, whose job it was to seal the tunnel over so that no sign of the entrance was visible once the wooden horse was removed. Once he had done this, McKay, along with the horse, went back inside one of the huts.

The three men waited for just over an hour before exiting the other end of the tunnel, which was only some 15 feet outside the camp's wire fence, at 18:00, by which time it was already dark. They could not risk leaving it any later as part of their plan included catching a train from Sagan railway station at 19:00, which would take them to Frankfurt.

They reached the woods without been seen by the camp guards and once safely out of sight, the three men removed their black camouflage suits and hoods, before cleaning each other down. They then walked to the railway station together, where Codner purchased two tickets to Frankfurt, whilst Philpot bought his own. In the station's booking hall, Williams came face to face with the German doctor who had treated him in the camp hospital just two days prior to the escape. Williams had fortunately cut off his rather large, bushy moustache, and luckily the doctor did not recognise him. Panic over.

When the train arrived, it was already packed, and it was standing room only. Due to the fear of Allied air raids, there were no lights on inside the train, which was a big help to the three men and ensured the rest of their journey was uneventful.

It had already been agreed that three men travelling together was likely to draw too much unwanted attention, so the plan was that they split up. Posing as French labourers, Williams and Codner's ultimate destination was the port Stettin (now Szczecin, northwest Poland). When their train first arrived in Frankfurt at 20:50, the two men failed to find a hotel room and so spent the night sleeping in a storm drain. Although it was a cold an uncomfortable night, it was at least dry and sheltered.

The next train, bound for Kustrin, left at 8:50 the following morning with Codner and Williams on board. The first carriage they entered was full of Russian POWs, and they were quickly ordered out by the German soldiers guarding them. Neither man needed telling a second time. The journey to Kustrin took just over an hour and then it was a case of killing time until the train for Stettin left at 17:08. The pair had realised that catching local trains that stopped at every station was the better and safer option, because they were usually full of workers and labourers, which meant there was less chance of them being stopped and questioned by German police.

They had spent the day waiting for the train alternating between sitting in a café and a cinema, to keep themselves as warm as they possibly could. The train arrived in Stettin at 20:00 on Saturday, 30 October, and, after once again failing to find a hotel room for the night, the two men slept in an air raid shelter in somebody's back garden, unbeknown to the owners of the house.

At 09:30 the following morning, Codner and Williams managed to book a room in the town's Hotel Schobel, where they stayed for the following two nights, checking out on the morning of Tuesday, 2 November. After leaving the hotel the pair walked to the docks at Freihaven, and on arrival took an amazing risk. There were a number of French workers employed there, and despite not knowing any of them personally, Codner and Williams decided to tell them that they were escaped POWs and were looking to make contact with Swedish sailors in the hope of being allowed on one of their vessels. They returned to Stettin that evening and managed to find accommodation at the Hotel Gust. They felt that it was best not to stay anywhere for too long a period of time, just in case news of two men staying at one location for four or five days came to the attention of the local civilian police or the local Gestapo.

They had spoken with a number of Frenchmen in the town's cafés and bars in their attempts to make contact with the Swedes, but one of the major hurdles was a lack of trust. Codner and Williams never knew if they were actually speaking to helpful Frenchmen or members of the Gestapo masquerading as French workers, while the Frenchmen themselves presumably had the exact same thoughts and were unsure if Codner and Williams were escaped POWs, as they claimed, or plain-clothed Gestapo officers trying to catch them out for helping escaped Allied POWs. The penalty for doing the latter was extremely serious.

Although no help had been forthcoming in finding a contact who could get them onto a ship due to sail for a neutral country, the two men knew that Swedish sailors who had come ashore tended to frequent the Café de l'Accordion, so on the evening of Friday, 5 November, that is precisely where Codner and Williams decided to head. Whilst there they met a Frenchman, Andre Henri Daix, a former sergeant in the French army, who told them he was leaving for Denmark the following evening, but he did not believe there would be room on the boat for them.

At 07:30 the following morning, another Frenchman they had made contact with came and found them on the outskirts of Stettin, where they had stayed the night before, to inform them that he had managed to find a Danish sailor who had room on his ship for them. Codner and Williams then hurried down to the dock, where they met the Danish sailor who took them on board the boat. Once on board they saw the Frenchman they had met at the Café de l'Accordion the night before, Daix, and were hidden away in a tiny compartment until the ship had been searched and cleared to leave by German soldiers. Once the search had been completed, the Germans had left the ship, and the vessel had left the harbour and was out at sea, Codner and Williams were let out, fed and provided with somewhere to sleep.

Their journey first took them to Copenhagen, where they arrived at noon on Sunday, 7 November, and remained for three days. They did not remain on the boat, however, as some of the crew took them ashore for a meal and some drinks. By the time they returned to the ship, Codner, Williams and their newfound group of friends were all suitably refreshed. The next stage of the journey began at noon on Wednesday, 10 November when the ship sailed for the Swedish capital, Stockholm, and then on to the final destination of Gothenburg, but plans were changed as the captain felt that it would be safer to get them off his boat before it arrived. Instead, they were dropped off at Strömstad at just after 17:00 on Thursday, 11 November, where they were handed over to the police and spent the night in the cells. The following day Codner and Williams were met by officials from the British Consulate in Gothenburg, who in turn sent them on to Stockholm where they met up with Philpot, who had already been there a week. They would have no doubt been elated to see each other and have confirmation that they had all successfully completed their escape.

After the men had been given time to relax and unwind, they were sent back home to England, where they arrived just before Christmas 1943, some two months after they had escaped.

The following is Codner's description of the equipment and documents he took with him on his escape.

Clothes. Converted naval tunic, converted naval battledress trousers, standard brown shoes, civilian shirt and collar and tie, R.A.F. mackintosh, home-made beret and woollen gloves, light underclothes. I was also carrying a home-made canvas valise containing washing, shaving, and boot-cleaning tackle, food, a polo-collar woollen dicky and spare socks. I am sure that for this type of escape it is necessary at all costs to look respectable and clean and to be carrying reasonable luggage. I think it would be an advantage to be able superficially to change one's appearance, ie. sometimes to wear a hat, sometimes a collar and tie, and to change by removing the hat and wearing a choker or high-necked sweater, as this work entails a great deal of hanging about in rather suspicious areas.

On this particular escape there were just three men. If both Williams and Philpot had a similar amount of clothing, it would have meant a mammoth combined effort from the camp's escape committee. Compare that to the more than 260 POWs who were part of the Great Escape and waiting their turn in line.

Codner also had in his possession a *Vorlaufiger Ausweis* (temporary ID), an *Arbeitskarte* (work card), police permission to travel, the reason for travelling, which had to be supplied by a German named firm, and a Swedish seaman's pass, which Codner described as being 'highly questionable'. He also had 50 Reichmarks in cash. He was fortunate because at no time during his escape did he ever have to show any of his papers, other than the *Vorlaufiger Ausweis*. Foodwise, he had with him five tins of concentrated food stuffs which had been prepared in the camp, as well as a bit of chocolate. He realised afterwards that he should have taken more food with him, such as biscuits, not for dietary needs but because he realised that it was normal for civilians and German military personnel to produce food from their pockets to eat when in cafés, restaurants or even in the best hotels, to have with their drinks.

Meanwhile, as for Philpot, his cover story after escaping was that he was a Norwegian salesman, the only problem with this was he did not actually speak the language, although he did speak excellent German. He, too, caught the train from Sagan to Frankfurt but instead of heading to Stettin with Codner and Williams, Philpot intended to catch the night train to the town of Küstrin in western Poland, close to the border with Germany. However, the train was cancelled and so he had to wait until the following morning. Rather than risk trying to find somewhere to stay, he spent the night in some nearby woods but returned to the railway station the following morning in time to catch the train to Küstrin before continuing on to Danzig. Thankfully for Philpot, the forged identity documents he had been provided with before leaving Stalag Luft III were of a reasonably good quality, and more than sufficient to pass an inspection. He was stopped whilst on the train by a German police officer in plain clothes, produced his fake ID, told his prepared story in German and was allowed to carry on his way.

He arrived in the coastal town of Danzig less than a day after he had escaped from Stalag Luft III. All he then had to do to complete his escape was to find a ship that would take him a neutral country and freedom. He began his search of the harbour area looking for a vessel flying the flag of a neutral country. By 18:00, Philpot still had not found a suitable vessel, and so, conscious of not drawing any undue attention to himself, which was a more than likely outcome if he continued his search in the dark, he found a small family run hotel and was greatly looking forward to having a good night's sleep in a warm and comfortable bed. The only downside, and potentially dangerous consequence of this decision, was because hotel rooms were at a premium, Philpot was required to share his room with another male guest, a person who was not only a stranger, but someone who he had no desire to become involved in a conversation with.

The following day, Sunday, saw him carry on his search of the harbour area looking for a suitable vessel. He knew time was of the essence because the longer he hung about the more chance there was he would start drawing attention to himself. In the early evening, he eventually came across a Swedish cargo vessel called the *Aralizz*. The hard part was getting on board the vessel; he could not just walk up the gang plank and ask the captain for permission to come on board. For all he knew there were German soldiers on board to prevent such events from taking place. His only option was to climb up one of the ship's mooring cables and just hope that he was not spotted. Once safely on board he decided it would be better to hide away and wait until the ship was underway before revealing himself. He made his way below decks and hid out in the ship's coal bunker, not knowing how long he would have to wait in there before the ship set sail. He was spotted by some of the crew and taken to the captain, who asked him to leave as his presence on board the vessel was placing both himself and the rest of the crew in danger. Philpot, who was stoic rather than stubborn, and who had not come this far to give up at the final hurdle, refused.

The captain was not a happy man and ordered his crew to escort Philpot off the ship. Luckily for Philpot, a couple of the crew took pity on him and instead of following their captain's orders, him hid in the bowels of the ship. The *Aralizz* finally set sail two days later on the Tuesday morning. Once it was clear of Danzig harbour and out to sea, Philpot once again presented himself to the captain, who by then was not as stressed by his presence.

On Thursday, 4 November, the *Aralizz* arrived in Stockholm where Philpot was handed over to the Swedish police, who in turn handed him over to the city's British Legation. At last Philpot could relax. He was not quite home yet, but he knew he was safe and that it was only a matter of time before he would be back in England.

Philpot did not return to operational flying duties with the RAF, possibly because it was believed he had already 'done his bit'. Instead, he was posted to the Air Ministry where he took up a new role as a senior scientific officer.

For their escape from Stalag Luft III and their successful return to England, all three men were awarded the Military Cross in 1944.

After the war, in 1949, Eric Williams published his book, *The Wooden Horse*, which detailed the famous escape. The following year it was turned into a film of the same name, which Williams also wrote the screenplay for. He continued with his writing and went on to pen a number of successful books based on his wartime exploits.

CHAPTER TEN

Roger Joyce Bushell

Roger Joyce Bushell was born on 30 August 1910 in Springs, Transvaal, South Africa, to Benjamin and Dorothy Bushell. His parents were both English and Benjamin worked in the country as a mining engineer. It was a job that paid handsomely and ensured he could provide his son with a first-class education. Initially attending school in Johannesburg, in 1929 Roger was sent to England to continue his education, eventually ending up at Pembroke College, Cambridge in 1930, where he studied law. Besides being academically bright he was also an excellent sportsman who was equally good at rugby as he was at cricket, and as if that was not enough, he was also an excellent skier.

On 10 August 1932, Roger Bushell received a commission as a pilot officer with the Royal Air Force Volunteer Reserve and Joined No. 601 (City of London) (Bomber) Squadron, Auxiliary Air Force (AAF), which had been formed on 14 October 1925 at RAF Northolt, Middlesex, when a group of young amateur aviators came up with the idea of becoming a Reserve Squadron of the RAF. All the squadron's members came from either wealthy or aristocratic families who could well afford to indulge their sons' desire to fly.

Whilst honing his flying skills, Bushell also continued his legal studies to enable him to become the barrister he had always wanted to be, with his preferred area of expertise leaning him more towards criminal defence cases. His reputation as a bastion of legal proceedings was such that the RAF utilised his court room skills to both prosecute and defend RAF personnel charged with a plethora of both military and or criminal offences.

One of the high-profile cases Bushell became involved in was the Battle of Barking Creek, a friendly fire incident which resulted in the death of the first RAF pilot of the war, and the first aircraft to be shot down by a Spitfire.

The incident resulted in two pilots facing a court-martial, which took place at Bentley Priory in Harrow, the headquarters of Fighter Command in October 1939. At the hearing Bushell was assistant to the lead defence barrister, Sir Patrick Hastings, who successfully defended the two pilots, Byrne and Freeborn, who were both exonerated. The court ruled that the incident was an unfortunate accident. Later in the war, Paddy Byrne was shot down over France in 1940 and ended up alongside Bushell as a POW in Stalag Luft III.

In October 1939, Bushell was put in charge of the newly reformed No. 92 Squadron, which flew out of RAF Tangmere in West Sussex. The aircraft flown by the squadron was the Bristol Blenheim Mk. 1F light bomber, but these were replaced the following March by Supermarine Spitfire Mk. 1s.

The squadron saw its first wartime action on 23 May 1940, during the Dunkirk evacuations, with Bushell being credited with damaging two German Messerschmitt Bf 110 aircraft. However, the day did not end well for him and No. 92 Squadron lost three of their Spitfires that day. As for Bushell, he was forced to land his damaged aircraft in a field near Boulogne, but before he could escape, he was captured by German forces and sent to the Dulag Luft transit camp for all captured Allied airmen, just outside Frankfurt. But rather than wait around to find out what the future had in store for him, Bushell escaped by cutting his way through the camp's wire fence. He made it nearly all the way to the German/Swiss border before he was captured by a German border guard and sent back to the Dulag Luft. However, he was only there for a short period of time before he was sent to Oflag X-C, which was located in the city of Lübeck in northern Germany.

For whatever reason, on 8 October 1941 the decision was taken by the German High Command that all British and Commonwealth officers held at Oflag X-C were to be transferred nearly 250 miles to

Oflag VI-B at Warburg. The transfer of the men concerned, which included Bushell, was by train. In the early hours of 9 October, the train stopped at Hannover and with security measures on board somewhat slack, Bushell and Czechoslovakian Pilot Officer Jaroslav Zafouk took their opportunity and escaped.

With the help of Zafouk's knowledge of the region and individuals he knew, the two men made their way to the Smichov area of Prague in German-occupied Czechoslovakia. Once there they contacted Otto and Marie Zeithammel, who lived with their two grownup children, daughter Blažena, and son Otokar. Both children were members of the Czech Resistance. Bushell and Zafouk stayed with the family for some eight months, whilst arrangements were made to move them safely on in their attempts to ultimately return to England. Because of the amount of time the two airmen spent living in such close proximity with the family in their apartment, it was no surprise when a relationship subsequently blossomed between Bushell and Blažena.

On 19 May 1942, Bushell and Zafouk were betrayed by a family friend and young Czechoslovakian soldier by the name of Miroslav Kraus, who had discovered the two airmen were staying with the Zeithammels and had informed the local Gestapo office, who he was actually working for as a paid informant. It is quite possible that his reasons for informing on the two airmen was out of nothing more sinister than jealousy, as Kraus and Blažena had previously been romantically involved with one another. Bushell and Zafouk were arrested and taken in for questioning at the Gestapo headquarters, located in the magnificent splendour of the requisitioned Petschek Palace. After his interrogation was complete, Bushell was sent to Stalag Luft III, whilst Zafouk remained in Prague. Sadly, for the Zeithammel family, their punishment for hiding Bushell and Zafouk was more severe. Along with other members of the Czech underground movement, they were shot by a firing squad on 30 June 1942, at the Kobylisy shooting range in Prague.

Eight days after Bushell and Zafouk had been captured, Reinhard Heydrich, a high-ranking member of the SS as well as the acting Reich Protector of Bohemia and Moravia, was attacked whilst being driven through the Czech capital and subsequently died of his wounds. The SS were incandescent with rage and wanted revenge. They had concluded, without any actual evidence, that Bushell had somehow been involved in the planning of the attack on Heydrich. Bushell was collected from Stalag Luft III and taken to Gestapo headquarters in Berlin, where they interrogated him about the matter. Regardless of what they may have thought, they were unable to prove that Bushell had been involved in Heydrich's death, and he was consequently returned to Stalag Luft III. Before they had finished with him, the Gestapo let Bushell know, in no uncertain terms, that if he ever came to their attention again, he would be shot.

As for Zafouk, after the Gestapo had finished questioning him, he was sent to Oflag IV-C in Saxony, which was more commonly referred to by its location: Colditz Castle.

The senior officer in charge of Stalag Luft III when Bushell first arrived was Wing Commander Harry Day. Along with Bushell and Fleet Air Arm pilot Jimmy Buckley, Day formed what was known as the camp's permanent British staff, whose job it was to help newly captured airmen adjust to life as a POW. Buckley was in charge of escape operations, with Bushell as his deputy, and along with Day, the three men also served as the camp's all important escape committee.

In October 1942, soon after Bushell's return to Stalag Luft III, the German authorities decided that the camp was becoming overcrowded and that a number of officers would have to be transferred to Oflag XXI-B POW camp at Schubin in northern Poland. Both Harry Day and Jimmy Buckley were amongst those who were transferred out. Group Captain Herbert Massey took over from Harry Day as the senior British officer, and Bushell replaced Jimmy Buckley as head of escape operations.

On 5 March 1943, thirty-four POWs escaped from Oflag XXI-B, including both Day and Buckley. Of these, thirty-two were captured within a matter of days. Buckley and his travelling companion, a young Danish officer by the name of Jorgen Thalbitzer, made it to Denmark and then tried to cross into Sweden by canoe on the evening of 28 March. Thalbitzer's body was later recovered and he was buried at Tibirke in Tisvildeleje, on the north coast of Zealand in Denmark. Buckley's body was never recovered and he has no known grave.

In POW camps where British and Commonwealth officers and men were held, the man in charge of organising escapes was also known as 'Big X'. Bushell, along with all RAF officers, saw it as their duty to try to escape from captivity and then not only to try to get back to England, but also to try to tie up as many German resources as they possibly could. They saw it as their way of waging war, the only way that they could. Bushell determined that if an escape attempt should be made from Stalag Luft III, sufficient resources and effort should be put in so that it could be done on a massive scale. He did not want to get just one or two men out; he wanted to get hundreds out. He decided that three tunnels would be dug simultaneously, so that if one was discovered by the Germans, or for some reason or another if it was no longer possible to carry on digging, work could continue on the other tunnels. In some respects, if the Germans did discover one of the tunnels, it could prove to be advantageous because they would likely have no reason to believe that any others were being built at the same time.

After Bushell had worked out exactly how he was going to proceed with his escape plans, he called a meeting of the camp's escape committee to give them the details of what he had in mind:

Everyone here in this room is living on borrowed time. By rights we should all be dead. The only reason God allowed us this extra ration of life is so we can make life hell for the Hun. In the North Compound we are concentrating our efforts on completely escaping through one master tunnel. No private tunnels are allowed. Three bloody deep, bloody long tunnels will be dug, Tom, Dick, and Harry. One will succeed.

To make his speech as impactive as it could possibly be, he drew on all his court room experience of making opening and closing speeches.

Before the questions came the silence and the confusion, but most importantly of all, Bushell's plans would galvanise the entire North Compound, providing a collective purpose and boosting morale to a level it had never previously been. Nobody had ever planned such a large-scale escape, with most involving just a couple of individuals, possibly three or four at most. It was not just about the number of men who intended to escape, but also the identity cards, money, maps, clothes, cases, dyes, food, water, train and bus timetables, and a back story for each and every one man etc. Before a single man could escape, however, there was the 'small job' of digging the tunnels. That in itself took some planning. Where would the tunnels start from and how would they hide the entrances from the Germans? If they were started from under one of the huts, how would each of them be hidden from prying German eyes, considering there was a gap under each of the huts to prevent such escapes from taking place?

Security was a major consideration in the digging of the three tunnels, but by the very nature of what was being proposed, a large number of those held captive in the North Compound would have had some knowledge of what was going on. The main security objective was to ensure that the German guards did not find out about the existence, or the location, of each of the tunnels. This would test Bushell to the limit, but if one man was ever up to the task, it was him.

CHAPTER ELEVEN

The Tunnels – Tom, Dick and Harry

The three escape tunnels used in the Great Escape were code named 'Tom', 'Dick' and 'Harry'. The origins of the three names being used together as a means of emphasising commonality, or as a description of 'everybody', can be traced as far back as 1657, when they were used by English theologian, John Owen. The names were first mentioned in the Oxford English Dictionary in 1734. Why Bushell, who was in charge of the escape committee, used the names for his three tunnels has never been confirmed, but it is more than likely that the main reason was that he did not want anybody to mention the world 'tunnel' through fear that its very use, if heard by the Germans, would lead them to start searching for one. Bushell let it be known that this was such an important aspect of the escape that he would court-martial anybody he heard using it.

'Tom' began from Hut 123 and 'Dick' from Hut 122. They were situated to the west of the camp, with 'Tom' being the nearest to the camp's perimeter fence, which created concern due to the fact it had to pass right under one of the camp's sentry towers. The total distance of 'Harry' was 102 metres (neither 'Tom' nor 'Dick' were accurately measured as they were never completed: 'Tom' because it was discovered by the Germans and destroyed, and 'Dick' because it was abandoned and used purely for storage and as a workshop). The more obvious of the huts to have dug from would have been Hut 107. This was also on the west side of the camp but was of equal distance between two of the sentry towers.

'Harry', which was dug from Hut 104, was located in the middle of the front of the camp and was possibly the least plausible of the three due the fact it was the longest of the three tunnels and had to pass under an area known as the *Vorlager*, which included additional huts. One of these huts was used as a sick bay, another was a prison block, and a third was used by the Germans for administration purposes. 'Harry' then had to go under the roadway at the front of the camp and continue on to the treeline. It was because of this particular dynamic that Hut 104 was never really suspected by the Germans as being a starting point for a mass breakout.

To ensure the noise of the digging was not picked up by the microphones the Germans had placed below the ground throughout the camp, the shafts leading down to each of the tunnels were dug to a depth of about 30 feet and were no more than 2x2 feet in width and height. This meant that anybody above a certain size simply would not fit through the tunnel entrance. For those who had the job of digging the tunnels, it certainly was not glamorous work. The men were either stripped down to their underwear, or in some cases, naked. They were also not for any individuals who suffered from claustrophobia.

At the base of the entrance shaft was a storage area where supplies and bags of sand that needed to be taken up to the surface were stored. This was also the area used in the latter stages of the tunnelling for items needed on the night of the escape, such as documents, clothing and food and drink. It was almost large enough for a man to comfortably stand-up in. Alongside this there was a small workshop where running repairs could be carried out on equipment needed for use in the tunnel. Adjacent to this was an area for the tunnel's air pump to ensure the men had sufficient air to breathe.

By the time the digging of the tunnels had been completed, somewhere in the region of 100 tonnes of soil and sand had been excavated. Once brought up to the surface, this then had to be distributed around the camp by a number of the POWs. They would walk around with their hands in their pockets, visit one of the numerous little garden plots tended by their colleagues and deposit the load they were carrying, which would then be mixed in with the soil. All of this was done whilst under the constant gaze of the German guards.

To try to prevent the tunnels from caving in, the tunnellers shored them up with wooden slats taken from the prisoners' beds, as well as pieces of wood scavenged from anywhere they could be found, or from wooden furniture scattered around the camp's huts. This aspect of the escape was a massive undertaking. It is estimated that on average, each of the men's beds contained twenty wooden slats which their mattress lay on. Of these, most had to give up twelve for use on the sides and roof of the tunnel. In total, somewhere in the region of 4,000 of these slats were used in the tunnels.

To help with reducing the level of noise caused by the digging, hundreds of the men's blankets were used as a very basic form of sound proofing whilst the shaft and walls of the tunnels were being dug. Although they did not know it, the Red Cross also played their part in the digging of the tunnels as the tins of powdered milk they provided to the camp on a regular basis were used as lamp covers to help light the tunnels, as well as being used as the main digging tools.

One of the main elements which ultimately allowed the tunnels to be dug was the initiative, dogged determination, and combined ingenuity of those involved in the planning and implementation of the escape. Besides having a lighting system in each of the tunnels, there was also a system in place which allowed much-needed fresh air to be pumped in. This was achieved by a makeshift set of bellows put together using a number of different items, such as pieces of wood taken from the men's bunk beds, hockey sticks, knapsacks and tin cans. There was even a pully system in place which allowed the freshly dug soil to be ferried back to the entrance area using a wooden railway, sledge-type trolley. This same system was also used on the night of the escape to get the escapees through the tunnel as quickly as possible.

'Harry' had two change-over points along its length, which were evenly spread out. The first one was known as Piccadilly Circus, and the second, Leicester Square. These were slightly wider points of the tunnel which allowed for men and soil to move in alternative directions at the same time.

The entrance to 'Tom' was located in a corner of Hut 123 next to a stove. The Germans discovered the tunnel by sheer chance on Wednesday, 8 September 1943, when one of the guards had simply entered the hut to speak with some of the POWs and had dropped something on the floor. As he bent down to pick it up, it became stuck in the rim of the trap door that sat on top of the escape tunnel. The game was up. The first thing the Germans did after discovering the tunnel was to take photographs of it. Then, to ensure it could not be used again, they dropped dynamite down it. No more digging would take place underneath Hut 123.

After 'Tom's' discovery, the digging work increased in both 'Dick' and 'Harry'. 'Dick' was hidden in the floor of Hut 122's washroom. In some respects, the escape plans were made somewhat easier with the discovery of 'Tom' because the Germans believed they had prevented whatever escape had been going to take place. They had not considered the possibility that there were other tunnels, in addition to the one they had discovered.

As previously stated, one of the reasons the decision was taken to dig a tunnel from Hut 122 was the fact that it was so far away from the camp perimeter fence and that because of this, the Germans would never suspect prisoners would attempt to dig a tunnel from there.

Unfortunately, the decision to stop digging 'Dick' was taken out of the prisoners' hands following a planned expansion of the camp. The exit to the tunnel would have meant coming up in an area cleared by the Germans. Left with no alternative, the escape committee took the decision to stop work on it and concentrate all efforts on 'Harry'.

'Dick' did not go to waste, however. Although no further digging was carried out on extending the length of the tunnel, it came in very handy to store soil dug from 'Harry', as well as a place to keep supplies and clothes to be used by the men who would take part in the eventual escape. It was also used as a workshop to make a number of items the prisoners would need once they had tunnelled their way out of the camp.

'Harry', whose entrance was hidden under a stove in the middle of Hut 104, had suddenly become the POW's last chance of escape.

When digging was taking place in the tunnel, the stove was always kept on so that it was nice and hot and would therefore deter any of the camp guards from getting too close to it.

If it was felt the German guards were getting too close to one of the huts, or if it looked like they were actually going to enter one of them, an elaborate look out system was put in place. Warnings would be given by one of the lookouts, who would simply turn the page in the newspaper or book they were reading, or by bending down and pretending they were tying up a loosened shoelace.

Many, if not all, of the guards were older men, most of whom were not fit enough for front line service. This meant being a camp guard was a relatively safe environment and one that they were more than happy to have been allocated. If the truth be known, they could not wait for the war to end so that they could return to their families and live out the rest of their lives in peace. So, when any of the guards were offered items such as chocolate, coffee and sugar in return for a piece of information, equipment or some kind of document such as an identity card, they were more than happy to oblige. Documents were particularly valuable as they allowed the camp's forgers to replicate them to the exact standard required.

With the closure of 'Tom' and 'Dick', the 600 men who had been working on the three separate tunnels could now all focus their collective efforts on 'Harry', although the intention was that only 220 of them would have a place amongst those selected to be part of the escape. This decision in itself was no easy task. How did one man earn the right to become part of the escape over someone else?

Of those who had participated in some way in the preparation work, no matter what they had done, the camp's escape committee, led by Roger Bushell, had the unenviable task of coming up with a fair process of selecting those whose names would be added to the list. It was decided that the first 100 would be chosen by the escape committee based on either how much they had contributed, or those who it was felt had the best chance of escaping from the camp and eventually making it back to England. Considerations in this process would have included a man's age, his level of fitness and whether he could speak a foreign language such as French, German or Dutch. The remaining 120 places were chosen by the drawing of lots, to give everyone who had played their part in enabling the escape a fair chance of being a part of it.

For those who did not make the final cut, this would certainly have been a difficult pill to swallow. But the men were professionals and the escape was ultimately all about the greater good, and what would be achieved by managing to get so many men out of the camp in one escape. The effect on morale of those left in the camp would have been a very positive one, knowing that so many of their comrades had managed to succeed, leading to a large number of Germans being involved in trying to recapture them.

CHAPTER TWELVE

Oberst Friedrich Wilhelm von Lindeiner-Wildau, Commandant of Stalag Luft III

❖

At the time of the mass escape from Stalag Luft III in March 1944, the camp commandant was *Oberst* (Colonel) Friedrich Wilhelm von Lindeiner-Wildau, who by all accounts was a fair man and not someone prone to random acts of cruelty or acts of barbarism to those under his control.

The Allied POWs held at Stalag Luft III, nearly all of whom were airmen, were guarded by men from the German Luftwaffe, and not the SS or any other unit of the Nazi war machine. Generally, the relationship between the guards and the POWs was professional, although this is not to suggest that there was any kind of collusion between the two. By the end of 1943 there were seven companies of guards, each consisting of 150 men, allocated to the camp. Besides sentry duties they also had the responsibility of carrying out patrols within the camp, as well as providing escorts if men had to be transferred to outside locations or to another camp. These men were part of the German territorial army and were quite diverse in their military experience. Some were simply too old, or unfit, for front line military service, whilst others were either convalescing after long and arduous deployments or were recovering from wounds sustained in battle. Some were simply the sole surviving son of a

German family. Regardless of how they had come to be guards, most of them were trustworthy and dedicated to their duty.

Although they would never admit it, the Luftwaffe guards had a level of respect for their fellow airmen and treated them accordingly, and certainly to the standard required by the terms of the Geneva Convention. This helped the POWs greatly because the relatively relaxed environment this provided allowed them to continue with their escape attempts with less fear that their tunnelling efforts would be discovered. It was not only the guards who treated the POWs well, however, as the camp commandant also had a good working relationship with the senior British officers.

Because of the relatively close proximity of Stalag Luft III with other camps such as Stalag Luft VIII, and the ever increasing numbers of Allied POWs being held within the camps across the country, there was a concern amongst the German High Command and camp commandants, including von Lindeiner-Wildau, that there was the real possibility the Allies would consider parachuting their men into or near to the camps to liberate the POWs, and provide them with a ready-made army. To this end, in the autumn of 1943 Lindeiner-Wildau requested, and was granted, the provision of a staff officer to be located at Stalag Luft III who would be responsible for such an occurrence, and to look into how best to defend against such eventualities. The man who was eventually selected for the position was *Oberstleutnant* Erich Cordes.

Von Lindeiner-Wildau was born on 18 December 1880 in Glantz, Germany. He graduated from the Corps of Cadets on 15 March 1898 when he was 17 and became a *Leutnant* in the 3rd Foot Guards of the Army of the German Empire. On 2 May 1902 he joined the *Schutztruppe* which was the official name of German colonial troops stationed in the African territories of the German Empire. During this time, he fulfilled several different roles and saw active service during the Maji Maji Rebellion between 1905 and 1907. He re-joined the Prussian Army in July 1908 and later fought bravely during the First World War, being wounded on three separate occasions, and winning the Iron Cross twice.

After the war he left the army and went to work in the civilian sector. When the Nazis rose to power, he was not enamoured with their politics, but with political tensions increasing throughout Germany, it was clear to him that there would be an outbreak of war, sooner rather than later. Although an army veteran, he decided that if he was going to serve his country, he would do so in the Luftwaffe, which seemed to be the wing of the military least affected by his nation's politics. Nevertheless, Herman Göring, who was head of the Luftwaffe and whose general staff von Lindeiner-Wildau found himself a part of, was a high-ranking Nazi and part of Adolf Hitler's inner circle.

Von Lindeiner-Wildau was 58 at the outbreak of the Second World War. He decided that he would prefer to retire rather than fight, and in an attempt to have his request granted, he even suggested he was not well enough to continue serving. His request was refused and instead, he was put in charge of Stalag Luft III, where he took over from the camp's original commandant, *Oberst* Kurt Stephani.

One of the 'perks' of his role as camp commandant was the accommodation, which was allocated for him and his wife just 3 miles west of Stalag Luft III at Schloss Jeschkendorf. It was more like a castle than it was a home and was the type of place that would certainly help a man forget the day-to-day realities of war and the part he played in it.

Lindeiner-Wildau's deputy was *Major* Gustav Simoleit, an extremely intelligent and well-educated individual who in civilian life had been a professor of history. He was also multi-lingual, which included speaking English fluently. Both men were similar in their outlook towards the enemy airmen under their control, which was of a sympathetic and balanced nature; an attitude that in turn filtered down to the camp guards as well. A good example of this was when it came to funerals. Despite a German ban on enemy combatants who died whilst held as a POW receiving full military honours at their funeral, this was something Lindeiner-Wildau and Simoleit were supportive of on such occasions.

Although Lindeiner-Wildau was a compassionate and considerate man, he was not a push over by any stretch of the imagination and ran a relatively tight ship. He was well aware that a number of the prisoners under his control had a record of having escaped from previous camps and would do the same again if given the slightest opportunity to do so. At the end of the day, however, it was better, and easier, for all concerned to have a happy and contented camp rather than a disgruntled one. It is more than likely that not all POWs wanted to escape, especially if it meant having to do so via a tunnel that was 30 feet down and well over 100 feet in length. The feeling of claustrophobia and being trapped in a collapsed tunnel was a sufficient deterrent to prevent many from ever considering it.

At lunchtime on 25 March 1944, having heard that a number of the escapees who had taken part in the Great Escape had been captured and were being held by the police in Sagan, he did his best to have the men brought back to Stalag Luft III. To this end, he contacted the head of the *Kripoleitstelle* at Goerlitz, Special Agent Absalon, who was the person in overall charge of investigating the escape. But he was told that no information on the matter would be given to him, nor would any instruction or order given by him be accepted or actioned.

Once news of the mass escape from Stalag Luft III by the seventy-six Allied POWs became known to the German High Command, von Lindeiner-Wildau was always on borrowed time. He was an intelligent man and knew he would not be allowed to remain in command of the camp.

Von Lindeiner-Wildau was arrested on the evening of 25 March by the Gestapo and was briefly replaced by Major Cordes, his staff officer. He in turn was replaced by Major Gustav Simoleit, who had been the camp's deputy commander under von Lindeiner-Wildau. Simoleit was then replaced by *Oberst* Braune, who arrived to take up his post on 6 April. This process would not have been a shock to von Lindeiner-Wildau, on the contrary, he would have expected such action. He was certainly threatened with court martial, although when diagnosed as apparently suffering mental illness, he avoided being imprisoned and was instead placed under house arrest. This sentence must have been rescinded because in February 1945, he was acting as the second in command of an infantry unit defending Sagan against advancing Soviet forces. He was wounded during the action, but thankfully for him, he was not captured and later surrendered to British forces.

Von Lindeiner-Wildau was detained by the Allies and sent to England for interrogation, specifically about his knowledge of the Great Escape and what happened to those who were recaptured. He arrived at 'the Cage' (the location for the interrogation of prisoners thought to have important intelligence, including captured spies and/or POWs who were non-compliant with POW regulations) on 7 August 1945, and was interviewed by Lieutenant Colonel Alexander P. Scotland, a British intelligence officer who had been recalled to military service and who had also been an interrogator for British military intelligence during the First World War. Without the skills and experienced Scotland possessed, the London Cage would not have become a productive intelligence collection facility. Not only was Scotland a fluent German speaker, but he was also familiar with German culture in both social and military senses.

Von Lindeiner-Wildau spent two years in detention at the London Cage before he was repatriated, having freely provided evidence and information to the RAF's Special Investigation Branch (SIB) into the murdered airmen who had escaped from Stalag Luft III. The investigation was led by the SIB's Wilfred Bowes and Frank McKenna (see Chapter Seventeen). During his tenure as commandant of Stalag Luft III, von Lindeiner-Wildau treated prisoners under his control fairly and certainly adhered to the terms of the Geneva Convention. By the end of the war, he had certainly gained the respect of the senior British officers under his control.

Von Lindeiner-Wildau died on 22 May 1963, aged 82, in Frankfurt.

CHAPTER THIRTEEN

Howard Goolding Cundall and the Radio Transmitter

❖

Although there were POWs involved in the preparation of the mass breakout from Stalag Luft III who did not actually take part in the Great Escape itself, it does not mean that they are unworthy of a mention. One such man is Pilot Officer Howard Goolding Cundall, who was a member of the Telecommunications Research Establishment (TRE). He had volunteered to take part in a Special Signals Investigation nighttime bombing mission over German-occupied France to observe the aircraft's radio and radar systems. To keep their anonymity and to help prevent their real identity and purpose from being discovered by the Germans, the men in the TRE were provided with RAF commissions.

At 18:30 on 5 November 1941, Cundall was on board a Wellington bomber aircraft which took off from RAF Boscombe Down in Wiltshire. The mission was a special signals investigation flight over occupied France. At 20:46 that evening, the aircraft was over Pontivy, Brittany, when it suffered engine trouble. Soon, the propellor of the starboard engine flew off and Cundall and his colleagues had no option but to bail out.

On landing, Cundall hid his parachute and slipped away into the night before German forces arrived. He then managed to stay at large for thirteen days before he was finally spotted and captured in a rowing boat just off the coast at Le Viviers Bay, on 18 November. Fortunately for Cundall, the flight's second pilot was the only one of the crew not to be captured, which then allowed Cundall to masquerade as a pilot thus keeping his qualification, and real reason for being a member of the crew, a secret.

After spending time as a POW at two other camps, Cundall eventually ended up as a POW at Stalag Luft III, where he continued to keep his secret from the Germans. Because of his technical knowledge and abilities, he managed to build a radio transmitter from bits he salvaged from around the camp. This allowed him to contact British authorities in London and provide them with crucial information obtained from captured air crew arriving at the camp, who were able to pass on valuable intelligence about their particular experiences with German night. All this was done right under the Germans' noses and was never discovered. He even managed to continue this contact during the long march from the camp which began in January 1945.

After his liberation and return to the UK, he along with all returning British military personnel had to fill out a security-based questionnaire marked 'Top Secret'. His is dated 24 May 1945.

The front page of the form shows that he was attached to No. 109 Squadron RAF, TRE, and although he had been given an honorary commission as a flight lieutenant (49897) to allow him to carry out 'special flying duties' with the RAF, he was in fact a civil servant and was thus the only British civilian ever held captive as a POW at Stalag Luft III. If the Germans had ever found out his true identity, he would have no doubt been interrogated about the finite details of British radar systems, not to mention the possibility that he could have been shot as a spy.

Question No. 8 of the questionnaire asked whether he had any other matter he might wish to discuss. In reply, Cundall stated that he had been 'Engaged in receiving code messages from AM by W/T (Wireless Transmission) for Stalag Luft III intelligence (East Camp) from August 1943 to end of war with F/Lt Barry, F/Lt Brownson. AC2 Mace. Engaged in construction, maintenance and operation of radio equipment for above and for news service from November 1942.'

CHAPTER FOURTEEN

The Escape Committee and Workers

◆◆◆

The escape committee for any POW camp was made up from the most senior and experienced officers, and for any escape bid to take place, the committee had to approve any plans before any kind of work could begin. It was quickly recognised that if such a process was not put in place, anybody who wanted to escape would simply go off and do their own thing, which would end up in chaos.

Stalag Luft III's first senior British officer (SBO) was Group Captain Harry 'Wings' Day, who at the time of his capture was serving with No. 57 Squadron. In June 1942, Day was replaced as the SBO by the arrival of Herbert M. Massey, who although the same rank as Day, was the more senior group captain.

Squadron Leader Roger Bushell was placed in charge of all escapes from the camp, should any individual wish to progress from an idea to a reality. The rest of the escape committee was made up of Flying Officer Wally Floody, a Canadian who had served with No. 401 Squadron prior to his capture; Peter 'Hornblower' Fanshawe, who had served with No. 803 Squadron, Fleet Air Arm; and finally Flight Lieutenant George Harsh, who was a member of No. 102 Squadron, operating as a tail gunner in a Halifax bomber when he was shot down on a bombing mission over Germany on the night of 5/6 October 1942. Harsh was an American who had enlisted in the Royal Canadian Air Force, and it was fate and good fortune that resulted in him being a POW at Stalag Luft III.

By the time of the mass breakout, Harsh, along with nineteen other POWs, had already been moved to another camp because of suspicions by the German authorities that he and his colleagues were somehow involved in planning an escape.

It was one thing having an escape committee, but for any escape plan to be successful, especially one intended to break out more than 200 POWs, it also required an awful lot of men to carry out the planning and preparation work. This meant finding document forgers, tailors, engineers, tunnellers and intelligence officers. Bushell knew that if his plan was successful, it would have a major effect on Germany's manpower resources, potentially tying them up for months whilst they searched for the escapees. If the truth be known, this was the real intention of the escape and not about getting 200 men back to England.

The major ingredient of such an audacious escape was the tunnel by which the escapees would leave the camp. Fortunately for Bushell, and the escape in general, he had at his disposal Canadian Flight Lieutenant Wally Floody, who before the war had worked as a mining engineer. What better man to have in such a situation?

The man in charge of making escape kits for all the escapees was Johnny Travis, a hard-looking Rhodesian. Originally selected to be one of the tunnellers (back on civvy street he had been a mining engineer), it was soon decided that his brilliance of being able to make much-needed items for the escapees from the most innocuous items, was of more value to the overall success of the escape. With a team working under him, Travis put together items such as compasses skilfully made from melted-down gramophone records and razor blades.

An important piece of equipment for any escapee was a map, one that was as detailed as possible. This was an imperative item if anyone was going to have any kind of chance of staying at large for any period of time. The escape maps were produced by Flight Lieutenant Desmond Plunkett and a team of individuals working underneath him. Attention to detail was extremely important, and one of the things assuring this standard was adhered to was the fact that a number of those taking part in the escape were the same men who had made the maps.

Flight Lieutenant Gilbert William 'Tim' Walenn was in charge of a team of forgers who copied and faked passes and identification documents. Some of the originals were 'borrowed' from the German guards and returned to them before they even realised the items were missing. Some guards were also open to being bribed in return for such items as chocolate or cigarettes. Despite having some kind of idea what those items must have been wanted for, as far as it is known none of the guards informed the camp authorities that they had been approached in such a manner. Documents, especially ID passes, had to be as up to date as possible because the German authorities had a habit of changing them at short notice and without any prior warning to the guards. To make matters even worse, many of these documents were printed in different colours, and when the appearance of a particular document was changed, so was its colour.

Those men who did the tailoring and produced the civilian items of clothing for the escape were led by Flight Lieutenant Tommy Guest. In their original form they were pieces of military uniform that were recut and then dyed different colours, in keeping with civilian clothes of the day.

An extremely important role within the camp was that of internal security. Although the German guards did not know it, every time one of them entered the camp they were followed and watched until they left. POWs were in position at several locations round the camp, in such a way that they could signal ahead to one of their colleagues that a guard was coming their way. This ensured that if any of the POWs were involved in work connected to an escape, they had plenty of time to stop and hide things away before what they had been doing was discovered. The man in charge of the camp's security was Flight Lieutenant George Harsh.

CHAPTER FIFTEEN

The Fifty Murdered Escapees

❖

This chapter looks at the fifty brave airmen who were murdered by the Gestapo on the orders of Adolf Hitler. Where possible, a short biography has been provided for each man to show their life before the war, their capture and their eventual incarceration at Stalag Luft III.

Flight Lieutenant Henry J. Birkland

Born on 16 August 1917 in Caldwell, Manitoba, Canada, prior to the war Birkland had worked a number of different jobs before enlisting in the Royal Canadian Air Force in July 1940, with the intention of being an aircrew member. However, after successfully completing his initial training, he was deemed to be a suitable candidate to undertake pilot training. Having graduated in January 1941, he was promoted to the rank of sergeant and the very next day was commissioned as a pilot officer. Not long after this he was sent to the UK. On his arrival, and to bring him up to speed with the aircraft he would be flying, he was initially posted to No. 57 Operational Training Unit.

On 11 August 1941 Birkland was transferred to Fighter Command's No. 122 Squadron, where he flew Spitfires out of RAF Turnhouse, in Edinburgh. His time there was short lived, as just five weeks later he found himself at RAF Hornchurch as a member of No. 72 Squadron. On 7 November he was flying a mission over Etaples on the occupied French coast when he was shot down by a

German aircraft, captured, and became a POW ending up at Stalag Luft III.

Having previously worked as a miner, Birkland's skills were extremely useful when it came to digging escape tunnels, hence why he became one of the camps leading tunnellers.

Following the mass breakout on the night of 24/25 March 1944, Birkland was one of those who intended to escape solely on foot. Unfortunately, he and his comrades did not make it far from the camp before they were discovered and re-captured and taken to Görlitz prison. From 30-31 March, ten of the recaptured men, including Birkland, were removed from the prison by members of the Gestapo and never seen alive again. It is believed Birkland was murdered by Gestapo officers Lutz and Scharpwinkel (the two men who were primarily responsible for the murder of several of the captured escapees). What was slightly unusual was that the prison at Görlitz is some 35 miles south of the POW camp at Stalag Luft III, but the urn containing Birkland's ashes showed that his cremation had taken place at Liegnitz, 50 miles to the east of the camp.

His remains were reburied at the Old Garrison Cemetery in Poznan, Poland on 30 November 1948. At the time of his death, Birkland was 25 years of age. Like nearly all his fellow comrades who had been executed by the Nazis, he was mentioned in despatches in recognition of his 'conspicuous bravery' as a POW.

Flight Lieutenant Edward Gordon Brettell, DFC

Known as Gordon, Brettell was born on 19 March 1915 in Chertsey, Surrey. After leaving Cambridge University with a Bachelor of Arts degree, he decided on a career as a motor racing driver, but with the outbreak of the Second World War, he put his racing on hold and enlisted in the RAF in January 1940.

After successfully completing his pilot training he was commissioned as a pilot officer on 17 February 1941 and posted to No. 92 Squadron at RAF Tangmere, where he flew Supermarine Spitfires.

Sometime in the early months of 1942, Brettell faced a court martial for flying a single seater Spitfire to a squadron party at RAF

Biggin Hill with his girlfriend, who was in the WAAF, sat on his lap. Unfortunately for Brettell, his arrival at Biggin Hill was witnessed by the base commander, who was far from impressed and reported him for his actions. One of the charges he subsequently faced at his court martial was that of endangering the King's aircraft. In his defence he looked to his friend, colleague and Battle of Britain ace, Tony Bartley for help. Bartley, a test pilot for Supermarine Spitfires, had acquired some mathematical equations from one of the aircraft's chief designers to try to prove that Brettell's aircraft had never been in danger when he had flown it into Biggin Hill. When asked by the prosecution how his evidence could be proven, Bartley replied that he had also flown a Spitfire accompanied with a passenger, just as Brettell had done. This caused a problem for the RAF because they now faced the prospect of having to court martial two highly qualified and much needed pilots. Common sense prevailed and the case was dismissed, but Brettell's punishment was to be posted to another squadron.

By the summer of 1942, he found himself at RAF Lympne in Kent, having been posted to No. 133 (Eagle) Squadron, which other than himself, consisted purely of Americans who had volunteered to serve in Britain's RAF. On 19 August 1942, he was one of the pilots who provided air cover for the famous Allied Commando raid on Dieppe.

On 26 September 1942, he and his comrades were involved in escorting a group of B-17 USAAF aircraft on a bombing mission to Morlaix in northwest France. A combination of anti-aircraft fire and attacking Messerschmidt fighter aircraft saw eleven of the twelve Spitfires of No. 133 Squadron brought down over Brest. Bretell's was one of them. His aircraft crashed into the ground at an estimated speed of 200 miles per hour. He was captured and after spending time in a German military hospital, he ended up as a POW at Stalag Luft III.

Brettell became a member of the camp's escape committee, specifically as a member of the forged documents section, where rubber authenticate stamps were made from items such as heels from the men's own boots.

On 27 March 1943, a year before the mass escape, Brettell and a fellow prisoner, Kingsley Brown, escaped from Stalag Luft III and spent some time at large before being recaptured and returned to the camp.

After escaping from Stalag Luft III as part of the Great Escape, he teamed up with three other escapees and, posing as Lithuanian workers, caught a train travelling towards Danzig. Their luck ran out, however, and the men were recaptured at Schneidemühl (now Piła), in northwest Poland, on 26 March. Brettell and his three comrades were then taken to POW camp Stalag XXB, where they spent the night. The next morning the men were handed over to members of the Danzig Gestapo, who then drove them in two cars to a forest near the village of Pruśce, where they were shot. The bodies of the four men were cremated and their ashes returned to Stalag Luft III. Like most of the other murdered escapees, after the war Brettell's body was buried in the Old Garrison Cemetery in Poznan.

Flight Lieutenant Lester G. Bull, DFC

Born on 7 August 1916 in Highbury, North London, when he was 17 years of age Bull began training to be an architect, but in 1936 he had a change of heart and decided on a career in the RAF instead. He initially enlisted as an aircraftsman 2nd class, but by 1938 had qualified as a pilot and was posted to No. 75 (New Zealand) Squadron, which flew Wellington bomber aircraft out of RAF Marham in Norfolk.

In about June 1940, he was posted to the Aeroplane and Armament Experimental Establishment (AA&EE), located near to the Wiltshire town of Amesbury. As an experienced pilot, he was posted to the base's Blind Approach Training Development Unit to take part in testing and developing what was known as the 'blind approach aid', to help night bomber crews land in inclement weather when returning from missions across occupied Europe. It was on 10 December 1940 that this same unit became the newly formed No. 109 Squadron.

A couple of busy years followed which saw him serve with No. 9 and No. 109 squadrons, and by 13 June 1941 he had risen to the rank of flying officer. A month later, he was awarded the Distinguished Flying Cross in relation to a particularly dangerous tour of duty he had undertaken.

Bull took off in his Wellington bomber at 18:30 on the evening of 5 November 1941, on a special mission to discover the capabilities of Germany's radar sites located along the west coast of France. Whilst flying over the French port of Lorient, the starboard engine of his aircraft cut out, and to make matters worse, the propellor for the same engine fell away from the aircraft. With no other option, he held the aircraft steady to allow his five-man crew to bail out, quickly followed by himself. All six men survived and were captured soon after they had landed. Initially, Bull was sent to Stalag Luft I, which was where he first met Roger Bushell, and it was that same group of men who were moved from there to Stalag Luft III.

Bull's part in the escape was as a tunneller and he had the honour of being the first man out, which meant he was the one who then had to duck back down into the tunnel to let everybody else know they were still some 20 metres short of the treeline of the adjacent forest. Once out, and freedom was a reality, he was with a group of three others who managed to catch a train heading towards Hirschberg, near to the Czechoslovakian border, and then made it on foot into the Reichenberg mountain range where, on 27 March, they were stopped and arrested by a German mountain unit and taken to the local prison. In the early hours of 29 March, Bull, along with his three comrades, was collected from the prison by Gestapo officers and driven away in two cars, never to be seen alive again. An urn containing Bull's ashes subsequently arrived at Stalag Luft III, dated 29 March, with the name of the French town of Brux showing the location of where the cremation had taken place.

Squadron Leader Roger J. Bushell

Possibly one of the most well-known of the Stalag Luft III escapees, Bushell was born on 30 August 1910 in the South African city of Springs. From a wealthy family, his father was a mining engineer, and when he turned 18, Bushell was sent to live and study in England where he studied law at Pembroke College, Cambridge. Besides being academically gifted, he was also an excellent sportsman and excelled as a linguist, fluent in both French and German, the latter of which was extremely useful during his time spent as a POW.

He had first flown in 1932 after joining No. 601 Squadron of the Auxiliary Air Force (AAF), which was part of the Reserve Air Force. Nicknamed 'The Millionaires Mob', the majority of its members were well-to-do young men from wealthy families who paid to be taught how to fly and enjoyed the thrill and the buzz that went with it.

Whilst flying a Spitfire with No. 92 Squadron, he was shot down on 23 May 1940. After escaping from Stalag Luft III, he was recaptured at Saarbrucken and murdered on 29 March 1944 by Emil Schultz, a member of the Saarbrucken Gestapo. Bushell's body was cremated at Saarbrucken concentration camp.

A more detailed account of Bushell's early career, his time as a POW, and his involvement in the mass breakout from Stalag Luft III, can be found in Chapter Ten.

Flight Lieutenant Michael James Casey

Born on 19 February 1918 in Allahabad, India, his father was the inspector general for the province of Uttar Pradesh. After attending school in India, he finished his full-time education in Ireland, and then decided on a career in the RAF, starting off as a flight cadet at the RAF College Cranwell in Sleaford, Lincolnshire. He successfully passed his course and became an acting pilot officer when he passed out on 1 August 1936.

By the time he was 19, he was serving with No. 57 Squadron, who flew Hawker Hind bomber aircraft out of RAF Upper Heyford. By the outbreak of war, No. 57 Squadron had changed over to Blenheim aircraft and Casey had reached the rank of flying officer. Just a matter of days after getting married, in September 1939, Casey's squadron was sent out to France, but his operational wartime service was to be brief.

He took off at 11:00 on 16 October 1939 on a reconnaissance mission, the destination being the area of Wesel-Bocholt in Germany. This had been deemed to be a strategic target by Allied commanders due to it having a major rail bridge crossing the river Rhine, as well as being a major distribution centre for Germany's war effort. By the end of the war, 97% of the town had been destroyed, and its population had been reduced from 25,000 to less than 2,000.

Casey's aircraft was attacked by a Messerschmitt Bf109 fighter aircraft and shot down at Lingen. The aircraft crash landed but was still intact and all three members of the crew survived the impact but were later captured and became POWs.

Casey was initially sent to Stalag Luft I, where he met Roger Bushell, and became part of the group of prisoners known as the 'ghosts'. These men came up with the idea of hiding within the camp and did not attend daily roll calls, making the Germans believe they had escaped. This in turn tied up many German resources who then spent days searching the surrounding areas looking for them.

Along with Bushell and several others, Casey was eventually moved to Stalag Luft III, where he became a member of the camp's escape committee. In relation to the mass breakout in March 1944, his major involvement was the concealment of the forged documents which had been prepared for those taking part in the escape. Because of the frequency of the German searches of the camp and the unpredictability of when they would take place, there was a need not only to repeatedly move these documents to different hiding places around the camp, but also keep them in a number of separate bundles, so that if the Germans did manage to find one of the caches, not everything would be lost.

Having made good his escape, Casey teamed up with another prisoner and together they posed as foreign war workers. They managed to travel more than 37 miles before they were stopped by the local police on the outskirts of Görlitz. Their travel documents were examined but the officers were not happy with what they produced and so arrested them. They were then taken to the local gaol where several other recaptured escapees were already being held.

On the morning of 31 March, six of those being held at Görlitz, including Casey, were taken from the prison by members of the Breslau Gestapo, two of whom were Walter Lux and Wilhelm Scharpwinkel. The men were then driven out of the gaol for some 20 miles to the town of Halbau, where they were then told to get out of the cars before being shot by the side of the road.

Like all the other murdered escapees, Casey's ashes were subsequently returned to Stalag Luft III, before being buried at the Old Garrison Cemetery in Poznan.

Squadron Leader James Catanach, DFC

Born on 28 November 1921 in Melbourne, Australia, Catanach enlisted in the Royal Australian Air Force (RAAF) on 18 August 1940 and after completing his basic training, was sent to Canada to learn to fly. Having successfully completed his training he was commissioned as a pilot officer and in June 1941, and was then sent to England where he was initially posted to No. 144 Squadron, which flew Handley Page Hampden twin-engine medium bombers. He was not with the unit for long before being posted to No. 455 Squadron RAAF, based at RAF Swinderby in Lincolnshire.

At 20:40 on 4 September 1942, Catanach took off from RAF Sumburg in the Shetland Islands, on his way to Murmansk, Russia. His mission was to help protect the Artic convoys, but whilst flying over the North Sea his aircraft was fired upon by a German trawler and he had to make a forced landing near the town of Kirkenes in the north of Norway. Catanach and his crew were captured almost immediately by a German patrol and all ended up as POWs.

Being a fluent German speaker, his chances of staying at large once he had escaped from Stalag Luft III in March 1944 were better than those of his comrades. Catanach and one of the other escapees, a New Zealander called Arnold George Christensen, headed for the neutral country of Sweden. It is known they made it to Berlin by train where they changed trains and then made their way to Hamburg, from where they then caught a further train to Flensburg, close to the German/Danish border. But on the final leg of their journey, their luck finally ran out when they were approached by policemen on the train who began to examine their documents. Not happy, they took the search further and examined their luggage, and unfortunately for Catanach and Christensen, their bags contained escape food and rations. Both men were arrested, along with two others they had been travelling with. Eventually, all four men were arrested and when the train arrived at Flensburg, they were taken to the local prison and interrogated by members of the Kiel Gestapo. It was at this time that the four men were told they were to be driven back to Stalag Luft III the next day.

So, after spending the night in Flensburg prison, the four men were placed in the rear of separate Gestapo vehicles and driven away. Catanach was escorted by three members of the Kiel Gestapo, one of them being *SS-Sturmbannführer* Johannes Post, and another being *SS-Sturmbannführer* Hans Kähler. At about 16:30 on 29 March, the car Catanach was in pulled over to the side of the road on the outskirts of Kiel. Post, who was sat in the front passenger seat of the car, got out and walked a short way into the field, as if he was about to have a wee or smoke a cigarette. Moments later, he beckoned Catanach to join him. After walking only a few paces, Post drew his weapon, aimed it at Catanach's head and pulled the trigger; he was dead before he even hit the ground. A short while later, the cars carrying Flight Lieutenant Christensen, Lieutenant Espeid and Second Lieutenant Fuglesang pulled up behind Catanach's car, whereby the men were ordered to walk out into the field before being immediately shot dead.

For his war time bravery, Catanach was awarded the Distinguished Flying Cross in June 1942, and was also mentioned in despatches for his 'conspicuous bravery' for his time spent as a prisoner of war. His remains were eventually laid to rest in the Old Garrison Cemetery in Poznan.

Flight Lieutenant Arnold George Christensen

Born on 8 April 1922 in Hastings, New Zealand, after leaving full time education Christensen decided on a career in journalism and found employment with the *Hawke's Bay Daily Mail* newspaper. Wanting to be a pilot, he applied to enlist in the Royal New Zealand Air Force on 19 June 1940, just after his eighteenth birthday. He was accepted but it was a year before he began his training, which took place at New Plymouth, on the west coast of the nation's North Island. The aircraft he learned to fly in was the De Havilland Tiger Moth biplane, and although production of them only began in 1939, it was more in keeping with aircraft of the First World War era.

A further eight months of hard and determined training followed before he was awarded his wings, including four months at the No. 4 Service Flying Training School in Saskatchewan, Canada, between 20 October 1941 and 27 February 1942.

In March 1942, he found himself on the move again, this time to England, where he arrived on 2 June and was posted to No. 41 Operational Training Unit at RAF Old Sarum in Wiltshire, where he went to complete his fighter pilot training. Nine weeks later he was posted to No. 26 Squadron at RAF Lympne, which flew North American P-51 Mustangs on reconnaissance missions over occupied France. Just six days after arriving in Kent, he found himself taking part in the Dieppe Raid in August 1942. During the fighting his aircraft was struck by machine gun fire from the German defensive gun emplacements scattered in and around the centre of Dieppe. Realising his aircraft had sustained significant damage, he turned it around and headed for home as quickly as he could, all the time scanning the skies for the potential threat of any German aircraft looking for an easy target. He made it halfway across the English Channel before his engine seized and he had no option but to come down in the sea. Taking to his rubber dingy, he bobbed about in the water for nearly two days, but luck was most definitely not on his side. The Royal Navy did not come to his rescue, and instead, on 21 August, he once again found himself on dry land. Unfortunately for him, the tide had taken him the wrong way and he found himself washed ashore on the coast of France, where he was captured by German soldiers and taken to Stalag Luft III. There he became part of the camp's escape committee, specialising in intelligence. On the night of the Great Escape, once out of the tunnel he teamed up with James Catanach, but both men were later captured and murdered by the Gestapo.

His body was cremated at Kiel and his ashes returned to Stalag Luft III.

Flying Officer Dennis Herbert Cochran

Born on 13 August 1921 in Hackney, London, Cochran enlisted in the RAF in 1941 when he was 20 years of age and initially trained to become an aircrew man, specialising as a radio operator and air gunner. Having successfully completed his training, he decided that he wanted to become a pilot and so after being commissioned as a pilot officer, he was posted to RAF St Eval in Cornwall, where No. 10 Operational Training Unit was stationed. Their aircraft of choice was the Armstrong Whitworth Whitley medium bomber aircraft, with its main purpose being to carry out anti-submarine patrols.

On 8 October 1942, Cochran was on a mission heading for the Bay of Biscay when his aircraft was attacked and shot down by a Junkers Ju 88. The crew survived the crash and managed to find their way ashore on the French coast. Luckily for them, there were no German forces waiting and Cochran managed to stay at large for a month and a day before he was finally captured on 9 November and sent to Stalag Luft III.

He became involved in the preparation of the Great Escape mainly by being an enthusiastic tunneller. He also had the added ability of being able to speak almost fluent German, having started learning it as a small boy. This extremely useful attribute saw him allocated position No. 16 on the list of escapees. Once out of the tunnel, he decided his best chance of making it to a neutral country and then back home to England was by going it alone.

After escaping, his journey took him to Frankfurt and onto Freiburg before he was eventually recaptured at Lorrach, Germany, close to the borders of France and Switzerland, where he was taken to the local police station to be interrogated. The following morning, he was taken to Karlsruhe rather than back to Stalag Luft III. There, he was taken to the *Kriminalpolizei* prison, which was run by the Gestapo under the direct command of *Oberrgierrungsrat* Josef Gmeiner.

Gmeiner instructed one of his men, Walter Herberg, to take two of their colleagues, Heinrich Boschert and Otto Preiss, out into the countryside with Cochran and shoot him. On the morning of 31 March 1944, the three Gestapo officers collected Cochran from his cell and drove him to Natzweiller, where they stopped in a wooded area far from any prying eyes. After removing him from the car, they shot him dead. His body was then taken to the nearby Natsweiler-Struthof concentration camp and cremated, with his ashes being returned to Stalag Luft III before subsequently being buried in the Old Garrison Cemetery at Poznan.

Squadron Leader Ian Kingston Pembroke Cross, DFC

Born on 4 April 1918 in Cosham, Surrey, Cross attended the prestigious Churcher's School, located in the scenic market town of Petersfield, Hampshire, where he excelled both in academics and sports. After completing his education, Cross decided to follow his elder brother, Kenneth, into the RAF, wanting to become a pilot. Commissioned as probationary pilot officer on 21 December 1936, his training began at the No. 8 Flying Training School at RAF Montrose in Scotland on 16 January 1937.

Between 7 August 1937 and July 1940, Cross was a member of No. 38 (Bomber) Squadron, stationed at RAF Markham, and during this time was promoted to the rank of pilot officer on 12 October 1937, and further promoted to the rank of flying officer on 12 May 1939. In July 1940 he became an instructor with No. 11 Operational Training Unit at RAF Bassingbourne, where he remained until 8 August 1941. It was during this time that he was further promoted to the rank of flight lieutenant and awarded the Distinguished Flying Cross for gallantry and devotion to duty in the execution of air operations.

Having pushed his senior officers to allow him to return to operational flying, he was posted to No. 103 Squadron on 9 August 1941. At 14:52 on 12 February 1942, he took off from RAF Elsham Wolds as part of Operation Fuller, to locate and attack German battleships sailing up the English Channel in an attempt to return to their home ports.

During the operation, Cross' aircraft was struck by German naval anti-aircraft fire and was forced to crash land in the North Sea, some 40 miles off the Dutch coast at Rotterdam. Two of the six-man crew were drowned when they were unable to get into the aircraft's lifeboat.

Cross and the remainder of his crew spent twenty-four hours floating in their lifeboat before being rescued by German air-sea-rescue and taken prisoner. Cross was first sent to Oflag XXI-B POW camp, where met Roger Bushell, before both men were transferred to Stalag Luft III. As well as working on all of the 'Tom', 'Dick' and 'Harry' tunnels, he was also in charge of the group of men who carried the soil dug from the tunnels and spread onto the camp's numerous POW gardens and flower beds, as well as the space under the floor of the camps theatre, which was accessed by a hidden trap door placed under one of the seats.

After his escape from Stalag Luft III, Cross was recaptured relatively quickly near Görlitz. He was taken to the town's prison where, along with other recaptured escapees, he was interrogated. On the morning of 31 March, six of the men who had all escaped and been recaptured, including Cross, were driven away from by a number of Gestapo officers. None of the six men were ever seen alive again. Cross' ashes later arrived back at Stalag Luft III. Each of the named urns stated the men had died on 31 March 1944.

Subsequent post-war trials of the members of the Gestapo believed to be responsible for the murders of the fifty Allied airmen, suggested that Walter Lux and Wilhelm Scharpwinkel were jointly responsible for Cross' murder.

Sergeant Halldor Espelid

Born on 6 October 1920 in Askøy, Norway, after his country was occupied by German forces in April 1940, Espelid was determined that he would not just sit back, do nothing and see out the war as a prisoner in his own country. Instead, he wanted to do what he could to help release his country from the tyrannical control of Nazi Germany. His destination of choice was England so that he could join up with the Norwegian Armed Forces in exile and become part of the fight to help free his country. This was all well and good, but there was the small problem of the North Sea preventing him from doing so.

Despite the inherent dangers of what would happen to him if he was caught by the Germans trying to escape, Espelid managed to board the Norwegian merchant vessel *Traust* on 16 September 1940, which then made its way to Shetland, north of mainland Scotland. Once in the UK and cleared by British military intelligence for not being a German spy, he enlisted in the Norwegian Army Air Service.

Rather than undertake their training in the UK, Norwegian pilots and aircrews were sent to Canada, despite the dangers of crossing the Atlantic Ocean during the early months of the war. Espelid was an exceptional student who impressed his instructors with his application, and they recommended he received further training as a fighter pilot. He was also promoted to the rank of sergeant, having just turned 21.

By July 1942 he was serving with No. 331 Squadron who flew Supermarine Spitfires out of RAF North Weald in Essex. The unit consisted of mainly Norwegian pilots, and most of their work involved missions along the western coast of occupied France.

Espelid's aircraft was shot down over the French coast by German anti-aircraft guns on 27 August 1942, causing him to crash land near Dunkirk, where he was captured. He played two parts in the preparation of the mass breakout from Stalag Luft III on the evening of 24/25 March 1944. The first was being tasked by the camp's escape committee to collate any available information about Norway he could find to help those escapees considering heading there once they had tunnelled out of the camp. His other role was that of a tunneller on 'Harry'.

Once outside the camp, he teamed up with three other escapees. On 26 March, whilst on their third train journey, which was taking them from Hamburg to the coastal town of Flensburg, they were stopped by a diligent German police officer who, on scrutinising their documentation and searching their belongings, arrested Espelid and his three colleagues. All four men were taken to Flensburg prison and interrogated by members of the Kiel Gestapo. On the morning of 29 March, the four Allied airmen were told that they were going to be driven back to Stalag Luft III. During the journey, the Gestapo vehicles pulled over to the side of the road and the airmen were instructed to get out and stretch their legs. In a matter of seconds, all four were dead, having been shot in the head by their Gestapo captors. After their bodies were cremated at Kiel, the men's ashes were returned to Stalag Luft III, but their remains were subsequently reburied at the Old Garrison Cemetery in Poznan.

Flight Lieutenant Brian Herbert Evans

Born on 14 February 1920 at Shaldon, Devon, his father, Herbert Evans, was a captain for the Clan Line Steamer Company for what was then the Mercantile Marine.

Evans had become enamoured with flying in his early teens, and joined the Cardiff Aeroplane Club aged 18, where he subsequently qualified obtained his pilot's licence on 7 February 1939. Six months later he enlisted in the RAF and his operational service began in April 1940, when he was posted to No.14 Operational Training Unit, stationed at RAF Cottesmore in Rutland. The unit's purpose was to conduct anti-submarine patrols, mainly in the English Channel. On 30 September he was posted to RAF Scampton in Lincolnshire, where he became a member of No. 49 Squadron which flew Handley Page Hampden, twin-engine, medium bombers.

On 16 October, Evans was involved in a remarkable incident, made even more so because he was still only 20 years of age. While on a mine-laying mission directed on Bordeaux harbour, his aircraft was struck by ground-based anti-aircraft fire. Despite sustaining severe wounds, he still managed to fly his damaged aircraft back across the English Channel and make his way to RAF Lenham in Kent, where he crash landed. Despite the experience and his wounds, he was back flying the following month.

On the evening of 6 December 1940, Evans took part in a mission to bomb German airfields in occupied northern France. During the raid, his aircraft suffered anti-aircraft damage and to add insult to injury, the aircraft were forced to fly into a snowstorm, which was so bad and prolonged that it caused the engines to freeze and eventually stall. This resulted in the aircraft having to crash land near the town of Courville in northern France. All the crew survived the landing, although one or two of them sustained a few bumps and bruises. They were all arrested within a matter of hours and initially taken to Stalag Luft I POW camp in Barth, northeast Germany, although Evans was subsequently moved to Stalag Luft III.

Evans' involvement in the planning of the mass breakout from the camp came in the form of being a regular tunneller. After the escape, he was recaptured and then incarcerated in Görlitz prison where he and others were interrogated by members of the local Gestapo. On the morning of 30 March, Evans was one of a number of recaptured escapees who were collected from the prison and never seen alive again. When his ashes eventually arrived at Stalag Luft III, the urn was marked that cremation had taken place in the city of Liegnitz, in southwestern Poland.

Second Lieutenant Nils Jørgen Fuglesang

Born on 7 October 1918 in the Norwegian fishing village of Rasvåg, Fuglesang was a well-educated individual who, before the outbreak of the Second World War, was working as an apprentice in the shipping business. After the German invasion and subsequent occupation of his country, like many young Norwegians he was not prepared to sit back and suffer in silence. He wanted to make his way to England and enlist in the Norwegian Army Air Service (NAAS) and so obtained passage on board the Norwegian vessel *Heimjfell*, which sailed out of Kyammen on 12 March 1941, and made his way to Shetland.

After being interrogated by British military intelligence on his arrival and convincing them of his identity and intentions, he was released and was accepted by the NAAS and sent to Toronto, Canada for training. After successfully completing his course, not only had he been recommended for further training as a fighter pilot, but he had also been promoted to the rank of lieutenant. He was posted to No. 332 Squadron at RAF North Weald, flying Supermarine Spitfires along with other Norwegian pilots.

On the evening of 2 May 1943, Fuglesang and his colleagues set off on a mission to southwest Holland. On arrival, they were met by a group of Luftwaffe Focke-Wulf Fw 190 fighter aircraft, one of which shot down Fuglesang's aircraft, forcing him to crash land. After being captured by German ground troops, he became a POW.

His role in the preparation of the mass breakout from Stalag Luft III was as part of the tunnelling team on 'Harry', and more importantly, the boarding up of the tunnel.

After escaping, he teamed up with fellow Norwegian Halldor Espelid, James Catanach and Arnold Christensen and met the same fate. After being captured at Flensburg, he was murdered on 29 March 1944 by Johannes Post, a member of the Kiel Gestapo. He was cremated at Kiel and his ashes were returned to Stalag Luft III. In 1948 his ashes were returned to his hometown of Rasvåg, where he was finally laid to rest at Hildra cemetery.

Lieutenant Johannes Stephanus Gouws

Born on 13 August 1919 into an Afrikaans speaking family in Bultfontein, Orange Free State, South Africa, after finishing his full-time education Gouws applied to join the South African Air Force (SAAF) but was turned down because his ability to speak and understand English was not up to the required standard. Rather than give up on his dream, he returned to his education and improved his English skills sufficiently enough to be accepted on his second application in May 1940.

After successfully completing his aircrew training and having been commissioned as a second lieutenant, he was posted to No. 41 Squadron SAAF, who flew Hawker Hartbees aircraft, and sent to Abyssinia. Just five months later, however, in September 1941, he was back in South Africa having been posted to No. 40 Squadron SAAF, before being sent out to Borg El Arab in Egypt.

On 9 April 1942, whilst still in Egypt, Gouws was flying an American single-engine, single-seater P-40 Tomahawk on a mission over the Chichiba-Esseiat region, when his aircraft was attacked by two German Messerschmidt Bf 109 aircraft. Gouws was extremely fortunate. With his aircraft having sustained significant damage, he was out of the fight, but managed to keep control of his machine, which was already on fire, long enough to safely crash land it just south of Mteifel Chebir and survive the impact. Captured, he became a POW and ended up at Stalag Luft III.

Besides being able to speak and understand German, he played an active role in the mass escape preparation. His role was to hide the tunnelled soil in pouches on the inside of his trousers and disperse it at different locations around the camp. Most of the discarded soil was dropped onto flower gardens or vegetable plots and then dug in by those tending them before it could be spotted by the ever-watchful German camp guards. This action alone was sufficient to get him allocated as one of the first ten men into the tunnel. Having made it out of the camp into the surrounding forest, Gouws, who was teamed up with fellow South African Rupert Stevens, made his way to Breslau (now Wrocław) in southwest Poland. He was recaptured at Lindau, Bavaria, and then taken to Gestapo headquarters in Berlin to be interrogated. Neither Gouws nor Stevens was ever seen alive again.

At the subsequent post-war trial in relation to the murder of the fifty Allied airmen, it came to light that the person who murdered Gouws on 29 March 1944 was Johann Schneider of the Munich Gestapo.

Flight Lieutenant William Jack Grisman

Born on 30 August 1914 in Hereford, England, Grisman's father, William, had served as a private in the Norfolk Regiment during the First World War.

Grisman joined the RAF in 1931, prior to which he had worked as an engineer. He began his military service as an aircraft apprentice at RAF Halton, before graduating in December 1933. By 1936 he was working as a leading aircraftsman and was stationed in Iraq. In 1938 he was with No. 28 Squadron working as a rigger/fitter, before applying to begin aircrew training as an observer at RAF Mildenhall, Suffolk. Two months before the outbreak of the Second World War he was posted to No. 99 Squadron, whose aircraft of choice was the Wellington bomber, before being commissioned as a pilot officer on 20 December 1940. He was next posted to No. 109 Squadron at RAF Boscombe Down, where he helped in the development of the RAF'S Blind Approach Aids and Radio Counter Measures.

At 18:30 on 5 November 1941, he was an observer on board a Wellington aircraft to locate German radar facilities situated along the west coast of France. The pilot of the aircraft was Flying Officer Leslie George Bull, who also took part in the Great Escape from Stalag Luft III. After the aircraft's starboard engine failed over the port of Lorient, the six-man crew were forced to bail out. All of them survived the jump but were captured by the Germans, resulting in Grisman becoming a POW, initially at Stalag Luft I. It was there that Grisman first met Roger Bushell, and both men, along with Bull, were subsequently moved to Stalag Luft III. Grisman became a very popular figure in the camp when he brewed potato skins to make 'moonshine', which was drunk on special occasions such as Christmas.

He was one of the men involved in the digging of 'Harry', and was designated as one of the 'marshals' whose job it was to wait in the woods after he had exited the tunnel, gather up a pre-selected group of ten other escapees, and then lead them westwards.

He was recaptured by the Germans on the road to Görlitz and was taken to the town's prison, where he arrived on 28 March. One of the other recaptured escapees, Tony Bethell, heard a truck arrive at the prison on the morning of 6 April. He then heard the names of six of his recaptured colleagues called out, one of which was Grisham. No subsequent evidence has ever been found of when, where and by whom these six men were killed, although the ashes of all six were returned to Stalag Luft III, where they were initially buried. Grisman's remains were later reburied at the Poznan Old Garrison Cemetery.

For his 'conspicuous gallantry' as a POW, Grisham was later mentioned in despatches.

Flight Lieutenant Alastair Donald Mackintosh 'Sandy' Gunn

Born on 27 September 1919 in Auchterarder, Scotland, after completing his education Gunn became an apprentice engineer with Harland and Wolff ship builders in Glasgow. Just a year into the apprenticeship, he left to take up a place at Cambridge University to study mechanical sciences.

He enlisted in the RAF on 22 February 1940 and having completed his initial training, began his active service on 22 June as an airman 2nd class. On 18 January 1941, he was promoted to the rank of sergeant, and just one week later was commissioned as a pilot officer and joined No. 48 Squadron RAF, part of Coastal

Command, and spent most of his time flying photo reconnaissance missions. By January 1942 he was flying Spitfires out of RAF Wick in Scotland, most of his missions taking him towards occupied Norway.

Flying a Supermarine Spitfire, Gunn took off from RAF Wick on the morning of 5 March 1942 on a photo reconnaissance mission along the Norwegian coastline near Trondheim. On arrival he quickly came under attack by two German Messerschmitt Bf 109s. Knowing that his aircraft was badly damaged and partly on fire, he bailed out before it crashed into the ground near Langurda. On making it safely to the ground, he was captured by the Germans and eventually taken to Stalag Luft III.

Somewhat bizarrely, Gunn was promoted to the rank of flight lieutenant on 24 January 1943, some eleven months after becoming a POW, a promotion that was recorded in the edition of the *London Gazette* dated 24 January 1943.

Gunn was one of the six men who were removed from Görlitz prison on the morning of 6 April 1944 and never heard of again.

Warrant Officer Albert Horace Hake

Born on 30 June 1916 in Sydney, Australia, Hake enjoyed his school years and left with an ambition to do well for himself. But like most young men of his age, his ambitions were curtailed by his country's involvement in the Second World War. In July 1940 he joined the Royal Australian Air Force Reserve and was called up for wartime service the following January. Initially he was considered as potential aircrew, but his dogged determination saw him go on to qualify as a pilot on 20 August 1941. With the war quickly progressing, the following month he found himself on board the commandeered ocean-going liner, *Athlone Castle*, heading for England.

On his arrival, he was posted to No. 53 Operational Training Unit based at RAF Llandow in Wales, where he flew Supermarine Spitfires. After having successfully completed his training, he was posted to No. 72 Squadron at RAF Biggin Hill and escorted bomber aircraft as they carried out raids on nominated targets throughout northern France and the Netherlands.

Having taken off along with twelve other Spitfires from Biggin Hill at 09:36 on 4 April 1942, he was part of an operation known as a 'Circus 119' mission, which in essence was the escorting of daytime bomber raids against short-range targets across the English Channel. On this occasion, Hake and his colleagues were tasked with escorting twelve Boston light bomber aircraft from No. 88 Squadron, who had been sent to Saint-Omer in France to attack the town's railway station. On arrival at the target location, Hake's aircraft was hit by anti-aircraft ground fire, as well as the machine gun fire of a Focke-Wulf Fw 190. The attack caused irreparable damage to his aircraft and resulted in him having to bail out. As misfortune would have it, he landed right next to a group of German soldiers who had witnessed the dog fight in the skies above them. Having seen him bail out of his Spitfire, the Germans apparently assumed that Hake, who was a sergeant, was in fact an officer, and treated him accordingly, a mistake that Hake was certainly in no hurry to point out to his captors. After first having had some minor wounds and burns treated at a German military hospital, he was sent to Stalag Luft III, where after a short period of time he became involved with the camp's escape committee. His main duties involved forging German travel documents for use by the escapees once they had made it outside the wire. He also developed and produced several compasses that were carried by all of the escapees.

On the evening of 24 March 1944, Hake was one of those who nervously made their way through the tunnel some 30 feet under the ground, only to discover that when they climbed out of the other end, they were still some 20 feet or so away from the safety of the surrounding woods. Hake joined up with New Zealander Porkoru Patapu Pohe, who was more commonly known as 'John'. By the time the two men had been recaptured on 26 March, they were both badly frostbitten and bordering on the brink of exhaustion. They were initially taken to the police station at Sagan, where they were put in a cell with fellow escapee Flight Lieutenant Max Pemberton Ellis. On 29 March Hake and Pohe were seen at the civilian prison at Görlitz by Flight Lieutenant Shand, who survived the escape but was later returned to Stalag Luft III. Hake was one of those taken from the prison the following day and never seen alive again. When the urn containing his ashes was delivered to Stalag Luft III, its label stated that Hake's body had been cremated at Görlitz on 31 March 1944.

Flight Lieutenant Charles Piers Egerton Hall

Born on 25 July 1918 at Kings Norton, Birmingham, Hall enlisted in the RAF on 11 February 1935 and began training as a photographer at RAF Halton in Buckinghamshire. He remained on photographic duties until 19 August 1940, when he began his training to become a pilot at RAF Paignton in Devon. This was immediately followed by flight training at RAF Hullavington in Wiltshire and on the successful completion of this training, he was commissioned as a pilot officer on 17 April 1941 and posted to the 1st Photographic Reconnaissance Unit (PRU) based at RAF Benson in south Oxfordshire.

On 28 December 1941, Hall took off a mission to photograph bombed out factories in Dusseldorf and Essen but never reached his destination. Instead, his aircraft came down over Bergen op Zoom and Hall was taken prisoner.

Like other POWs at the camp, Hall was promoted whilst he was incarcerated, not once but twice. On 17 April 1942 he was promoted to the rank of flying officer, and exactly one year later was further promoted to flight lieutenant.

After being recaptured following the escape he was executed by the Gestapo on 31 March 1944 and his body cremated at Liegnitz. Whilst being held after his recapture, he wrote the following on the wall of his cell at Görlitz prison: 'We who are about to die, salute you.'

After the war, his remains were buried at the Old Garrison Cemetery in Poznan.

Flight Lieutenant Anthony Ross Henzell Hayter

Born on 20 May 1920 at Farnborough, Hampshire, Hayter's father, Herbert, had been a military man who retired at the rank of lieutenant colonel, having served in both the Second Boer War and the First World War, and who was awarded the Distinguished Service Order.

Hayter enlisted in the RAF in 1938, having first discovered a love for flying some nine years earlier when he had the opportunity to fly in a bi-plane owned by his elder stepbrother. He qualified as a pilot on 13 May 1939 and was commissioned as an acting pilot officer, the temporary promotion was announced in the *London Gazette* on 9 June 1939.

He was confirmed as a pilot officer on 6 November 1939, and in April the following year joined No. 57 Squadron, based in Montdidier in northern France. During the following three years Hayter was posted to several different squadrons, mainly flying bomber-type aircraft, such as the Wellington.

Stationed in Malta, and by then a flight lieutenant, Hayter took off from RAF Luqa at 20:45 on 23 April 1942, flying a Vickers Wellington bomber aircraft with No. 148 Squadron. The mission was to bomb strong enemy defensive positions at Comiso, Sicily. Both Hayter's aircraft and another involved in the operation were shot down, but out of both crews, Hayter was the only one to survive. Having parachuted to safety, he was captured and ended up at Stalag Luft III, where he was allocated to Hut 120 and joined the camp's escape committee. He took on the role of map maker and also learnt conversational German.

Having planned his escape route in detail, he intended to make his way to Switzerland either through Germany or France. Following the escape, he made his way to the French town of Mullhouse, with his cover story being that he was a Danish businessman. After resting for two days he moved on, his next destination being Basel in Switzerland. However, en route he was stopped in the town of Zillesheim and a close inspection of his documentation showed them to be forgeries. He ended up at Strasbourg police station where he was interviewed and revealed his true identity. He was then told that he was being taken back to the camp at Sagan and was placed in the back of a car. Sadly, Stalag Luft III was never the car's intended destination. As they approached the French town of Natzweiler, the car pulled over to the side of the road and a bullet to the back his head ended Hayter's life. His body was taken to a nearby concentration camp where it was cremated. It was only his ashes that made it back to Stalag Luft III.

Flight Lieutenant Edgar Spottiswoode Humphreys

Born on 5 December 1914 in Exmouth, Devon, Humphreys had a keen interest in flying from a young age, so keen in fact that he passed the required tests to gain his Class A pilot's licence before he was 17, making him the youngest pilot throughout Europe. On reaching his eighteenth birthday, he enlisted in the RAF and was sent to the No. 1 School of Technical Training at RAF Halton, and after having successfully completed his training, graduated as an aircraftman 2nd class in 1935.

Humphreys was commissioned as a pilot officer on 19 July 1940, having earned his pilot's wings and been promoted to the rank of sergeant. He was posted to No. 107 Squadron at RAF Wattisham in Suffolk, where he flew Bristol Blenheim light bomber aircraft.

Flying a Bristol Blenheim bomber, Humphreys took off from his home base on the evening of 19 December 1940 to bomb a German airfield in the town of Lannion, in the Brittany region of France. During the raid the aircraft was brought down and the crew, all of whom survived, were captured and became POWs. Although initially held at Stalag Lift 1, where he first met the likes of Bushell, Grisham and Bull, Humphreys eventually ended up at Stalag Luft III.

Having been one of those involved in the digging of 'Harry', Humphreys was allocated place number fifty-four in the queue of those escaping on the night of 24/25 March 1944. Once out of the tunnel, at just after 02:30 and safely in the surrounding woods, Humphreys joined a group of others before linking up with Paul Royle, who had been the man behind him in the tunnel. The pair started heading south but their luck soon ran out when, at 03:00 on 26 March, they were stopped and arrested just outside Tiefenfurt by members of the German Home Guard. They had travelled just 16 miles from the camp. Having initially been detained at the local police station along with a few other recaptured escapees, they were moved again, first to the police station at Sagan, and from there on to Görlitz prison.

On the morning of 31 March, a German military truck arrived at the prison and Humphreys, along with nine other captured escapees, climbed on board never to be seen again. The truck had not travelled far when it suddenly pulled over to the side of the road and the escapees were ordered out of the back and shot dead in a nearby clearing. The bodies of the murdered airmen were loaded back up onto the lorry and taken to nearby Liegnitz, where they were cremated.

Flight Lieutenant Gordon Arthur Kidder

Born in St. Catherines, Ontario on 9 December 1914, Kidder was an intelligent young man who particularly excelled when it came to languages; he studied French and German at the University of Toronto.

He enlisted in the Royal Canadian Air Force on 8 January 1941, specifically to train as aircrew rather than a pilot. However, by the time he had successfully finished his training, he had qualified as a navigator.

Having been sent to England soon after the completion of his training, he initially found himself stationed at RAF Pershore in Worcestershire as part of No. 23 Operational Training Unit. From there he found himself posted to RAF Mildenhall as a member of No. 149 Squadron, but due to a shortage of aircraft, his stay there was brief. By September 1942, Kidder found himself stationed at RAF Warboys in Huntingdonshire as part of No. 156 Squadron, which as part of the RAF's No. 8 Group, became one of the original pathfinder squadrons.

On the evening of 13 October 1942, Kidder and the crew of a Wellington Mark III medium bomber took off from RAF Warboys, along with seven other aircraft from No. 156 Squadron. They were part of a force of 288 RAF bombers on a mission to bomb the German coastal city of Kiel, but things did not quite go according to plan for Kidder and his comrades. Soon after dropping their bombs, they were caught by German searchlights and before they could escape, were hit by anti-aircraft fire that knocked out one of their engines. Now it was a race against time to get back to their base as quickly as possible due to the potential damage to their other engine. Their worst fears quickly became a reality whilst crossing the North Sea, when the remaining engine cut out leaving the aircraft nothing more than an extremely heavy glider. Not long afterwards, their aircraft crashed into the sea with such force that three of the five-man crew, flight sergeants Jack Taylor, William Wesley Lott and Donald Willard Congdon were killed. Only Kidder, who broke his ankle in the forced landing, and the air gunner, Sergeant Edward Earle MacDonald of the Royal Canadian Air Force, survived. Once the two men had established that they were the only ones who were still alive, they inflated a dingy and exited the aircraft before it sank. After spending several hours bobbing about in the icy cold waters of the North Sea, they were rescued by a German vessel. The bodies of Lott and Congdon were also recovered, but unfortunately Taylor's body was lost to the sea.

Kidder spent a period of time in a German military hospital whilst he recovered from his broken ankle, before eventually ending up as a POW at Stalag Luft III.

When it came to the mass escape on the evening of 24/25 March 1944, Kidder, who had originally been paired up with Dick Churchill for the escape, was number twenty of those through the tunnel. Immediately behind him was Squadron Leader Thomas Gresham Kirby-Green, who it was latterly decided Kidder would pair up with for the escape. Once out of the tunnel and into the nearby woods, Kidder and Kirby-Green, who were posing as Spanish labourers, headed for the nearby railway station at Sagan, where there were also several others who had escaped from the camp. They all caught the 03:30 train headed for Breslau and after arriving later that morning, they proceeded to catch another train heading towards Czechoslovakia, with the idea to then catch a further train on to either Yugoslavia or Hungary. However, they were arrested at Hodonin in southern Moravia, close to the Austrian border, on 28 March, and taken to the nearby prison at Zlín. Having been interrogated by local Gestapo officers, they were placed in the rear of separate cars and taken towards Moravská Ostrava, where they were shot by the side of the road. Their bodies were then cremated at a nearby crematorium and their ashes returned to Stalag Luft III.

The circumstances surrounding the deaths of both Kidder and Kirby-Green came out during the hearing of a British Military Court case which took place in Hamburg between 1 July and 3 September

1947. A total of eighteen Germans, mainly members of the Gestapo, were put on trial and faced a total of nine charges, six of which were to do with the murder of the fifty Allied officers. Charge number nine directly related to the murders of both Kidder and Kirby-Green, and saw Erich Hermann August Zacharias, a former member of the Zlín Gestapo, charged with the murders of both men.

Zacharias made a statement to the British authorities that Berlin had ordered the two British officers were to be shot because they were saboteurs and spies. In his evidence to the court, Zacharias claimed that he did not carry out the killing because he had been ordered to do it, but because the British officer he was responsible for had 'made a determined attempt to escape'. Zacharias' driver, a man by the name of Friedrich Kiowsky, also made a similar statement. It is believed that Kidder was the British officer that Zacharias shot. Zacharias was found guilty of murder and was sentenced to death by hanging. He was subsequently executed at Hamelin prison at 10:50 on 26 February 1948.

Flight Lieutenant Reginald Victor 'Rusty' Kierath

Born on 20 February 1915 in Narrowmine, New South Wales, Australia, Kierath's father, William, owned the town's general store and was of German descent.

He had worked in banking before enlisting in the Australian Army after the start of the Second World War. First posted to the 17th Battalion, a year into the war he decided he wanted to become a pilot. After having completed his preliminary flight training in Australia, he was then sent to Rhodesia to undertake his full flight training, which he successfully completed on 10 June 1941. Two months later he was posted to No. 33 Squadron at Amriyah, Egypt, where he flew Hawker Hurricanes. On 8 January 1942, Kierath was posted to No. 450 Squadron RAAF, which at the time was an operational training unit located in Borg El Arab in Egypt, before moving on to RAF Gambut in Libya in February.

On 23 April 1943, whilst flying a P-40 Kittyhawk fighter bomber aircraft, Kierath was involved in attack on German shipping off Cape Bon in northeast Tunisia when his aircraft was struck by

German anti-aircraft fire, causing its engine to seize and Kierath to parachute to safety. He was in the water for more than two hours before he was rescued and taken prisoner.

On the night of the mass escape from the camp, Kierath was part of a group of twelve escapees posing as lumber mill workers on their way home on leave. When they arrived at Tschiebsdorf railway station, one of the group, Polish navigator Jerzy Mondschein, bought tickets for the 06:00 train to Boberrohrsdorf. Having arrived there at 09:00, the group split up and Kierath and three others, Willy Williams, Leslie George Bull and Jerzy Mondschein, made their way through the Riesengebirge mountain range with the intention of crossing into Czechoslovakia. Before they could make it, however, they were stopped and arrested by a German mountain patrol and taken to Richenberg prison.

In the early hours of 29 March, Kierath, Mondschein, Williams and Bull were handed over to members of the local Gestapo, believing they were going to be taken back to Stalag Luft III. However, when they reached Hirschberg, they were told to get out of the vehicle and were shot. Their bodies were cremated and their ashes returned to the camp at Sagan.

Major Antoni Wladyslaw Kiewnarski

Affectionately known by his RAF colleagues as 'Tony', Kiewnarski was born in Moscow in 1899, but had served in the Polish Army during the First World War.

By the time the Second World War began, Kiewnarski had become part of the Polish Air Force. After his nation had been invaded by both Germany and Russia, rather than allow himself to be detained and placed in a POW camp, or worse, he decided to make his way to England. To this end he joined the Free Polish Air Force and served as a flight lieutenant with No. 305 Polish Bomber Squadron *Ziemia Wielkopolsa*, who flew Wellington bombers out of RAF Ingham.

On the evening of 27 August 1942, he took off from his base at RAF Ingham in his Mark IV Vickers Wellington bomber, on a mission to take out a nominated target at Kassel in Germany, but on the way there, his aircraft was shot down over Eindhoven in the Netherlands by a German fighter aircraft. Three members of the five-man crew were killed. Only Kiewnarski and the aircraft's wireless operator, Sergeant Frankowski, survived, with the latter being wounded in the attack. Both men were captured and became POWs. After receiving hospital treatment for his wounds, Frankowski not only managed to escape but made his way safely back to England. As for Kiewnarski, he ended up at Stalag Luft III and was one of those who escaped on the evening of 24/25 March 1944. Once out of the tunnel, he was in a group of men which included Reginald Kierath.

After the group had caught a train as far as Boberrohrsdorf, they split up into pairs and Kiewnarski found himself with fellow Polish airman, Kaz Pawluk. After catching another train, they made it as far as Hirschberg only to be arrested by local civilian police as they walked through the town. They were taken to the police station where they were interrogated about who they were, where they had come from, and what they were doing in the town. They were then moved to the local prison where other recaptured escapees were being held, but two days later, on 31 March 1944, they were suddenly removed from the jail by members of the local Gestapo. After a short drive they were told to get out of the vehicle and were both shot dead with a single bullet to the back of their heads. Kiewnarski's remains are now buried in Poznan's Old Garrison Cemetery, while his name is commemorated on the Polish Air Force Memorial at RAF Northolt.

Squadron Leader Thomas Gresham Kirby-Green

Born on 27 February 1918 in what was then the British Protectorate of Nyasaland, now Malawi, Kirby-Green's father, Sir William, was the British District Governor in Dowa, where Kirby-Green junior was born.

During his early teenage years his father sent him to boarding school at Dover College in England, and after finishing his education, he went to live with his parents, who at that time were living in Tangier. Whilst there he took flying lessons and qualified as a pilot, before going on to receive a commission in the RAF on

24 August 1936. He undertook his initial training at the No. 8 Flying Training School in Montrose, Scotland, before going on to serve with No. 216 Squadron in Egypt. His confirmation as a pilot officer was announced in the *London Gazette* dated 29 June 1937.

The next couple of years saw him attached to several different RAF squadrons, including No. 99 Squadron, who operated Wellington bomber aircraft out of RAF Mildenhall; No. 9 Squadron, who also flew Wellingtons, out of RAF Honington; and No. 311 Squadron, who flew Wellington bombers out of RAF East Wretham as part of Bomber Command's No. 3 Group.

In September 1941 he returned to operational duties after being on training duties for the previous six months. After reaching the rank of acting squadron leader, he found himself a member of No. 40 Squadron, who operated Wellington Mark lc bomber aircraft out of RAF Alconbury.

At 01:06 on 17 October 1941, Kirby-Green took off on his thirty-seventh mission to bomb German factories in Duisburg. Having dropped their bombs on the intended target, Kirby-Green and his crew turned for home, but their Wellington was shot down by anti-aircraft fire and crashed landed at Kirchellen, Germany. Kirby-Green was the only member of the crew to survive. The other five men were all killed and buried at the Reichswald Forest War Cemetery.

Kirby-Green's capture was deemed to be somewhat of a coup by the Germans, to such a degree that on 16 November, they had the American-born Irish-British Nazi collaborator, William Joyce (also known as Lord Haw Haw, because of his upper-class English accent), announce it over German radio.

Kirby-Green eventually found himself a POW at Stalag Luft III, where he became the senior security officer for the camp's escape committee. He also took his turn at tunnelling duties.

After escaping in March 1944, he shared the same fate as Gordon Kidder.

Flying Officer Włodzimierz Adam Kolanowski

Born on 11 August 1913 in Pawlowice, Poland, less than 60 miles away from the location of Stalag Luft III, in 1934 Kolanowski enlisted in the Polish Army and by October 1937 had received a commission with the 66th Polish Infantry Regiment. A year later, for reasons unknown, he decided to transfer to the Polish Air Force, where after successfully completing his training, he qualified as an air observer and was posted to No. 222 Squadron.

Rather than allow themselves to become POWs following the invasion of Poland in September 1939, Kolanowski and his comrades escaped to Romania before making their way across Europe to France, where on 13 November 1939, he enlisted in the French Air Force in Marseille and became a member of No. 11 (Polish Air Force) Squadron. Once France fell to the Germans in June 1940, Kolanowski made his way to England and enlisted in the Free Polish Air Force as part of No. 301 (Polish) Bomber Squadron, who flew Wellington Bombers out of RAF Hemswell, Lincolnshire.

At 18:47 on 7 November 1941, Kolanowski and his colleagues left their Lincolnshire base and headed towards the German city of Mannheim to bomb designated military targets. Having dropped its bombs and beginning its journey back to England, their Wellington bomber sustained flak damage from German anti-aircraft batteries and was subsequently forced to land near Maldegem, Belgium, where the entire crew were captured by German ground forces.

Kolanowski ended up as a POW at Stalag Luft III, where he became part of the camp's escape committee and helped to produce coloured maps of the surrounding towns and villages to assist those taking part in the mass escape. On the night of the escape, he managed to travel some 20 miles from the camp, which in the deep snow and extremely cold weather conditions was no mean feat. His initial plan had been to catch a train from Sagan, but by the time he arrived at the station, the train had already left. Instead, he joined a group of English escapees whose intention it was to make their way to Czechoslovakia. Starting off again the following day, he made his way the best that he could, but on 28 March was detained and arrested by German auxiliary police and taken to Görlitz prison, where a number of other recaptured escaped POWs from Stalag Luft III were already being held.

On the morning of 31 March, Kolanowski and nine other escapees were placed in the back of a covered military truck and driven out of the prison. None of the men were ever seen alive again. Their bodies were subsequently cremated, and their ashes returned to the POW camp at Stalag Luft III.

After the war's end, Kolanowski's remains were reburied at the Old Garrison Cemetery in Poznan. His name is commemorated on the Polish Air Force Memorial at RAF Northolt.

Flying Officer Stanisław Zygmunt 'Danny' Król

Born in Zagorzyce, Poland, on 22 March 1916, Król joined the Corps of Cadets, No. 3 Squadron Polish Air Force, when he was 21, and after completing his initial military training in January 1938, attended the Aviation Cadet School in the town of Dęblin to begin training as a fighter pilot.

Król was certainly a determined young man. On the very day that German forces invaded his country, he was commissioned as a second lieutenant and so he and a number of his colleagues made their way to Romania where they were placed in an internment camp to sit out the war. Rather than sit and await his fate, Król escaped and made his way to the Bulgarian coastal town of Balchik. There he managed to board a Greek merchant vessel, the *Aghios Nikolaos*, which then made its way to Beirut.

In Beirut, Król boarded the French merchant vessel, the *Ville de Strasbourg*, which then sailed to Marseille. After his arrival, Król joined the Free Polish Air Force and was soon undergoing training on the French Morane fighter aircraft in Lyon. On 10 May 1940, German forces began their land invasion of France and once again Król found himself having to escape rather than surrender to the Germans. On 23 June he managed to find passage on the French merchant vessel, *Président Del Piaz*, which sailed out of Bordeaux to Oran, Algeria, before he next sailed to England on board an unknown British merchant vessel. Once his story of escape had satisfied British military intelligence, he again teamed up with the Free Polish Air Force as a pilot officer and was posted to RAF Hawarden in Flintshire, Wales, where he learnt how to fly Supermarine Spitfires. Having successfully completed his training he was posted to No. 74 Squadron and posted to RAF Gravesend in Kent.

Król took off from his home base in the afternoon of 2 July 1941, and whilst flying his aircraft over Saint-Omer, he was attacked by a German Messerschmitt Bf 109 and shot down. After spending time in a number of POW camps, he eventually ended up at Stalag Luft III in spring 1942, not too long after the North Compound had opened. Before the year was at an end, Król had already made an attempt at escaping. Along with Flight Lieutenant Sydney Dowse, who later went on to be one of the Great Escapers who survived the Gestapo's systematic murder of fifty of his fellow escapees in March 1944, Król tried to escape by cutting through the barbed wire perimeter fence. Thankfully for both men, none of the guards had a desire to open fire on them. Instead, they were captured before they could escape and placed in the camp's 'cooler'. The same two men were undeterred by their previously failed attempt, and within a matter of months they tried again. This time their attempt at freedom was via a tunnel, but it was subsequently discovered by the camp guards, and it was back to the cooler for Król and Dowse.

When it came to the mass escape on the evening of 24/25 March 1944, Król was one of the first escapees out of the tunnel, with his immediate destination being the railway station at Sagan. However, because of a nearby Allied air raid, the railway station had closed, and so Król and Dowse had to change their plans. With no train, their only other option was to walk, with their new destination being Poland. Luck and good fortune were on their side as they managed to stay at large for nearly two weeks, but on 6 April, their luck ran out after they took refuge from the severe weather in a barn, just 2 miles from the Polish border, and were discovered by members of the German Home Guard. On 11 April they were interrogated by Gestapo officers from the Breslau office and once their true identities had been discovered, the two men were separated. Because Dowse had escaped four times from German POW camps, he was sent to Berlin for further interrogation before ending up at Sachsenhausen concentration camp, but he survived the war. Unfortunately, Król had already been marked for death by *SS-Gruppenführer* Arthur Nebe. The last time Król was seen alive was on 12 April 1944. His remains now rest at the Old Garrison Cemetery in Poznan, and his name is commemorated on the Polish Air Force Memorial at RAF Northolt.

Flight Lieutenant Patrick Wilson Langford

Born on 4 November 1919 in Edmonton, Alberta, Canada, three months after his twentieth birthday Langford enlisted in the Royal Canadian Airforce and was commissioned as a regular service officer.

Having arrived in England on 9 April 1942 he became a member of No. 16 Operational Training Unit at RAF Upper Heyford, which formed part of the RAF's No. 6 Group of Bomber Command. The unit had a dual purpose of training night bomber crews flying Wellington aircraft, as well as undertaking operation missions.

At 22:14 on 28 July 1942, Langford was on board a Wellington Mark 1c bomber that left its base at Upper Heyford on a mission to bomb the shipyards of Hamburg. Having dropped its bombs, the Wellington had begun its return journey to England when it was attacked by a German fighter aircraft and crash landed near Lübeck in northern Germany. Three of the crew, Sergeant Trevor Haughton Cray, Sergeant William John Atchison, and Pilot Officer Arthur Ferdinand Litzow, were all killed and are buried at Kiel War Cemetery. Langford, Pilot Officer Francis Lowe and Sergeant William White, all survived. Lowe was uninjured, but Langford and White were badly wounded. In Langford's case, he had bailed out of the aircraft, but his parachute was on fire and he was badly burnt as a result. Langford's wounds were so severe that he spent the first two months of his captivity in a German military hospital having his burns treated. Both Langford and White ended up as POWs at Stalag Luft III.

Langford played an important role in the mass escape as not only was he involved in the planning and excavation of 'Harry', but he was also responsible for making sure that the stove in Block 104 was always back in place over the tunnel entrance whenever the camp guards came near the hut.

Come the night of the mass escape he was one of those selected to take part. Having made his way out of the tunnel, he like all the other escapees was met with snow and freezing cold weather. Somewhat miraculously given the circumstances, Langford and his colleagues managed to stay at large until 28 March when they were recaptured and taken to the civilian prison at Görlitz. On the morning of 31 March Langford was one of eleven prisoners who were taken in the back of a covered military vehicle on the pretence that they were going to be returned to Stalag Luft III. Whether any of them had any idea of what was about to happen to them, we will never know. After being shot in a clearing off the main Görlitz road by members of the Gestapo, their bodies were cremated at nearby Liegnitz and their ashes returned to Stalag Luft III.

After the war Langford's remains were transferred to the Old Garrison Cemetery at Poznan. For the 'conspicuous gallantry' he displayed whilst a POW, he was mentioned in despatches. He could not have received any type of military award, however, because at the time such awards were not awarded posthumously.

Flight Lieutenant Thomas Barker Leigh

Born on 11 February 1919 in Sydney, Leigh's father was British and his mother Australian, although just prior to Leigh's birth the family home had been in Shanghai. Leigh was just 7 when his mother died in 1926, so along with his two siblings he returned to England where all three attended boarding school.

After completing his full-time secondary education, he sat and passed the entrance exam for the Merchant Navy training ship *Mercury*, but less than a year later, he decided that rather than a life at sea he wanted one that took him up into the clouds. So it was that on 20 August 1935, he began his apprentice training with the RAF at the No. 1 School of Technical Training. So good was he at his newfound career, and so quick was he to learn, that he was promoted to leading apprentice. After nearly three years of study and hard graft, he graduated on 26 July 1938 and was posted to No. 48 Squadron at RAF Bicester as an aircraftman 2nd class. The squadron was part of the RAF's Coastal Command and took part in general reconnaissance missions along the south coast of England, flying Avron Anson twin-engined aircraft.

In May 1941, having successfully completed his aircrew training, he joined No. 76 Squadron based at RAF Linton-on-Ouse in Yorkshire as a sergeant air gunner. Only a matter of weeks after joining, the squadron moved to RAF Middleton St. George, near Darlington, County Durham.

At about 21:45 on 5 August 1941, Leigh, who just three days earlier had been promoted to the rank of pilot officer, was a rear gunner on a Handley Page Halifax bomber aircraft which took off on a mission to bomb railway workshops at Karlsruhe in Germany. After dropping its bombs on its intended target, Leigh's Halifax was caught in the glare of a number of searchlights, which in turn made it an immediate target for the anti-aircraft guns who wasted no time in opening fire. One of the shots found its target and blew off the bomber's tail section, causing the aircraft to become unstable. Miraculously, the seven-man crew all managed to bail out before it crashed into the ground below. Six of them, including Leigh, survived, whilst the seventh was killed. Leigh remained at large for about five hours before he was captured and initially interrogated at the Dulag Luft at Oberusel and then sent to Stalag Luft I. It was there that he first met Roger Bushell and several other men who, like him, would eventually be sent to Stalag Luft III.

Leigh was one of those heavily involved in the planning and execution of what became known as the Great Escape. Because of his involvement he was high on the list of those who were the first to leave the 'Harry' tunnel on the evening of 24 March 1944. Leigh and some of his colleagues managed to stay at large for five days, despite the heavy snow and freezing conditions, before being recaptured and taken to Görlitz prison. On the morning of 30 March, Leigh and five others were placed in the back of three Gestapo cars and driven away and were never seen alive again.

Leigh was mentioned in despatches for 'conspicuous gallantry' during his time spent as a prisoner of war. This was recorded in the *London Gazette* newspaper on 8 June 1944.

Flight Lieutenant James Leslie Robert 'Cookie' Long

Born on 21 February 1915 in Bournemouth, England, Long joined the Civil Air Guard and soon after war broke out in 1939, was called up and applied to join the RAF so as to continue his flying training. After achieving this, he was posted to No. 9 Squadron on 3 March 1941.

Stalag Luft III was a German POW camp located at Sagan, Poland, for Allied airmen and was run by the Luftwaffe.

A Stalag Luft III sign including the Wehrmacht symbol sitting on top of a Nazi swastika, written in a German gothic style font.

A pilot admiring the artwork of a Stalag Luft III 'Donald Duck' image. The artwork was carried out by artists working for Walt Disney. During the Second World War, more than 1,000 such pieces were produced, helping to raise the morale and spirit of the American military.

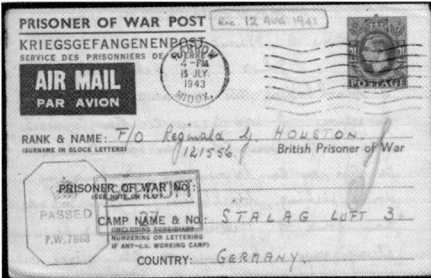

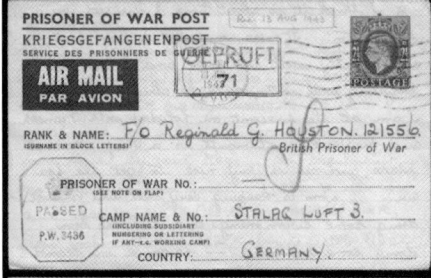

Above: Captured POWs arriving at Stalag Luft III. Their faces show a combination of happiness that they are still alive, but uncertainty as to what lay ahead.

Left: Letters dated 1943 and 1944 sent to Reginald Gordon Houston at Stalag Luft III. Houston, a member of No. 35 Squadron, failed to return from an operational flight to Limbricht, Netherlands, on 30 May 1943.

A photograph of day-to-day camp life at Stalag Luft III. Notice the clothing and uniform hanging out to dry on the side of the hut.

Above and below: POWs taking part in numerous events during a 'Sports Day' at Stalag Luft III, August 1942.

POWs tending their gardens at Stalag Luft III. Besides growing their own fruit and vegetables, gardening also allowed dirt excavated from the tunnels to be mixed in with the mud of the flowerbeds.

Above left: A programme from the 1943 New Year's Day football match that took place at Stalag Luft III between English and Scottish POWs.

Above right: Henri Albert Picard was a Belgian pilot serving with the RAF. Shot down over France in August 1942, he was captured and sent to Stalag Luft III. After taking part in the Great Escape, he was recaptured and was one of the fifty murdered airmen.

Above left: Second Lieutenant Michael Codner, Royal Artillery, was captured whilst serving in North Africa on 14 December 1942. On the evening of 29 October 1943, he escaped with two others in what was known as the Trojan Horse escape.

Above right: Alfred Burke Thompson was a Canadian serving with the RAF. After experiencing engine trouble on a bombing mission over Germany, he bailed out and was captured by German forces, becoming the first Canadian prisoner of war of the Second World War. He was recaptured after escaping in March 1944 but survived the war.

Squadron Leader Leonard Henry Trent, VC (left), a New Zealand pilot flying for the RAF. On the night of the Great Escape, he was only halfway out of the escape tunnel when he was captured by a German guard.

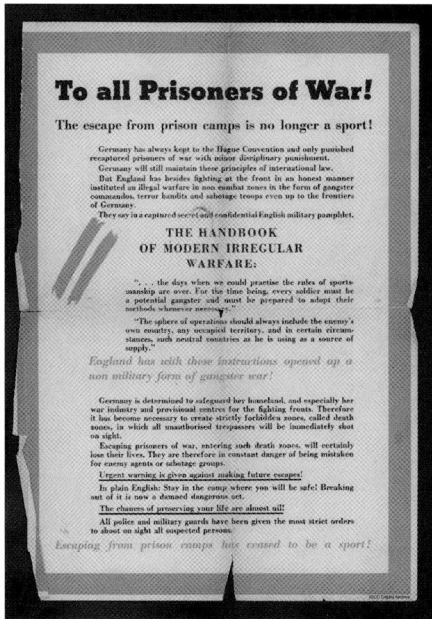

To all Prisoners of War!

The escape from prison camps is no longer a sport!

Germany has always kept to the Hague Convention and only punished recaptured prisoners of war with minor disciplinary punishment.

Germany will still maintain these principles of international law.

But England has besides fighting at the front in an honest manner instituted an illegal warfare in non combat zones in the form of gangster commandos, terror bandits and sabotage troops even up to the frontiers of Germany.

They say in a captured secret and confidential English military pamphlet.

THE HANDBOOK
OF MODERN IRREGULAR
WARFARE:

"... the days when we could practise the rules of sportsmanship are over. For the time being, every soldier must be a potential gangster and must be prepared to adopt their methods whenever necessary."

"The sphere of operations should always include the enemy's own country, any occupied territory, and in certain circumstances, such neutral countries as he is using as a source of supply."

England has with these instructions opened up a non military form of gangster war!

Germany is determined to safeguard her homeland, and especially her war industry and provisional centres for the fighting fronts. Therefore it has become necessary to create strictly forbidden zones, called death zones, in which all unauthorised trespassers will be immediately shot on sight.

Escaping prisoners of war, entering such death zones, will certainly lose their lives. They are therefore in constant danger of being mistaken for enemy agents or sabotage groups.

Urgent warning is given against making future escapes!

In plain English: Stay in the camp where you will be safe! Breaking out of it is now a damned dangerous act.

The chances of preserving your life are almost nil!

All police and military guards have been given the most strict orders to shoot on sight all suspected persons.

Escaping from prison camps has ceased to be a sport!

Left: A poster issued by the camp commandant at Stalag Luft III in the immediate aftermath of the Great Escape to try to impress upon POWs that trying to escape was a dangerous pastime.

Below: A diagram of the 'Harry' escape tunnel at Stalag Luft III. Its depth and length highlights just how much time and effort went into its construction.

Bottom: A detailed map of the 'Harry' escape tunnel showing its complexity. A bellows system kept the air circulating and a mini 'railway line' allowed individuals to be pulled along the tunnel on a pully system.

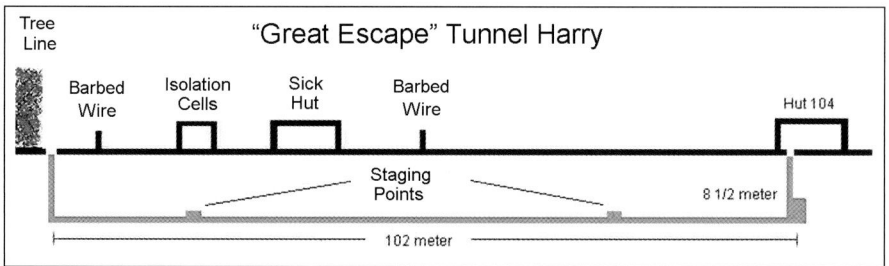

"Great Escape" Tunnel Harry

Tree Line | Barbed Wire | Isolation Cells | Sick Hut | Barbed Wire | Hut 104

Staging Points — 8 1/2 meter

102 meter

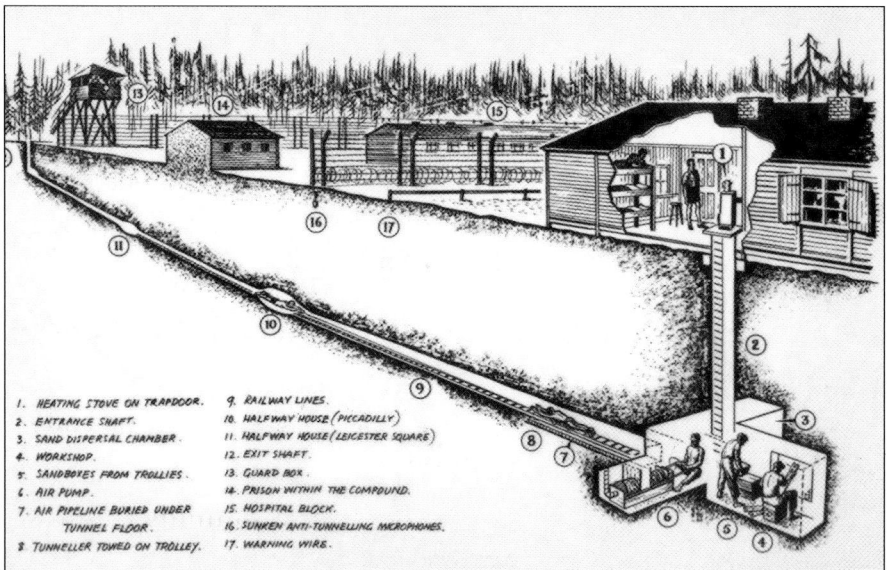

1. HEATING STOVE ON TRAPDOOR.
2. ENTRANCE SHAFT.
3. SAND DISPERSAL CHAMBER.
4. WORKSHOP.
5. SANDBOXES FROM TROLLIES.
6. AIR PUMP.
7. AIR PIPELINE BURIED UNDER TUNNEL FLOOR.
8. TUNNELLER TOWED ON TROLLEY.
9. RAILWAY LINES.
10. HALFWAY HOUSE (PICCADILLY).
11. HALFWAY HOUSE (LEICESTER SQUARE).
12. EXIT SHAFT.
13. GUARD BOX.
14. PRISON WITHIN THE COMPOUND.
15. HOSPITAL BLOCK.
16. SUNKEN ANTI-TUNNELLING MICROPHONES.
17. WARNING WIRE.

Above left: SS-Gruppenführer Arthur Nebe, the man behind the decision to execute the fifty captured escapees. He was subsequently executed by the Nazis on 21 March 1945 over his involvement in a failed attempt to kill Adolf Hitler in July 1944.

Above right: Romualdas Marcinkus, a Lithuanian-born pilot who served with No. 1 Squadron RAF. After his aircraft was shot down on 12 February 1942, he became a POW at Stalag Luft III and was later one of the murdered escapees.

Below: Norwegian pilot Jens Einar Muller was escapee number forty-three out of the tunnel and was one of only three men who made it safely back to the UK. His contribution to the digging of 'Harry' was the construction of an air pump and the ventilation system in the tunnel.

Above left: Johnnie Bigelow Dodge, DSO, DSC, MC was an American-born British Army officer who served in both the First and Second World Wars. He was one of those who escaped from Stalag Luft III but was recaptured a few days later and returned to the camp.

Above right: After the Second World War, Australian airmen Paul Brickhill, one of the POWs at Stalag Luft III, wrote a best-selling book about what became known as the Great Escape. Published in 1950, it was subsequently turned into a Hollywood film in 1963. However, Brickhill did not take part in the escape himself as he suffered from claustrophobia.

Below: Stalag Luft III memorial to the fifty murdered escapees.

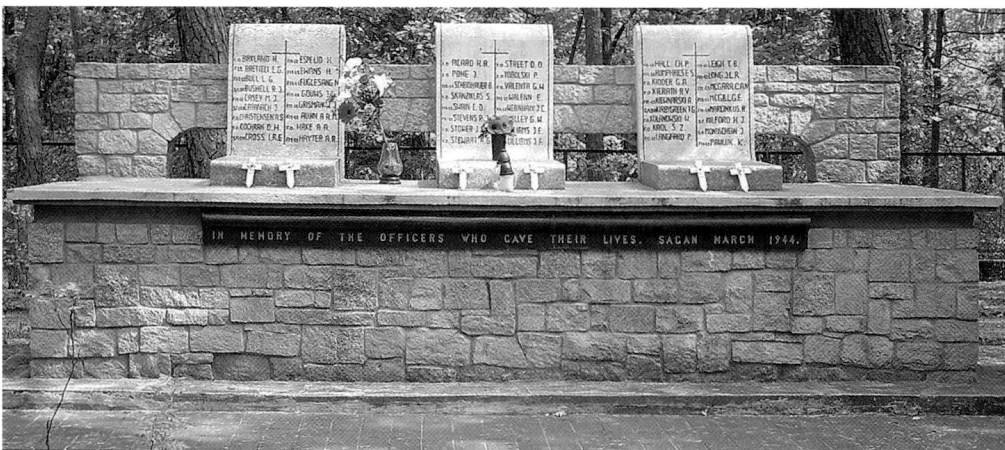

On 27 March, just over three weeks after being posted to No. 9 Squadron, he took off from RAF Honington at 19:43 in a Wellington Mark lc bomber. The mission was to attack a target in Cologne, but after having dropped its bombs and starting its journey home, the plane was attacked by a German fighter aircraft and was so badly damaged that it was forced to crash land in the Netherlands. The crew survived but were captured and became POWs, initially at Stalag Luft I. Long had no intention of sitting the rest of the war out in a POW camp, and along with John Shore, another captured crew member, he set about trying to escape. Shore was successful in one such attempt and made it back home to England, via Sweden. As for Long, he was transferred to Stalag Luft III on 21 March 1942, but he even had the audacity to try to escape whilst he was making his way between the two camps. Ultimately, he was recaptured before he got too far away. Once in his new 'home', he wasted no time involving himself in the business of digging tunnels and trying to escape. He was particularly involved with the digging undertaken in relation to the tunnel codenamed 'Tom'.

On the night of the mass escape there were a number of delays as the men made their way through the tunnel. Two of these occasions were due to cave ins, which Long was responsible for repairing to enable the escape to continue. Once out of the tunnel and into the nearby woods, Long joined the group known as the 'hard arsers', so named because their intention was to escape purely on foot. To ensure they were heading in the right direction, Long's group walked adjacent to the railway line so as not to get lost in the woods. After three days at large, Long and fellow escapee Tony Bethell were recaptured by members of the German Home Guard and initially taken to Sagan police station before being forwarded on Görlitz prison, where they arrived on 29 March. Long was last seen alive at Görlitz by a fellow prisoner on 11 April. It has never been confirmed what happened to him, but like a number of his colleagues it is almost certain he was shot dead by members of the Gestapo. Nevertheless, his remains have never been recovered.

The list of names of escapees who had been 'shot while attempting to escape' that was handed over to the senior British officer at Stalag Luft III on 18 May 1944, Group Captain Douglas

Ernest Lancelot Wilson, included Long's name, although when a similar list was reported in the British press on 22 May, Long's name was not included.

Flight Lieutenant Romualdas Marcinkus

Born in Jurbarkas, Lithuania on 22 July 1907, Marcinkus moved to the city of Kaunas when he was just 17 to further his education. After this he attended the Kaunas Military School and graduated in 1928 as an infantry second lieutenant.

In 1930 Marcinkus decided that he wanted to become an aviator and so attended the Vytautas the Great Military Institute's aviation department. Two years later he had qualified as a military pilot, and the following year saw him promoted to the rank of lieutenant. In 1934 he transferred to the air reconnaissance section, which culminated with him learning a wide range of skills and resulted in him becoming a more rounded aviator.

He left his home country in March 1940, just before it was occupied by the Soviet Union, and made his way to France where he eventually became a pilot in the French Air Force. However, it was not long before the French capitulated and so Marcinkus found himself on the move again, this time to North Africa, where he was finally demobbed from the French military in August 1940. After acquiring the required documentation, Marcinkus was allowed to make his way to England, eventually arriving by boat at Liverpool in October 1940.

After lying about his age, which he lowered by three years, he joined the RAF in December 1940. After completing his operational pilot training, he was posted to No. 1 Squadron at RAF Wittering, where he became the only Lithuanian to become a pilot in the RAF and flew Hawker Hurricane Mk. 1 aircraft.

On 12 February 1942, Marcinkus and five of his colleagues were tasked with locating and attacking the German battleships *Scharnhorst* and *Gneisenau* and the heavy cruiser *Prinz Eugen*, who were attempting to sail to their home bases at Kiel and Wilhelmshaven, via the English Channel. During the subsequent fighting, Marcinkus' Hurricane aircraft, which was attacking the

Scharnhorst, was shot down by the ship's anti-aircraft guns and crashed into the sea. He survived but was badly injured when he fractured his spine. He was plucked from the water by the crew of a German convoy vessel and was admitted to a military hospital on their arrival at Wilhelmshaven. After some weeks of medical treatment by German doctors, Marcinkus was released and sent to Stalag Luft III.

Having been accepted by the rest of the camp, Marcinkus was informed of the upcoming mass breakout, and more than played his part in the planning of the escape. He was allocated to the group involved in compiling the forged documents that the escapees would need once in the outside world, which included the much-needed local railway schedules. He had the added attribute of being able to speak fluent German.

One of those who survived the escape was Squadron Leader Bertram Arthur 'Jimmy' James. When interviewed some years after the war about the Great Escape, he had the following to say about Marcinkus:

> While I didn't know Marcinkus directly, I remember him very well. I remember him as a friendly guy, having a good character, he also had a phenomenal memory. He was especially good at memorising numbers, dates, and after analysing a pile of information, he made a precise compilation of the Reich's railway schedules. These were used by men, who during the Great Escape travelled by train, including me. He was fluent in German, perhaps this allowed him to bribe or negotiate with German officials in order to get needed information, but I know for sure, that Marcinkus analysed vast amounts of information and became very useful during the Great Escape.

When it came to the actual escape, Marcinkus was amongst the first ten men to exit the escape tunnel. He and three others were making their way to Lithuania and from there on into neutral Sweden. By 26 March they had made it as far as Schneidemühl (Piła), which today is located in northwest Poland. The four men were arrested and sent to the German POW camp Stalag XX-B, where they spent the night before being handed over to members of the Danzig Gestapo the following morning. On 29 March, Marcinkus was taken to a clearing in the forest near to the Polish village of Pruśce and executed with a single bullet to the back of the head. His body was cremated later the same day.

Second Lieutenant Clement Aldwyn Neville McGarr

Born in Johannesburg, South Africa, on 24 November 1917, McGarr enlisted in the South African Air Force (SAAF) on 23 May 1940 and was commissioned as a second lieutenant. In October 1941, having completed his pilot training, he found himself attached to SAAF's No. 2 Squadron, stationed in North Africa.

On 6 October, two P-40 Tomahawks, including the one flown by McGarr, were intercepted and shot down by a formation of German Messerschmitt Bf 109s while undertaking a patrol of Sidi Omar in the Egyptian desert. McGarr was able to bail out of his stricken aircraft and parachuted safely to the ground. Escaping from a desert was never going to be easy, but McGarr managed to avoid capture for three days, during which time he had neither food nor water, before eventually being detained by members of the German *Afrika Korps* on 9 October. After initially been held in a POW camp in Libya, he was sent to Germany where he eventually ended up at Stalag Luft III.

McGarr was quick to volunteer for tunnelling duties once he became aware of the plans for the mass breakout. The problem was his size, both in height and build, to such an extent that he was physically too big to take part in such work. Instead, he settled for being part of the security team who ensured the tunnels remained undiscovered by the German guards as they walked around the camp.

When it came to the breakout, despite his size, McGarr was included in the list of those who would take part in the escape. This nearly proved to be a questionable decision when at one stage during the escape he became stuck in the tunnel. Despite initial concerns, he, along with the help of others, was able to release himself from the restrictions, continue along the tunnel, and make his way into the nearby woods. After surviving in the cold outdoors for nearly three days, he was discovered and arrested, and along with other recaptured escapees, ended up in Görlitz prison. In the early hours of 6 April, McGarr and five others were taken from their cells and shot soon afterwards on the road out of Görlitz. His body was cremated at Breslau and his ashes returned to Stalag Luft III. After the war his remains were reburied at the Old Garrison Cemetery in Poznan.

Like a number of his fellow escapees, McGarr received a mention in dispatches for his 'conspicuous bravery' whilst incarcerated as a POW.

Flight Lieutenant George Edward McGill

Born on 14 April 1918 in Toronto, Canada, McGill enlisted in the Royal Canadian Air Force on 3 September 1940. Prior to sailing to England on 14 July 1941, he had been promoted to leading aircraftman on 8 December 1940, further promoted to the rank of sergeant on 12 April, and commissioned as a pilot officer on 13 May. After completing his operational pilot training at No. 21 Operational Training Unit at RAF Moreton-in-Marsh, Gloucestershire, he was posted to the RAF's No. 103 Squadron at RAF Elsham Wolds in Lincolnshire, on 17 October 1941.

McGill became a POW on 10 January 1942 after being captured when his Wellington bomber caught fire during a raid on the German naval port city of Wilhelmshaven.

Like a number of his colleagues, McGill was promoted whilst been held in captivity as a POW: on 13 May 1942 he was promoted to the rank of flying officer and exactly a year later became a flight lieutenant.

After escaping from Stalag Luft III on the evening of 24 March 1944, he did not make it far before being captured. Rather than being taken back to Stalag Luft III, he was taken to the prison at Görlitz along with a number of other recaptured escapees. In the early hours of 31 March, McGill was one of eleven other recaptured POWs who were collected from Görlitz by ten Gestapo officers, never to be seen alive again. It is more than likely that all eleven were shot dead on the outskirts of Görlitz shortly after they had been removed from the prison.

When urns containing the murdered men's ashes were returned to Stalag Luft III, they contained no date of when they had been killed, although they did show that their cremations had taken place at Liegnitz.

McGill's remains were also moved to the Old Garrison Cemetery in Poznan in November 1948. Like a number of his comrades, he was also mentioned in despatches for 'conspicuous gallantry' for his time spent as a POW.

Flight Lieutenant Harold John Milford

Born on 16 August 1914 in Streatham, southwest London, Milford enlisted in the RAF in June 1940 and began his training to become an aircraftman, before being promoted to the rank of leading aircraftman. On subsequently completing his flight training he received a commission as a pilot officer in August 1941, and was posted to No. 226 Squadron, who were stationed at RAF Swanton Morley, Norfolk.

On the morning of 22 September 1942, Milford was part of the three-man crew who took off from RAF Swanton Morley in their Douglas Boston aircraft. Sergeant Morris Collins was the pilot; Sergeant G.A. Nicolls, the wireless operator and air gunner, and Milford the co-pilot. Their mission, along with other aircraft from No. 226 Squadron, was to attack a power station at Chocques in the Pas-de-Calais region of France. Milford's aircraft was attacked by a German fighter and rather than crash into the ground with the stricken aircraft, the three men all bailed out and landed safely on the ground. Once down, the three men decided they should split up and in doing so make the chances of them being captured less likely. Milford and Nicolls went off together but were eventually arrested after hiding out in a haystack. Both men were eventually taken to Stalag Luft III, whilst Collins, who had gone off on his own, managed to avoid capture and make it safely back to England.

At Stalag Luft III, Milford met an old acquaintance in the form of Johnny Williams, with whom he had gone through his initial training. This friendship allowed him to be more readily accepted by the others already at the camp. Milford's main role in the escape process was as a tunneller. On the night of the escape, once out of the tunnel Milford teamed up with fellow escapers Alastair 'Sandy' Gunn and John F. Williams. One of the main difficulties the escapees had to deal with was the extreme cold and heavy snow fall. At that time of the year, it was quite normal to have nighttime temperatures reaching as low as -10°C. The three men managed to remain at large for three days, but when they were captured on the afternoon of 27 March, they were still in the Sagan area. Initially they were taken to the Sagan prison where they were held overnight before been taken to Görlitz prison the following morning.

On the morning of 6 April 1944, a canvas-covered German military truck arrived at the prison along with a number of members of the Breslau Gestapo. Six prisoners' names were called out, one of which was Milford's. All the men were instructed to climb up onto the back of the truck and within a matter of minutes they were gone. Like others before them who had left the prison in similar circumstances, they were never seen alive again. In fact, the truck carrying the six men did not travel that far from the camp at all before they were all shot dead in a clearing on the side of the road.

The bodies of Milford and his comrades were cremated at Breslau crematorium and their ashes returned to Stalag Luft III. After the war, Milford's ashes were buried at the Old Garrison Cemetery in Poznan. Like a number of his fellow murdered escapees, he was mentioned in despatches in recognition of his 'conspicuous bravery' whilst being held as a POW by the Germans.

Flying Officer Jerzy Tomasz Mondschein

Born on 18 March 1909 in Warsaw to a German father, prior to the Second World War Mondschein was already a member of the Polish Air Force, but with the fall of Poland to German and Soviet forces in September 1939, he had no desire to become a POW and so escaped to France. His time there was short lived due to the nation's capitulation on 25 June 1940, but with a strong desire to continue the fight against Nazi Germany, he managed to make his way to England. After convincing the British authorities he was who he claimed to be, he was accepted by the Free Polish Air Force, retrained as an observer/navigator crew member on Wellington bombers and was posted to No. 304 (Polish Bomber) Squadron RAF Lindholme in South Yorkshire.

At 18:03 on 7 August 1941, the all-Polish crew of a Wellington bomber took off from its home base at RAF Lindholme and headed towards its intended target, the German city of Mannheim. The aircraft was last heard of at 20:55, when it radioed its base to inform them that they had successfully bombed their target. However, when it failed to return home at the expected time, confusion reigned. It transpired that with his aircraft quickly running out of fuel, the pilot, Sergeant Blicharz, took the decision to land at St Trond airfield, near Liège, Belgium, failing to realise that it was in fact a German base for Luftwaffe fighter aircraft. No sooner had the aircraft landed than it was surrounded by German ground forces and the six-man crew were arrested. It is unclear, and not recorded, as to who was the most shocked: the Polish aircrew or the Germans. On realising their mistake, and before they were detained, the Polish crew not only managed to destroy all their papers and documents, and anything else that might be considered useful to the Germans, but also set fire to the aircraft.

Mondschein ended up as a POW at Stalag Luft III where he became an active member of the escape committee. He helped to convert camp uniforms into civilian clothes, and blankets into much-needed thick coats. He was also involved in gathering important intelligence from any German-language magazine and newspapers he could get his hands on. His ability to be able to speak, read and write German was a massive help towards the escape plans, both during the planning stages as well as once he had escaped from the camp. He was part of a group of twelve whose cover story was that they were a group of lumber mill workers on their way home on leave. When they reached the railway station at Tschiebsdorf it was Mondschein who bought the tickets for the group using his forged travel pass. If the ticket master was suspicious of this large group of men, he did not say anything, nor did he raise any alarm. The tickets were for the 06:00 train to Boberrohsdorf, which was a three-hour journey, giving them all the opportunity not only to keep warm, but to grab some much-needed sleep as well. On arriving at their destination, the men felt it was more sensible to split up into smaller groups so as not to draw attention to themselves. Mondschein and three others left on foot with the help of members of the Czech Resistance and made their way through the Reisengebirge mountain range, which they hoped would ultimately take them into Czechoslovakia. It was an arduous journey of nearly 13 miles through snow, which on some occasions was so deep that it came up to the men's waists. However, on route they bumped into a German mountain patrol and were arrested and taken to the civilian prison at Reichenberg.

In the early hours of 29 March, Mondschein and his three comrades were collected from the prison by Gestapo officers, who they believed were going to take them back to Stalag Luft III. Instead, having travelled a few miles away from the prison, the two cars the men were in pulled over to the side of the road on the outskirts of the Polish city of Hirschberg. The men were told to get out of the vehicles and were quickly executed. Their bodies were cremated in the city of Brux in Czechoslovakia and their ashes returned to Stalag Luft III.

Mondschein was another who was mentioned in despatches for his 'conspicuous bravery' as a POW. Besides numerous other locations where Mondschein's name is commemorated, it is also recorded on the Polish Air Force Memorial at RAF Northolt.

Flying Officer Kazimierz 'Kaz' Pawluk

Born on 1 July 1906 in Warsaw, in 1929 Pawluk enlisted in the Polish Army, but later transferred to the Polish Air Force, where he rose through the ranks to become a commissioned officer.

Like a number of his compatriots, after Poland was invaded in September 1939, Pawluk made his way to first France, and then on to England. There, he joined the Free Polish Air Force as a flying officer and was allocated to No. 305 (Polish Bomber) Squadron who flew Wellington bomber aircraft out of RAF Cammeringham in Lincolnshire.

At 21:23 on 28 March 1942, Pawluk was the navigator/bomb aimer on board a Wellington bomber that left RAF Lindholme on a mission to bomb the German city of Lübeck. What was notable about this particular raid was that it was the first such attack on a

German city during the course of the war. This was not an attack on a designated military target, or industrial units that were supporting the German war effort, it was a raid on the civilian population in an attempt to impact public morale.

Pawluk's Wellington bomber was hit and damaged by the city's anti-aircraft batteries, forcing the entire crew to bail out. Pawluk and his five comrades were all captured and became POWs. Once he had been interrogated by the Germans, he was then placed into the prison camp system and ended up being sent to Stalag Luft III.

Pawluk was one of those selected to be part of the mass escape. Come the night of the actual breakout, he was one of the early ones out of the tunnel as he was one of those who had a train to catch. His allocated group of escapees included seven others whose cover story was that they were a group of lumber mill workers. Along with several of his fellow escapees, he caught his intended train on the morning of 25 March and by later that afternoon, with the group having split up, he was alone with Antoni Kiewnarski. Having made it to town of Hirschberg, they were stopped by civilian police as they strolled through the streets, arrested and taken back to the local police station. Unbeknown to the two men the authorities were already on the lookout for escapees from Stalag Luft III, and when they were later taken to the local prison, they discovered that they were not the first to have been recaptured. On the morning of 31 March, they were collected by two members of the local Gestapo and removed from the prison. Like those who had been removed before them, they were never seen alive again. Their bodies were cremated and their ashes subsequently returned to Stalag Luft III.

After the war Pawluk's ashes were taken to the Old Garrison Cemetery in Poznan. He is another whose name is commemorated on the Polish Air Force memorial at RAF Northolt, and who was mentioned in despatches for his 'conspicuous bravery' whilst held as a POW.

Flight Lieutenant Henri Albert Picard, Croix de Guerre

Born on 17 April 1916 in Etterbeek, a suburb of Brussels, Picard began his training to become an army officer when he was 20.

Having successfully completed the course he decided to continue his military training, but this time as an observer in the air force. He graduated in June 1939 and in January 1940, began training to be a pilot. He was still undergoing his training when the German invasion of Belgium in May 1940 forced his school to close and relocate to Morocco. The following month Picard and his fellow trainee pilots set sail for Gibraltar, and then onto England, where they eventually arrived on 14 July and were sent to RAF Gloucester. On 8 November 1940 he was commissioned as a pilot officer in the Royal Air Force Volunteer Reserve and after completing his operational training in Scotland, was posted to No. 131 (Belgian) Squadron at RAF Atcham in Shropshire.

In November 1941, Picard was posted to No. 350 (Belgian) Squadron who flew out of RAF Kenley on the edge of Greater London. On 27 August 1942, he flew one of the Supermarine Spitfires which provided air support for the ground forces who took part in the amphibious raid on Dieppe by British and Canadian forces. His involvement in the raid resulted in him being shot down over the English Channel near Abbeville. Despite being wounded, he managed to parachute out of his aircraft before it crashed into the sea but spent six days in a life raft bobbing about in the English Channel. Unfortunately for Picard, the tide took him towards France instead of the south coast of England, where he was captured by German forces and became a POW. He had his wounds treated in a German military hospital in France, before being sent to Stalag Luft III.

Picard was an accomplished artist and often completed pencil drawings of his fellow camp mates at Stalag Luft III. On Wednesday, 1 November 1944, nine of his drawings appeared in the *Tatler and Bystander* newspaper. Most of the drawings were completed in the early months of 1943 and had been posted to the wife of Picard's hut mate, Squadron Leader V.T.L. Wood, although they did not reach her until October 1944.

It was because of his artistic skills that Picard became one of the escape committee's camp forgers, working on the documentation the escapees would need on the outside after their escape.

Picard teamed up with three others after escaping the camp and together they posed as foreign labourers, but their taste of freedom came to an abrupt end when they were arrested by the Gestapo on 26 March at Schneidemühl in northwest Poland. From there they were taken to the German POW camp, Stalag XX-B in Wielbark, Poland, where they spent the night before being collected by members of the Danzig Gestapo the following morning. Picard and his three fellow escapees were taken to a wooded area near Prusce where they were murdered with a bullet to the back of their heads.

Picard's remains were eventually laid to rest at the Old Garrison Cemetery in Poznan. His name is also commemorated on the memorial at St Andrew's Church, North Weald.

Flying Officer Porokoru Patapu 'John' Pohe

Born on 10 December 1914 in Wanganui, New Zealand, after finishing his education Pohe divided his time between working on his parents' farm and being a member of the Manawatu Mounted Rifles, which was a unit of the New Zealand Territorial Army.

After deciding that he wanted to be a pilot, he volunteered to enlist in the Royal New Zealand Air Force (RNZAF) on 12 September 1939, but was not called up until 1 September 1940, when he commenced his training, initially at No. 3 Elementary Flying Training School, in Harewood, and at No. 2 Flying Training School, in Blenheim. When he qualified as a pilot on 18 January 1941, he became the first Māori to serve in the RNZAF. He was promoted to the rank of sergeant on 1 March 1941.

On 18 May 1941, having successfully completed further training in Canada, he arrived at RAF Abingdon in Oxfordshire, where he became part of No. 10 Operational Training Unit. Just three months later, on 24 August, he was on the move again. This time he was posted to No. 51 Squadron at Dishforth, Yorkshire and flew Armstrong Whitworth Whitley aircraft. Over the following eight months he took part in twenty-two operational missions on targets throughout occupied Europe.

In February 1942, he helped drop British paratroopers who were part of the raid on Bruneval, and the following month he piloted one of the Whitley bombers that helped provide air support for the successful Allied raid at St. Nazaire. The following eighteen months saw him flying with other squadrons, both on training courses and as an instructor, before he returned to No. 51 Squadron for a second time on 21 September 1943, who were then based at Snaith, Yorkshire.

The following night, 22 September, Pohe, who was the captain of a Halifax bomber, took off from RAF Snaith at 18:44 on a raid on the German city of Hanover, in Lower Saxony. Pohe's aircraft was struck by German anti-aircraft fire whilst over its intended target and turned for home, despite being badly damaged. Pohe managed to ditch his aircraft in the English Channel and so good was his control that not only did the aircraft stay afloat on landing, but none of the crew was injured in the action. They made it into two dinghies and were in the water for two days before being spotted. Unfortunately for Pohe and his crew, it was a German aircraft that had seen them, and the pilot radioed the sighting to his home base. A few hours later a German naval vessel came to their rescue and took them to France. Pohe was sent to Stalag Luft III, where he arrived on 6 October 1943.

His involvement in the preparation of the mass escape was as a tunneller, initially in 'Dick' and then afterwards in 'Harry'. On the night of 24/25 March 1944, Pohe's partner in crime was Albert Horace Hake, whose escape story has been told earlier in this chapter.

Pohe's remains are to be found at the Old Garrison Cemetery in Poznan, and for his 'conspicuous bravery' during his time spent as a POW, he was mentioned in despatches in the 1944 King's Birthday Honours, the notice of which was published in a supplement of the *London Gazette* newspaper dated 8 June 1944.

Sous Lieutenant Bernard William Martial Scheidhauer

Born in Landau, Germany on 28 August 1921, despite his German ancestry Scheidhauer was actually a French pilot serving with the RAF prior to his capture and incarceration as a POW at Stalag Luft III.

The youngest of seven children, at the time of his birth Scheidhauer's father was the head of the 1st Battalion of the Infantry Regiment of Morocco, which led to the family living in a number of different countries. In the early 1920s the family moved to Brest, which, fortunately for Scheidhauer, was not too far away from the Brest-Guipavas aerodrome. His attempts at becoming a pilot began at the Ecole de l'Air (The Air Force School) near Brest but were curtailed with the outbreak of the Second World War and the occupation of France. Like so many others, Scheidhauer decided to make his way to England, although this was easier said than done. On the evening of 20 October 1940, he and five of his colleagues managed to find passage on board a small sailing vessel leaving from the French coastal town of Douarnenez. The boat's intended destination was Cornwall, with an expected journey time of about a day, but a combination of bad weather, high seas, and a lack of fuel instead meant it lasted eleven days, before the men eventually arrived at Milford Haven.

Scheidhauer and his comrades were handed over to a representative of the Free French Navy, but much to his surprise, Scheidhauer was assigned as an anti-aircraft gunner on board the French naval vessel, *Courbet*. As he had dearly wanted to be a pilot, Scheidhauer was extremely disappointed and made his feelings known to his senior officers, who on discovering he was an experienced flyer, re-assigned him for pilot training with the RAF. To this end he was sent to the No. 6 Elementary Flying Training School at Sywell in Northamptonshire, along with further training at Ternhill in Shropshire.

Schneidhauer qualified as a pilot in April 1942 and then spent a period of time with No. 52 Operational Training Unit at Aston Down, Gloucestershire before being posted to No. 242 Squadron who were stationed at Drem, in Scotland. He saw active service as part of the August 1942 raid on Dieppe, before being transferred the following month to No. 131 Squadron, who were stationed in Wickham at Westhampnett.

He took off from RAF Westhampnett at 14:10 on 18 November 1943, on what was known as a 'Rhubarb' mission. This was when RAF fighters or fighter-bombers would cross the English Channel during periods of low cloud and poor visibility, then drop down below cloud level to search for random targets such as trains and rolling stock, enemy troops, transports or aircraft on the ground.

On 18 November, Scheidhauer made his way across the English Channel and crossed the French coast at St-Aubin-Sur-Mer, before turning west and following the Caen-Cherbourg railway. At Carentan he successfully attacked a locomotive, although in return the

Germans unleashed a heavy barrage of anti-aircraft fire. Scheidhauer continued on towards Ouistreham in northwest France, where he was confronted with even more anti-aircraft fire. Damaged, he turned for home but, realising that he was losing fuel, he knew that he would not make it back to his base. Deciding his best option was to head for the Isle of Wight and land there, the only problem with his plan was that in his desire to make it back across the English Channel, he had lost his bearings. This meant that what he believed to be the Isle of Wight was in fact the occupied Channel Island of Jersey.

After landing in a field some 4 miles north of St. Helier and realising his mistake, he quickly set about smashing as many of the cockpit instruments as possible. German forces were soon on the scene and arrested him. Unfortunately for Scheidhauer, the Germans were able to repair his otherwise intact, and flyable Spitfire.

Ending up at Stalag Luft III, Scheidhauer was utilised as an intelligence officer, with instructions to find out as much as he could about anything to do with France. On the night of the mass breakout, Scheidhauer was in the first group of twenty to escape and was teamed up with Squadron Leader Roger Bushell. Once out of the tunnel, the two men made their way to Sagan railway station where they bought tickets for Breslau. Upon arrival, they were about to leave the train when a Gestapo officer calmly said to Bushell, 'Good luck' in perfect English. Without thinking, Bushell replied, 'Thank you', and both he and Scheidhauer were immediately arrested.

At a subsequent trial, evidence was provided that Bushell and Scheidhauer were collected from the local civilian prison at Saarbruken, driven along the autobahn towards Mannheim, and after having travelled for about 25 miles, the car they were in was stopped, their handcuffs were removed and they instructed to stretch their legs and go to the toilet.

One of the Gestapo officers, Dr Spann, the *Kriminaldirektor* (Criminal Director) of the Gestapo regional headquarters at Saarbrucken, then stepped forward and shot both men in the back. Scheidhauer was killed outright whilst Bushell was wounded and fell to his knees. His body was cremated and his ashes were subsequently returned to Stalag Luft III, before being eventually laid to rest at the Poznan Old Garrison Cemetery in Poland.

Pilot Officer Sotiris 'Skan' Skanzikas

Born on 6 August 1921 in Athens, sadly very little is known about Skanzikas' childhood or early life. When Crete fell to the Germans in April 1941, Skanzikas managed to avoid being captured and made his way to the Middle East, where he flew as a member of No. 336 Fighter Squadron, of the Royal Hellenic Airforce, which was stationed at Sidi Barrani, Egypt. He had previously taken part in several 'dogfights' against Axis aircraft from the cockpit of his Hurricane fighter aircraft.

At 07:10 on Friday, 23 July 1943, Skanzikas took off along with thirty-six other aircraft when he was shot down over the eastern end of Crete, during the ill-fated Operation Thesis. The intention had been to strafe targets such as camps, vehicles and personnel located across the occupied island. It was an operation that had little or no impact upon German forces stationed there, and its purpose is still questioned by some historians to this very day.

Skanzikas was captured by the Germans and eventually found himself incarcerated as a POW at Stalag Luft III. It is unclear what part he actually played in the planning of the escape, but because he was the twenty-eighth man to exit the tunnel, he must have played a fairly significant role. Once out of the camp he was one of a group of ten who made their way to the local railway station and caught a train at 05:00 on 25 March. Six hours later the train arrived at Ober Rohrsdorf and the group decided it was best to split into smaller groups so as not to attract any unwanted attention.

Skanzikas paired off with Flight Lieutenant Bertram Arthur James, and the men decided to travel on foot and across country, which was a very brave decision. They headed up into the surrounding hills of the Riesengebirge, where they were confronted with a heavy snow fall. To give themselves some respite from the extreme cold, they decided to head back to the town of Hirschberg, where they made for the railway station. Their appearance soon brought them to the attention of the local police, who were instantly highly suspicious and arrested them. They were then taken to the town's civilian prison to be interrogated, and it was during this time that Skanzikas and

James were separated, with James being sent to Sachsenhausen concentration camp, where he arrived on 6 April 1944.

The complete circumstances of Skanzikas' death are unknown, but he is believed to have been murdered on 30 March 1944 by a member of the Gestapo.

Lieutenant Rupert John Stevens

Born on 21 February 1919 in South Africa, the son of George Reuben and Patricia Stevens. He served with No. 12 Squadron of the South African Air Force (SAAF), who in November 1941 were stationed at El Daba airfield in Egypt. At 11:25 on 14 November 1943, Stevens was piloting a Maryland bomber aircraft on a mission to bomb the Derna airfield in northern Libya, which was a seaplane base. The journey to their intended target took Simpson and his men two hours. On their arrival they encountered heavy enemy anti-aircraft fire and four of the squadron's aircraft, including that of Stevens, were damaged. Three of these aircraft managed to make it back to their home base, but after being hit, Stevens had attempted to land his damaged aircraft, but in doing so he had mistaken the German-held Bardia – El Ahmar airfield rather than the Allied one at Tobruk. This resulted in Stevens' aircraft being struck again by German gun fire, causing it to crash land. He survived but was sent to a German military hospital, before ending up at Stalag Luft III.

Stevens was involved in both the Trojan Horse Escape of October 1943 and the Great Escape of March 1944. His part in the Trojan Horse Escape was that of the gym instructor, showing the men how best to vault the wooden horse used to hide the men inside and underneath. His part in the mass escape of March 1944 is unknown, but it must have been reasonably important as he was the sixth man out of the tunnel.

Stevens was paired up with fellow south African Johannes Gouws and the information concerning his escape can be found in Gouws' entry.

Flying Officer Robert Campbell Stewart

Born on 7 July 1911, Stewart was the son of Alexander Campbell and Augusta Campbell Stewart, who at the time of his birth were living in north London. Stewart had two older sisters, Mary and Lily, and an older brother, Alexander Jnr. When the Second World War broke out, Stewart's brother was too old for wartime service (he was 40) and so instead served as a stretcher bearer for the ARP.

A married man, Stewart served as a member of No. 77 Squadron. Having taken off from RAF Elvington, Yorkshire, as a navigator on board a Halifax bomber aircraft at 00:39 on 27 April 1943, on a mission to bomb Duisburg, he was subsequently shot down by German anti-aircraft fire later that morning over Haarzopf, Essen, and crash landed in Scheidstrasse. Two members of the crew, Pilot Officer John Downing Pye and rear gunner Sergeant John Raymond Wells, were killed, the other five, including Stewart, were captured and became POWs. Both Stewart and Flying Officer Douglas William Atter ended up in Stalag Luft III, whilst the others were sent to Stalag 357 at Thorn, Poland. Although Atter was one of those who took part in the subsequent mass escape, he was not subsequently executed and instead was returned to Stalag Luft III on 17 May 1944. He was finally liberated from the camp on 28 January 1945.

Stewart did not get far during the escape and was recaptured close to Sagan. Instead of being immediately returned to the camp, he was instead taken to Görlitz prison. He was last seen alive on 31 March, when he and nine others who had escaped were removed from the prison by Gestapo officers. Stewart is believed to have been murdered by the Gestapo officer Walter Lux under the instruction of his fellow Gestapo officer, Scharpwinkel. Stewart was cremated at Lignitz and his ashes returned to Stalag Luft III. His remains were later reburied at the Poznan Old Garrison Cemetery, Poland.

Flying Officer John Gifford Stower

Born on 15 September 1916 in Buenos Aires, unfortunately little is known of Stower's prewar life. However, it is known that at 17:14 on 16 November 1942, while flying a Wellington bomber as part of

No. 142 Squadron, Stower took off from RAF Waltham in Grimsby on a mission to lay mines in the North Sea. Stower and the other four members of his crew took part in the mission along with five other Wellingtons from Stower's squadron and sixty-five other aircraft. Stower's aircraft was one of three that did not make it back to their base, having been hit by German anti-aircraft fire off the coast of Büsum at about 20:00 and crash landing in mud flats just south of the town. The crew all made it safely out of their stricken aircraft and into one of their dinghies and came ashore at Friedrichskoog. After being captured Stower eventually ended up in Stalag Luft III.

The mass escape from the camp on the night of 24/25 March 1944 was not his first attempt at escaping. On 12 June 1943, two large working parties of POWs were being escorted out of the camp by two uniformed German guards, only in this case the two escorting guards were actually Allied POWs dressed in homemade German uniforms. Stower was in the first working party, who manged to escape, but the second group were stopped before they made it out of the camp.

Stower's story, should he be stopped by any of the local authorities, was that he was a Spanish labourer. He managed to make his way to Czechoslovakia, entirely on foot, where he made contact with the Czech Resistance, hoping they would be able to get him across the border into Switzerland. Unfortunately, he instead returned to Germany hoping that he would be able to cross into Switzerland from there, but before he could do so he was stopped by a German border patrol, arrested and interrogated by the Gestapo, before finally being returned to Stalag Luft III.

On 13 September 1943 he was promoted to the rank of flight lieutenant, an announcement of which was recorded in the *London Gazette* of 17 September.

On the night of the Great Escape and once having made it out of the tunnel and into the nearby woods, Stower teamed up with Flight Lieutenant Ivo Tonder, a Czechoslovakian member of the RAF, and headed south. By the morning of 27 March, the two men had made their way to the Polish town of Kohlfurt, from where they caught a train to Görlitz before heading towards Reichenberg. During the journey they were stopped and questioned by members of the German civilian police and when the two men were searched, their POW identity tags were discovered, and they were subsequently arrested. When the train reached its destination, they were taken to the civilian prison, where they met five other escapees from Stalag Luft III.

Tonder later described how he had seen Stower driven out of the prison on the morning of 31 March. This was the last time that he ever saw him. Tonder was given no explanation as to why he had been left in the prison or why Stower had been removed. Within a matter of days of Stower's departure from the prison, Tonder was sent to Colditz Castle and told that he was facing a death sentence. Whether that was ever actually the case is debateable. He was more likely told this to scare and intimidate him, because if he had been one of the men nominated to be killed by the Germans, he would have no doubt left the camp with the others who were executed.

Flight Lieutenant Denys Oliver Street

Born on 1 April 1922 to Sir Arthur and Lady Street, of Mill Hill, Middlesex, Street was a member of the Royal Air Force Volunteer Reserve's No. 207 Squadron and took off from his home base at RAF Langar in Nottinghamshire at 21:35 on Monday, 29 March 1943 to bomb Berlin. Street's aircraft was attacked as it approached the German coast near the town of Rerik, but Street and his crew managed to bail out before it crashed into the ground. Captured on landing, four of the crew ended up as POWs in Stalag 357, a further two were sent to Stalag Luft VI, and Street was sent to Stalag Luft III.

Very little is known about his journey once he escaped from the camp on the evening of 24/25 March 1944. His body was later cremated in Breslau and his ashes were then returned to Stalag Luft III. Unlike the remains of most of the other murdered escapees, his remains were not interred at the Old Garrison Cemetery in Poznan but instead were buried in the grounds of the Berlin 1939-1945 War Cemetery, where his gravestone records the date of his death as being 6 April 1944, and his age just 21. His internment at his final resting place was in fact a reburial which took place during the week of 22-29 May 1959. Where his remains had been between the time Stalag Luft III was liberated and their reburial, is unclear.

Flight Lieutenant Cyril Douglas Swain

Born on 15 December 1911 in the market town of Wem, Shropshire, Swain had enlisted in the RAF before the war, having earned his wings on 29 August 1936 after successfully completing his training at No. 6 Elementary Flying Training School at RAF Sywell.

By the outbreak of the Second World War, Swain was serving with No. 105 Squadron, who flew Blenheim bombers out of RAF Swanton Morley as part of No. 2 Group RAF, Bomber Command.

At 17:28 on 28 November 1940, the Blenheim aircraft Swain was piloting took off from RAF Swanton Morley on a bombing raid over Düsseldorf and Antwerp. On the return journey, Swain's aircraft got into difficulty and they were left with no other option but to abandon it. Swain and his crew all managed to bail out safely before it crashed near Morlaix, France. Swain and another member of his crew, Pilot Officer Clelland, managed to remain at large for three days before being captured. Swain was initially incarcerated at Stalag Luft I, before being transferred to Stalag Luft III.

After being recaptured near the town of Görlitz, Swain was imprisoned there and was last seen alive when he was taken from the prison on 31 March 1944. Having been cremated at Leignitz, Swain's ashes were returned to Stalag Luft III some weeks after his murder, and subsequently buried in the Old Garrison Cemetery, Poznan.

Flying Officer Paweł W. 'Peter' Tobolski

Born on 21 March 1906 in Poland, Tobolski was a member of No. 301 (Polish) Squadron, which was a bomber squadron. On the night of 25/26 June 1942, he was a member of crew on board a Wellington bomber aircraft that took part in one of bomber command's thousand-bomber raids over Bremen; it was Tobolski's second mission. The aircraft was shot down by German anti-aircraft guns over the village of Dornumergrode in East Frisia, Germany.

Managing to bail out of the stricken aircraft, he was captured by ground forces and sent to Stalag Luft III. Having taken part in the mass breakout on the evening of 24/25 March 1944, his was an elaborate plan by any stretch of the imagination. He was dressed as a German soldier and was in company with fellow escapee Harry Day. Their story was that Tobolski was taking Day to Berlin to be interrogated at Gestapo headquarters. Before the pair could get very far, Tobolski needed his travel documents stamped and authenticated by the local German army barracks in Sagan. If this was not done and he was stopped and searched, he ran the risk of being treated as a deserter, the sentence for which was death by firing squad. The pair made it as far as Stettin, a city in northern Poland, where they were betrayed by some French workers.

Where the pair were actually executed is unclear, but the remains of both men eventually ended up at the Old Garrison Cemetery, Poznan.

Flight Lieutenant Arnošt Valenta

Born on 25 October 1912 in the small mountain village of Svébohov, in what was then Austria-Hungary, Valenta's father, Adolf, had served during the First World War in the Austro-Hungarian army, but was killed in 1915.

Valenta completed his education in June 1933 but after wanting to go to university to study philosophy, his family could not afford to send him. Instead, he enlisted in the armed forces, commencing his compulsory two-year military service and becoming an officer in the Czechoslovakian army on 31 July 1933. Sometime before 1941, he became a radio operator in the Royal Air Force Volunteer Reserve. The unit he was allocated to was No. 311 (Czechoslovak) Squadron, which flew Wellington bomber aircraft out of RAF East Wretham.

On 6 February 1941, he was the radio operator on a Wellington bomber which took off from RAF East Wretham on a bombing mission over Boulogne-Sur-Mer in occupied France. Valenta was not initially due to take part but replaced Pilot Officer Jaroslav Partyk after he was taken ill at the last minute. On the return journey the Wellington incurred radio problems, which meant that it was difficult for the pilot and the crew to work out with any degree of certainty where they were. As if that was not bad enough for the crew, they also had to battle extremely strong winds. The pilot, Pilot Officer František Cigoš, misjudged his actual location to such a degree that after landing in what he believed to be at an airfield on the south coast of England, it was actually in Flers, in occupied northern France.

Valenta and the rest of the crew were all captured and became POWs, with Valenta ending up at Stalag Luft III. Having settled into camp life and being fully trusted by his fellow POWs, Valenta became part of the escape committee. His role was what was known as the 'Head of Contacts', which was more commonly referred to as the 'scrounger'. It was his job to get hold of everything that would be needed to help the escapees once they had made it out of the camp, such as documents, ID papers, train timetables, money, official stamps, clothes dyes, and even compasses. His part in the escape ensured that he was amongst the early groups of POWs who exited the tunnel.

Valenta did not remain at large for long and was eventually recaptured near the town of Görlitz. He was taken to the town's prison and interrogated. On 31 March Valenta, along with nine other recaptured escapees, was taken from the camp by members of the Gestapo and was never seen alive again.

Flight Lieutenant Gilbert William Walenn

Also known as Tim Wallen, he was born on 24 February 1916 in Hendon, London. His love of flying had come from his father, who had served as a pilot with the Royal Flying Corps during the First World War.

Walenn decided on a position working in a bank as a way of earning sufficient money to pay for flying lessons, and so dedicated was he to achieving his goal that he became one of a small group of individuals who helped form the Midland Bank Flying Club. In 1937 he enrolled in the Royal Air Force Volunteer Reserve, which had only been formed the year before, in support of the RAF in the event of another war.

At 19:55 on 10 September 1941, the same day he had been promoted to the rank of flight lieutenant, Walenn, serving as a flying officer with No. 25 Operational Training Unit, took off from his home base at RAF Finningley in South Yorkshire on a night-time bombing mission. At 05:31 the following morning, having dropped his bombs on his intended target, he had turned for home and was over the Dutch city of Rotterdam when his aircraft was struck by anti-aircraft fire. It was so badly damaged that he and his crew had no other option other than to bail out, which they all successfully did. Walenn was captured and sent to Stalag Luft III. He was an immediately recognisable character as he had a big bushy handlebar style moustache – the sort that immediately identified a man as being a member of the RAF.

He played an active part in the preparation of the mass escape from the camp, particularly in the forgery department, producing all kinds of documents that an escaped man might possibly require having made it under the wire and out of the camp. He left the camp as part of a group of four who masqueraded as French and Lithuanian workers. They managed to catch a train on the morning of 25 March from the railway station at Sagan heading towards the city of Danzig. They made it as far as Schneidemühl, in northwest Poland, before they were captured by the Gestapo and taken to Stalag Luft XX-B POW camp, where they were kept overnight. The following morning, Walenn and his three fellow escapees were taken from the camp, driven to a dense wooded area near Gross Tramken, and shot. The bodies of the four men were taken to the crematorium in Danzig where they were cremated on 29 March, and their ashes returned to the camp at Stalag Luft III before eventually being buried at the Old Garrison Cemetery at Poznan.

Flight Lieutenant James Chrystall Wernham

Born on 15 October 1917 in Scotland, Wernham's family later immigrated to Canada, where they set up home in Winnipeg, Manitoba.

During the Second World War Wernham enlisted in the Royal Canadian Air Force, and on his arrival in the UK became a pilot officer with No. 405 Squadron, stationed at RAF Pocklington, Yorkshire.

At 22:57 on 8 June 1942, Wernham, acting as an air observer, took off in a Halifax bomber as part of a large bombing mission on the German city of Essen. The aircraft is known to have crashed at Gelderland after a mayday was received at 03:40 the following morning. It is believed that it had been hit by anti-aircraft fire, and although the aircraft was badly damaged, there was still sufficient time for Wernham and the rest of the crew to bail out over Zaltbommel, Holland. They were all captured and Wernham ended up as a POW at Stalag Luft III.

After his escape, Wernham made it as far as Hirschberg, Germany, before being recaptured. He was later murdered by the Gestapo.

Flight Lieutenant George William Wiley

Born on 24 January 1922 in London, Ontario, Canada, with the war just four months old Wiley enlisted in the Royal Canadian Air Force on 4 December 1940.

At 15:45 on 10 March 1943, whilst serving with No. 112 (Fighter) Squadron, Wiley took off from an Advanced Landing Ground at Neffatia in Tunisia, in his Kittyhawk aircraft, along with eleven of his colleagues. Their mission was to provide top cover for aircraft from No. 250 and No. 260 Squadrons, who had been detailed to attack enemy transport and armoured vehicles in southern Tunisia. At 16:48, just over an hour after he had taken off, his aircraft was shot down, but he managed to bail out and land safely in the desert. He survived for two days before he was spotted by an enemy patrol. Initially he was sent to Italy, before eventually ending up at Stalag Luft III on 4 April 1943.

Although not a great deal is known about Wiley after he escaped from Stalag Luft III, or whilst he was at large, it is known that after his recapture he was incarcerated at Görlitz prison. Along with five other recaptured airmen from Stalag Luft III, he was removed from the prison on 31 March 1944 and shot dead later that day in the vicinity of Halbau, near Görlitz, by members of the Breslau and Görlitz Gestapo.

Squadron Leader John Edwin Ashley 'Willy' Williams, DFC

Born on 6 May 1919 in Wellington, New Zealand, Williams spent most of his younger years growing up in the Sydney suburb of Manly, Australia.

With tensions mounting throughout most of Europe, the potential for war was never far from most people's minds. Williams was no exception. He travelled to the UK in early 1938, enlisted in the RAF and was given a short service commission as a pilot officer, which was announced in the *London Gazette* of 12 April 1938. By August 1941, he had been promoted to the rank of flight lieutenant.

Between 11 April and 14 June 1942, Williams served with No. 112, No. 94, No. 260, and No. 450 squadrons. Whilst serving with the latter he shot down four, and damaged a further two, German aircraft in less than a month. For his efforts he was awarded the Distinguished Flying Cross.

On 31 October 1942, when he was the commanding officer of No. 450 Squadron, he was involved in strafing a ground target at Buq Buq, Egypt, along with eleven other Kittyhawks, during the Second Battle of El Alamein. During the confusion of battle, he was accidentally shot down by one of his own aircraft. Williams was seen to crash land on rough ground but appeared to be uninjured and climbed out his aircraft. He was subsequently captured and became a POW, but it was not until the early months of 1944 that he ended up at Stalag Luft III.

Sadly, little is known about what happened to Williams after he escaped from the camp during the mass breakout, other than at the time he was recaptured, he was in the company of three other escapees. His remains eventually ended up at the Old Garrison Cemetery, Poznan, and his gravestone shows that he died on 29 March 1944.

Flight Lieutenant John Francis Williams

Born in 1918 in Ewell, Surrey to parents John and Bertha, Williams was a member of the RAF's No. 107 Squadron, Bomber Command, which flew out of RAF Great Massingham in Norfolk. From March

1942, the squadron had specifically begun carrying out daytime operations against designated targets in occupied Europe.

At 14:22 on 27 April 1942, Williams was the navigator of the three-man crew of a Douglas Boston Mk III bomber aircraft on its way to bomb a German-controlled power station in the town of Sequedin situated in northern France. Having dropped its bombs, the aircraft was attacked and shot down by a German Fw 190 near Bourbourg at 15:50. All three crew members managed to bail out and were captured by German ground forces. The aircraft's pilot, Sergeant Kenneth Nicholas Carpenter, ended up in Stalag Luft VI, whilst W/02 Gordon Samuel Guy Black, of the Royal Canadian Air Force, and the rear gunner on the flight, ended up as a POW at Stalag 357. Williams, meanwhile, was sent to Stalag Luft III.

Sadly, not that much is known about Williams' time spent as a POW at Stalag Luft III, and what part he played in the planning of the mass escape. After being re-captured and then executed by the Gestapo, his body was cremated at Breslau.

Like all those whose ashes were brought back to Stalag Luft III, he is buried at the Old Barrack cemetery in Poznan.

CHAPTER SIXTEEN

The Escapees Who Survived

The following is a list of the men who escaped from Stalag Luft III on the evening of 24/25 March 1944, but who were either returned there or detained at another POW or concentration camp following their recapture.

Every one of these men had an individual history, which although not connected before the outbreak of the war, certainly helped to bring them together afterwards. Their lives were spared by the simple stroke of one man's pen.

Flight Lieutenant Albert Armstrong

Born on 14 July 1920 in Bolton, Lancashire, Armstrong worked as an electrical engineer before the war. He was also member of the General Duties Branch of the Royal Air Force Volunteer Reserve and as such was called up after war was declared.

Having left its home base at RAF Kabrit, Egypt, Armstrong's Wellington bomber was shot down on a mission to Tobruk, Libya, on the evening of 10 August 1942. After being captured, Armstrong was sent to Germany where he was initially incarcerated at Dulag Luft until 27 August. He was then transferred to Stalag Luft III, arriving on 29 August.

Armstrong was the forty-second man out of the tunnel on the evening of the escape and managed to stay at large until 26 March, when he was stopped and recaptured by a detachment of the

Volksturm, Germany's version of the Home Guard. He was returned to Stalag Luft III on the morning of 5 April, where he remained until the forced march of 27 January 1945. He was finally liberated on 10 April.

On his return to the UK, he married Florence May Cocker in Bolton on 12 July 1945 and the couple would go on to have two children: David, who was born in 1947, and Janet, who was born in 1948.

Flight Lieutenant Richard Anthony Bethell

Born on 9 April 1922 in Dar es Salaam, Bethell's parents served with the British Colonial Service in East Africa, which meant he and his brothers were sent to the prestigious Junior King's School, in Sturry, Kent.

Aged 18, he enlisted in the RAF in February 1941 as an airman 2nd class but was sent to America to complete his pilot training. On his return to England with the rank of pilot officer, he was eventually posted to No. 268 (Fighter) Squadron, who flew American P-51 Mustangs out of RAF Snailwell, in Cambridgeshire. On 26 November 1942, whilst still a member of No. 268 Squadron, and having reached the rank of flying officer, he registered the unit's first recorded air-to-air combat victories when he shot down two German aircraft near Elburg and Oldebroek, during a mission over the Netherlands.

The squadron's main purpose was to attack German shipping off the Dutch coast and inland ground targets, such as trains, ground forces or military vehicles. On 7 December 1942, whilst carrying out such an attack over Alkmaar, Bethell's aircraft was struck by anti-aircraft fire and he was forced to crash land. He survived and was captured by German troops. He was initially interrogated at a nearby Dulag Luft, before being sent to Stalag Luft III, where he quickly settled into camp life.

Bethell became an active member in the escape's preparation, being both a tunneller and a 'penguin', one of those who dispersed the soil from the tunnels at different locations around the camp. During the actual escape he was positioned at the tunnel's second staging point, an enlarged area that allowed for wider movement.

This involved helping to pull other escapees through the tunnel until he in turn was relieved to continue with his own escape. At one point, whilst he was pulling the other escapees through, there was a collapse in the tunnel and he had to wait at his location for nearly an hour before the cave-in had been repaired.

Bethell was one of the last dozen men to exit the tunnel before the escape was discovered. He and some of the other escapees had only been in the woods for a matter of minutes when they heard a gunshot and instinctively knew that the Germans had somehow discovered a breakout was taking place.

Having escaped from the camp, Bethell teamed up with Flight Lieutenant James Long, known by his camp mates as 'Cookie'. Their original plan was to head for Czechoslovakia, which meant they would have to travel some 40 miles, but because of inclement weather, they had no option but to change their plans and head for Frankfurt instead. Unfortunately, luck was not on their side and while travelling during the day, they were captured at Bernau. Both men were taken to the prison at Görlitz, and by nothing other than the luck of the draw, Bethell was one of those who was returned to Stalag Luft III, whilst Long was sadly to become one of the fifty murdered escapees.

Bethell was one of the POWs who were force-marched out of the camp in January 1945, as Soviet forces approached the Sagan area. He returned to civvy street after the end of the war, but on 7 December 1949, he re-joined the RAF at his old rank of flight lieutenant and became a navigator instructor. He also spent time as the personal assistant to the then Air Chief Marshal Sir George Pirie. He remained in the RAF until June 1955, when he immigrated to Canada. He died on 17 February 2004, aged 81.

Flight Lieutenant Leslie C.J. Broderick

Born 19 May 1921 in Wandsworth, London, in 1939 he enlisted in the Territorial Army and was stationed on Canvey Island in Essex as part of a searchlight unit. By 1940, and with the war under way, Broderick had had a change of heart and transferred to the RAF.

He was commissioned as an officer before being posted to No. 106 (Bomber) Squadron, which flew Lancasters from RAF Cottesmore in Rutland.

At 22:00 on 14 April 1943, Broderick took off from RAF Syerston on what was his nineteenth bombing mission, this time to Stuttgart. After dropping his bombs over the designated target, he was returning to England when his aircraft was struck by German anti-aircraft fire and he was forced to crash land at Sauvillers-Mongival in northeast France. Four members of his crew were killed in the crash, but Broderick survived and ended up as a POW at Stalag Luft III.

Once at the camp, he became one of the tunnellers in both 'Dick' and 'Harry'. On the night of the escape, he was number fifty-two in the queue as the escapees patiently and somewhat nervously made their way through the tunnel. Once outside, he teamed up with Henry Birkland and Denys Street and decided to escape on foot. This decision turned out to be their downfall as the inclement weather was not conducive to being outdoors for long periods of time. With the elements taking their toll on the three men, they saw a cottage and decided to knock to see if they could stay the night to escape the worsening weather. Unfortunately for the three escapees, when the cottage door was opened they found several German soldiers living there. They were arrested and taken to the local police station before being sent on to Gestapo headquarters at Görlitz, some 35 miles from Sagan, where they were interrogated. On 31 March, Birkland, Street and a number of other recaptured POWs were taken from the camp and never seen alive again.

Meanwhile, Broderick was returned to Stalag Luft III and subsequently survived the 'Long March', which began on 27 January 1945, when the remaining fit and healthy inmates were force-marched out of the camp as Soviet forces approached from the east. As if the journey for Broderick and his comrades was not perilous enough, it nearly became a lot worse when they were fired upon by a Spitfire, who quickly broke off the attack when he realised who he was firing at. Broderick and the others eventually reached a tobacco plantation near Lübeck, from where they were liberated on 2 May 1945.

Demobbed in 1945, Broderick took up a teaching job at Leigh Beck Primary school on Canvey Island, where he remained until 1955 before immigrating to South Africa. He died on 8 April 2013, aged 91.

Flight Lieutenant William J. Cameron

Born in Canada, on 26 July 1943 Cameron was serving with No. 72 Squadron on a reconnaissance mission over the northern coast of Sicily, specifically on the lookout for shipping in the waters of the Strait of Messina. The Strait was heavily defended on both sides with several strategically placed anti-aircraft batteries, who opened fire on Cameron's aircraft as well as the other three Spitfires he was with. When his aircraft was struck, he had no option but to bail out. Upon landing he was captured and so began his life as a POW, initially in camps in Italy, but by September 1943 he had been moved to Germany and eventually arrived at Stalag Luft III on 1 November 1943.

Having been one of those who escaped from the camp, Cameron only managed to remain at large for two days before he was recaptured at Halbau. From there he was taken to the prison at Görlitz where he was interrogated by the Gestapo. He was then returned to Stalag Luft III, where he remained until 28 January 1945 before being part of the enforced march. His eventual destination was the German POW camp known as Marlag und Milag Nord, situated near the village of Westertimke, where he arrived on 4 February. He was liberated three months later on 3 May.

Of the seven members of the Royal Canadian Air Force who took part in the Great Escape, Cameron would be the only one to survive.

Flight Lieutenant Richard S.A. Churchill

Churchill was a member of No. 144 Squadron. In September 1940, his aircraft was shot down by German night fighters over the Netherlands, on what was his twenty-sixth operational mission. He was forced to bail out and upon landing, was captured and became a

POW. He was initially sent to the Dulag Luft near Frankfurt, before moving to Stalag Luft I and eventually Stalag Luft III.

By the time it came to the digging of 'Harry', he was already an experienced tunneller, which made him an extremely useful addition to the camp. When it came to the night of the escape, he was the fiftieth man to make his way through the tunnel to freedom.

After escaping from the camp disguised as a Romanian worker, Churchill teamed up with fellow escapee, Gordon Kidder. Together the two men, who had planned to make it to Czechoslovakia, managed to remain at large for two nights before they were recaptured after being discovered by a farmer hiding in his barn. What they could not have known was that Adolf Hitler had ordered every barn within 100 miles of Stalag Luft III to be searched in case any of the escapees tried to use them to hide. The deep snow and freezing temperatures had left the two men cold, wet through, exhausted and in desperate need of shelter and respite from the inclement weather.

Despite their cover story, neither of the men could speak Romanian other repeating a few phrases they had managed to remember verbatim. The reason they chose Romanian was that they had estimated there would not be any German soldiers who could speak the language, and that trying to get somebody to translate would simply take too long.

After the two men had been recaptured, they both ended up at the Gestapo prison in Görlitz. Although Kidder was one of the fifty escapees to be murdered, Churchill later said in an interview he gave to the *Daily Telegraph* in March 2014 that he believed he had been one of those spared because the Germans thought him to be related to Prime Minister Winston Churchill, which in turn meant he could be used as a potential hostage in any future negotiations with the British.

Churchill went on to become the last surviving member of those involved in the Great Escape, dying on 13 February 2019, aged 99.

Wing Commander Harry Melville Arbuthnot Day, GC, DSO, OBE

Born on 3 August 1898 in Sarawak, Malaysia, as a teenager Day was sent to England to continue his education at Haileybury College, where he joined their Officers Cadet Corps. During the First World

War he served in the Royal Marines, having been commissioned as a second lieutenant on 31 August 1916. On 9 November 1918, just two days before the end of the war, his ship HMS *Britannia* was struck by a German torpedo and sank. Before the ship went down, Day twice went below decks to rescue two trapped, injured men. For his actions that day he was awarded the Albert Medal, which in 1971 he exchanged for the George Cross.

After the end of the First World War, Day remained with the Royal Marines until 1924, when he decided to transfer to the Fleet Air Arm. In June that same year he received a commission as a flying officer in the RAF.

With the Second World War was just two months away, Day was promoted to the rank of wing commander and put in command of No. 57 Squadron, who flew Bristol Blenheim twin-engine bomber aircraft out of RAF Upper Heyford.

When war broke out, the squadron was sent to Metz in northeast France in direct support of the British Expeditionary Force. It operated out of an airfield located at Roye/Amy, where its main purpose was to act as a reconnaissance unit. On 13 October 1939, Day went on a mission to reconnoitre the areas around Hamm, near Dortmund, Hannover and Soest, but his Blenheim aircraft was attacked and shot down by a Messerschmitt over the German town of Birkenfeld. With his aircraft on fire and the other two members of his crew already dead, Day bailed out and was arrested as he landed on the ground. His face and hands had been burned before he had been able to parachute out, resulting in him being admitted to a German military hospital.

Following his release from hospital, he was initially sent to a POW camp in Oberusel, northwest of Frankfurt, but only spent a few weeks there before he was on the move again, this time to Oflag IX-A/H POW camp in Spangenberg Castle. His time at the castle lasted only a couple of months before he was sent to the transit camp at Dulag Luft, where it would be fair to say he gained a certain reputation, but not one he would have particularly wanted to embrace. Because of his apparent friendship with several German guards, as well as the camp's commandant, Major Rumpel, some of his fellow POWs suspected him, and other senior British officers, of collaborating with the Germans. Nothing could have been further from the truth. The reality was that Day, along with other senior officers including Roger Bushell, Jimmy Buckley and Johnnie Dodge, had not only been gathering intelligence, but had used the 'privileges' they had gained from their 'friendships' with the guards and commandants to build an escape tunnel, which started from right underneath the very bed Day slept in.

In June 1941, Day and seventeen other POWs activated their escape plan and tunnelled their way out of the camp, at the time making it the first Allied mass escape of the war. Once out of the camp Day went it alone and made his way on foot. He was at large for five days before he was recaptured, as was everyone else who had taken part in the escape. Part of their punishment was to be transferred to Stalag Luft I POW camp, but this was no deterrent for Day, who went about arranging an escape committee. Another tunnel was dug, and twelve officers made their way through it. After only three of them had exited the tunnel, however, the escape attempt was discovered and the three men were quickly recaptured.

In March 1942 the German authorities took the decision that Stalag Luft I was to be closed and all prisoners moved to Stalag Luft III. The move to a different camp was no deterrent to Day and his attempts at escaping: between March and October 1942 he made two further bids but was unsuccessful in both. This resulted in him being transferred to Oflag XXI-B, but five months later he was up to his old tricks once again when on the night of 5/6 March 1943, he was one of thirty-five men to escape from the camp via a tunnel. Day was recaptured and ended up back at Stalag Luft III.

Day subsequently helped plan and organise the mass escape from the camp on the night of 24/25 March 1944, and was one of those who made it through the tunnel before the breakout was discovered. His story should he be stopped was that he was a British colonel who was under escort by a German soldier, fellow escapee Flying Officer Pavel Tobolski. The pair made their way by train to Berlin and then on to Stettin, where they arrived on the evening of 25 March. Unfortunately, after asking for help from a group of French workers, they were betrayed and arrested the following morning.

Day was taken to Berlin where he was interrogated by Arthur Nebe, head of Germany's Criminal Police, the individual responsible for selecting the fifty escapees from Stalag Luft III who were to be murdered. One of those men was Pavel Tobolski. Day would later claim that Hitler had personally ordered his execution but was saved when Hermann Göring intervened on his behalf, concerned at the potential reaction as Day was so well known to the British public. Instead, he was sent to Sachsenhausen concentration camp. It was not long, however, before he and four others had managed to tunnel their way out and escape. After being recaptured, Day was returned to Sachsenhausen, but to insure he did not escape again, he was placed in solitary confinement in one of the camp's death cells.

In February 1945, as the war was coming to an end and Germany faced the daunting task of being overrun by British and American forces from the west and Soviet forces from the east, the decision was taken to move Day yet again. Initially he was transferred to concentration camps at Flossenburg and Dachau, but on 27 April 1945, Day was one of 139 high-profile prisoners who were moved to the Hotel Pragser Wildsee in South Tyrol, northern Italy.

Day and his group were eventually liberated on 4 May 1945 by elements of the United States 85th Division's 339th Infantry Regiment. On 1 May, Day and another prisoner had left the Hotel Pragser Wildsee, stolen a vehicle, and two days later came into contact with elements of the US Fifth Army. In the early hours of 4 May, G Company, 339th Infantry Regiment arrived at the hotel, whereby the German soldiers laid down their arms and surrendered.

For his actions as a POW, Day was awarded the Distinguished Service Order, appointed an Officer of the Order of the British Empire, and the United States Legion of Merit. He remained in the RAF after the war, finally retiring in 1950 at the rank of group captain. He died in Malta on 11 March 1977, aged 78.

Major John Bigelow Dodge, DSO, DSC, MC

Born on 15 May 1894 in New York City, Dodge made his way to England in August 1914 and received a commission into the Royal Naval Division, even though he did not become a naturalised British citizen until the following year. This was likely because the First Lord of the Admiralty at the time was none other than Winston

Churchill, and Dodge's sister, Lucie, was married to Lionel George William Guest, a cousin of Churchill's.

Dodge saw active service at Gallipoli in 1915 where he served with the 7th (Hood) Battalion of the Royal Naval Division. He was awarded the Distinguished Service Medal in recognition of his service during the Gallipoli campaign.

On 14 April 1916 Dodge transferred to the British Army with the rank of temporary captain and was posted to the 10th (Battersea) Battalion, Queens Royal West Surrey Regiment. He later went on to command the 16th Battalion, Royal West Surrey and was decorated with the Distinguished Service Order.

He was demobilised from the British Army on 18 December 1920 but kept the rank of major. At the outbreak of the Second World War Dodge was already 45, but once again he wanted to do his bit and so re-enlisted. Keeping his rank of major, he served with the Middlesex Regiment but was attached to the 51st (Highland) Infantry Division, who had been given the task of holding off advancing German forces during the mass evacuations from Dunkirk. The outcome for those officers and men of the 51st was either to be killed or captured. Dodge, along hundreds of other members of the division, was captured at Saint-Valery-en-Caux and became a POW.

Whilst being transported on a barge along the River Scheldt to a POW camp in Germany, he escaped by jumping overboard. When he reached the river bank, however, he came across a Dutch civilian who handed him over to a Luftwaffe officer. This explains how Dodge ended up in Stalag Luft III, because despite being an army officer and not an RAF one, he now found himself as a prisoner of the Luftwaffe. Initially he was held at Dulag Luft and was one of the seventeen British officers who escaped from there in June 1941. After this he was sent to Stalag Luft I, before arriving at Stalag Luft III in April 1942, where he became second in command to Wing Commander Harry Day, before being transferred out to Oflag XXI-B in November the same year. He had not even arrived at his new home before attempting to escape once again. During the journey, he jumped from the train but was spotted by one of the guards and quickly recaptured. He was only at XXI-B for six months before he was transferred back to Stalag Luft III, where he became part of the camp's escape committee. His part in the preparation of the escape was not as a tunneller but to create distractions, covering any noise that might have been audible from the digging of the tunnels.

Having escaped some four hours before the Germans discovered a mass breakout was taking place, Dodge teamed up with Canadian Flight Lieutenant James Wernham, but the pair was re-captured at Hirschberg railway station later that same day. They were interrogated at the local police station, after which Dodge was sent to Sachsenhausen concentration camp, while Wernham became one of the fifty recaptured escapees who were subsequently murdered by the Gestapo.

On his arrival at Sachsenhausen, Dodge made another escape attempt on the evening of 23 September 1944, when he and four other British officers managed to escape. He remained at large for more than four weeks before being recaptured and returned to Sachsenhausen, where he was placed in one of the camp's death cells. This time, however, he was chained to the floor in solitary confinement so as to prevent him from making any further escape attempts.

After being held like this for nearly four months, Dodge was suddenly removed from the camp in February 1945 and taken to Berlin. Uncertain of his fate, he would no doubt have been somewhat surprised when he was taken to two unnamed senior German officers, who, knowing of his relationship to Winston Churchill, wanted him to act as a go between for the German and British governments. After offering a German surrender to British and American forces, but not to the Soviets, Dodge returned to England and on 6 May met with Churchill and America's ambassador to the UK, John Gilbert Winant, whose own son was being held by the Nazis. Dodge passed on the German offer of surrender, but it was not acted upon by either Churchill or Winant. Churchill in particular wanted a complete defeat of Germany and would accept nothing less than an unconditional surrender.

On 18 April 1946, it was announced in the *London Gazette* that Dodge had been awarded the Military Cross for his services and actions as a POW. He died in London on 2 November 1960, aged 66.

Flight Lieutenant Sydney Hastings Dowse

Born on 21 November 1918 in Hammersmith, London, Dowse was affectionately known as 'laughing boy' because he always had a smile on his face.

Enthralled by flying since he had been a young boy, when he was 19 Dowse decided to enlist in the Royal Naval Volunteer Reserve so that he could learn to fly at the weekends. When the Second World War began in September 1939, he was called up to the RAF.

When Dowse completed his training on 21 October 1940, he was commissioned as a pilot officer and posted to No. 608 Squadron, which flew Avro Ansons and were part of No. 16 Group RAF Coastal Command, flying as convoy escorts and on anti-submarine operations.

By the beginning of 1941 Dowse had transferred to the No.1 Photographic Reconnaissance Unit, flying Supermarine Spitfires out of Heston aerodrome. On 15 August he was flying over Brest, attempting to photograph the German battleships *Scharnhorst* and *Gneisenau*, which had been located in that area. Whilst carrying out his mission, Dowse's Spitfire was struck by groundfire, and although wounded in one leg, he managed to bail out and was captured soon after landing. Four months later Dowse was still in a German military hospital recovering from his wounds. He had quite clearly recovered much better than he had let on because on 1 December 1941, he escaped from the hospital and remained at large for three days before he was recaptured whilst attempting to cross the border into the Netherlands.

After having been recaptured. he was sent to the nearby Stalag IX-C POW camp at Bad Sulza, but on 21 January 1942, just a matter of weeks after his arrival, Dowse was up to his old tricks once again. He escaped by joining a work party tasked with conducting work outside of the camp. He then somehow managed to separate himself from his fellow campmates, without being noticed, and escaped. He was a free man for five days before being recaptured close to Germany's border with Belgium. By the time he was recaptured, he had hardly eaten or slept since his escape and the extreme cold weather had left him close to frostbite. His physical condition was so bad that he required a short stay in hospital to recover fully. On his release, instead of being returned to Stalag IX-C, he found himself being sent to Oflag VI-B, a camp for officers near the town of Warburg.

Being sent to another camp made absolutely no difference to Dowse. No sooner had he settled into life in his new home than he was looking at ways to escape. Plans were made, a tunnel was dug, and on the evening of 18 April 1942, the conditions were right for the breakout to go ahead. The plan was for a total of thirty-five men to make their way along an excavated tunnel under the camp's fence. As was the case with the subsequent mass escape from Stalag Luft III, the estimation of how long the tunnel needed to be was way off the mark. Instead of coming up in the woods surrounding the camp, it finished in the open, which also happened to be exactly in line with the route taken by the German sentry who patrolled on the outside of the camp. Only six of the POWs managed to escape before the tunnel's exit was spotted by the patrolling guard.

The following month, Dowse and several other POWs were transferred to Stalag Luft III, where the German authorities had started sending all its 'problem' POWs and prolific escapers to. As far as they were concerned, Stalag Luft III was escape proof. On 30 November 1942, Dowse and fellow POW Flight Lieutenant Stanisław 'Danny' Król, tried to make their way out of the camp by simply cutting through the perimeter wire, after having already made their way through the wire that separated their own part of the main camp into the central section. The two men were caught before they could ultimately make their escape to freedom. Their escape attempt cost both men fourteen days in a solitary confinement cell.

Dowse eventually returned to his role of working in the camp's postal censor office, not because he was a fluent German speaker, because he was not, but because of his affable character and personality. This was an invaluable character trait to have, especially in such an environment. He was a man who could easily make friends and if they just happened to be German, then any such friendships had the potential to become an extremely valuable commodity. And so it proved to be when Dowse managed to obtain a German soldier's gate pass long enough for it to be copied by the

POW's forgery section. This was no mean feat as Dowse had to do this without the German soldier knowing he had temporarily lost it.

The copying of the pass lead directly to an escape from the camp on 12 June 1943, when twenty-four POWs were escorted from the camp by two others, disguised as German soldiers, on the pretence that they were on their way to a neighbouring compound to be deloused. The men were at large for just a few hours before they were all re-captured.

Dowse's involvement in the preparation of the mass breakout of the night of 24/25 March 1944 was to have assisted in the building and tunnelling of 'Harry'. On the night in question, he was the twenty-first escapee to leave the tunnel. His cover story was that he, along with his companion and old friend Król, were Danish workers. The pair were on the run for nearly two weeks before they were recaptured and initially held in the gaol at the police station at Oleśnica. They were subsequently interrogated by members of the Breslau Gestapo. On 12 April both men left the police station, but while Dowse was informed that he was going to Berlin for further interrogation, Król was told he was being returned to Stalag Luft III, but was never seen alive again.

Dowse ended up at Sachsenhausen concentration camp, from where he escaped along with four others on the evening of 23 September 1944. All five men were subsequently recaptured and returned to Sachsenhausen, where they remained until April 1945 when they moved on to the Tyrol region of Italy, staying at Flossenburg and Dachau concentration camps on route.

For his actions and services whilst held in captivity as a POW, Dowse was awarded the Military Cross. He died in Hampshire on 10 April 2008, aged 89.

Flight Lieutenant Bedřich 'Freddy' Dvořák

Born on 18 December 1912 in Chotěnov, Czechoslovakia, Dvořák graduated from the military aviation school in Prostějov in 1936 and was posted to No. 33 Squadron of the 2nd Aviation Regiment. Following the annexation of the Sudetenland in Dvořák first travelled to Poland, before moving on to France and finally, England.

He was serving with No. 312 (Czechoslovakian) Squadron, whose duties included coastal patrols and shipping reconnaissance flights out of RAF Fairwood Common, in Glamorgan, Wales, when he was shot down over Cherbourg on 3 June 1942. He was captured and incarcerated at Stalag Luft III POW camp, where in the build-up and preparation of the Great Escape, he was involved in the digging of 'Harry'.

After having exited the escape tunnel in around fourteenth place, he made his way safely into the adjoining woods and teamed up with Desmond Lancelot Plunkett. After being recaptured and interrogated by the Gestapo, Dvořák, never made it back to Stalag Luft III. Instead, he was first taken to Stalag Luft I, before ending up at Oflag IV-C, better known as Colditz Castle.

Returning to his native country after the end of the war, he remained in military service in the reformed Czechoslovakian Air Force, but in February 1948, everything changed when the KSČ, (the Czech Communist Party) came to power following a coup d'état. Dvořák was demoted from major to private and then discharged from the military. He died in 1971 and is buried a family tomb in Mladočov, near Litomyšl.

Flight Lieutenant Bernard Green

Born on 23 December 1887 in Oxfordshire, during the First World War Green served with the 1st Battalion, Oxfordshire and Buckinghamshire Light Infantry, at the ranks of 2nd lieutenant and captain, as well as with the Machine Gun Corps as a temporary major. He first arrived in France on 31 March 1915 and was subsequently wounded when he was struck in the groin by shrapnel. After recovering from his wounds, he returned to action, having transferred to the Machine Gun Corps, with whom he saw service at both the Battle of the Somme and the Battle of Passchendaele. It was whilst on a Lewis and Vickers machine gun course in 1916 that he met Johnny Dodge, who also went on to be one of those who would later escape from Stalag Luft III.

Green was wounded for a second time in October 1918 when he was again struck by shrapnel, this time in the heel, which saw an end to his involvement in the war. For his wartime service, he was mentioned in despatches in early 1917 for his actions during the Battle of the Somme and was awarded the Military Cross in the King's Birthday Honours List in 1918.

With the outbreak of the Second World War, and despite being 52 years of age, Green was accepted into the RAF Volunteer Reserve and after passing his air gunnery course at RAF Aldergrove, he was posted to Bomber Command's No. 44 Squadron at RAF Waddington in Lincolnshire, where he served as a rear gunner on board a Hampden bomber aircraft. Because of his age, he was affectionately known by his colleagues as 'Pop'.

On 19 July 1940, Green took off on his first mission to drop mines in the waters off occupied Denmark at Frederikshavn. In the early hours of the following day, his aircraft was struck by anti-aircraft flak and caught fire. The pilot, Sergeant Edward Farrands, decided he would have to crash land in the sea. Green and Farrands were the only members of the four-man crew to survive.

Fortunately, Green was a strong swimmer and despite the cold and choppy seas, he made it ashore. Within a matter of hours, he had been discovered by locals and taken to the police station at Skagen, where he was then handed over to German forces to begin his time as a POW, eventually ending up at Stalag Luft III.

His part in the preparation of the mass escape was to become a 'penguin' and help to disperse the excavated soil removed from 'Harry'.

Having escaped from the camp, he and twelve other prisoners pretended to be a group of Czechoslovakian workmen. They caught a train to the village of Hirschberg some 50 miles away but were stopped and arrested. Green was one of those returned to Stalag Luft III. At the age of 56, he was the oldest of the escapees.

Having been one of those who were force-marched from the camp in January 1945, Green was finally liberated on 2 May 1945 near Lübeck by elements of the British 11th Armoured Division. He died on 2 November 1971, aged 83.

Pilot Officer Bertram Arthur 'Jimmy' James, MC

Born on 17 April 1915 in India, James' father, Herbert, was a tea-planter. After the death of both his parents, and the loss of a tea importing business he and his father had started together, James decided to leave England and try his luck, first in America, and then in Canada, where he had relatives. But with the depression of the early 1930s affecting businesses on both sides of the Atlantic, it was hard to find a job anywhere. He lived mainly outdoors for a time in America, sleeping wherever he could, his lifestyle that of a homeless tramp. Whilst working in British Colombia in Canada in 1939, he saw a recruiting advert to join the RAF and so made his way back across the Atlantic to England to enlist. By 9 December 1939, he had completed his basic training and had received a commission as an acting pilot officer.

In April 1940, after having finally completed his initial training, he was posted to No. 9 Squadron. On the evening of 6 June 1940, James and his colleagues took off on a bombing mission over occupied Europe, but as they crossed the Dutch coast on their way to Berlin, they experienced heavy and sustained anti-aircraft fire. Their aircraft came down at Geervliet and although James and three of his colleagues survived, they were captured and became POWs. The remaining two crew members were killed.

Rather than being taken straight to a POW camp, James and several other captured Allied airmen were taken to Berlin; not for interrogation by the Gestapo, but to be marched through the city for all to see.

Still unclear as to what his ultimate fate was going to be, James' levels of anxiety and uncertainty would have been sky high. As it transpired, other than being sent to a POW camp, his worst fears never came to fruition. He was first sent to the still-unfinished Stalag Luft I, which is where he took part in his first attempt at an escape, although he did not even make it out of the camp.

During the build up to the escape from Stalag Luft III, his role had been that of a 'penguin', and once out of the tunnel, James and his fellow escapee, the Greek Pilot Officer Sotiris Skanzikas, made their way on foot. Having reached Hirschberg, the two men were detained at the local railway station whilst trying to purchase travel tickets and conveyed to the town's Gestapo office. The two men were separated, the gravity of which would not have dawned on either man. For James it was salvation, and a journey to Sachsenhausen concentration camp, but sadly for Skanzikas, it meant death by execution.

James was, if nothing else, a determined individual, hellbent on doing his duty to the best of his ability, despite the fact that by September 1944, he been a POW for more than four years. He simply saw a POW camp as somewhere to escape from. The tougher the Germans tried to make it for him, the more ingenious it made him in his attempts. Sachsenhausen was no different a challenge for him. As if to prove a point, he escaped from there, along with four others, on 23 September 1944. Together the men had dug a tunnel more than 10 feet deep and 100 metres in length, with nothing bigger than pieces of cutlery they used to eat what meagre food rations they were given. James managed to stay at large for a number of weeks before he was recaptured and returned to Sachsenhausen, but this time it would be extremely difficult for him to escape. His new cell was so small he could literarily only stand up in it, regardless of whether he was awake or asleep. If he had a 'call of nature', he went standing up. This was his very existence for nearly four months of his life, and it only stopped because with Soviet forces fast approaching, it was decided that any important prisoners were to be moved to the South Tyrol. James' eventual liberation and freedom took place on 6 May 1944.

On 17 May 1946, James was awarded the Military Cross and was mentioned in despatches for the number of times he had attempted to escape during his wartime incarceration. He remained in the RAF after the war, before transferring to the RAF Regiment on 9 December 1952, then finally retiring on 11 June 1958. He next went on to work for British Intelligence and the Diplomatic Service, which took him to countries all over the world. He died on 18 January 2008, aged 92.

Flight Lieutenant Roy Brouard Langlois, DFC

Born on 10 May 1917 in St. Peter Port, Guernsey, at some point during the war Langlois appears to have acquired the nickname of 'Daddy Long Legs'.

Initially serving at the rank of flying officer with No. 6 (Bomber) Squadron in Palestine, on 22 December 1939 he was awarded the

Distinguished Flying Cross (DFC) for his combined actions and service during the two years he had spent in the region until that time. He was promoted to flight lieutenant on 3 September 1940, and soon afterwards was posted to No. 12 Squadron, before subsequently moving on to RAF Binbrook, which was a base primarily used by Bomber Command.

At 22:25 on 5 August 1941, Langlois left on a bombing mission to attack the railway marshalling yards in Aachen. Not far from the intended target, Langlois' Wellington suddenly developed engine trouble. Without hesitation, Langlois took the decision to drop his bombs, despite being some 15-20 miles from their intended target. Whilst heading for home, the aircraft's starboard engine burst into flames, forcing Langlois to fly at a much lower altitude than he would have liked. Indeed, they were at such a low height that it meant it was impossible for Langlois or any of his crew to bail out, and so his only option was to get his burning aircraft on the ground as quickly as possible.

Left with no other option, he crash-landed his stricken Wellington bomber at Antwerp-Deurne airport in Belgium at 02:19 on 6 August. The aircraft remained in one piece and none of the crew was injured. Exiting the aircraft as quickly as they could, Langlois instructed his crew to set it on fire so that it did not fall into German hands. Luckily, the enemy did not arrive at the airport until the following morning because it was too dangerous for them to be above ground level during the nightly air raids, and seeing the flames they had assumed the aircraft had exploded on impact anyway, killing all of the crew in the process. Fortunately, this poor judgement by the Germans gave Langlois and his crew sufficient time to escape.

They split into two groups, but Langlois and his radio operator, Flight Sergeant Andrew Copley, were hiding up in an apartment in Brussels when they were arrested on 2 October. Although Langlois was sent to Stalag Luft III, four other members of the crew were sent to different POW camps in Germany, whilst Sergeant Jack Lamport Newton managed to make it back home to England.

Langlois was allocated number sixty of those who made their way through the tunnel to freedom on the evening of 24/25 March

1944. He was subsequently recaptured and returned to Stalag Luft III, where he remained until the forced march of January 1945.

He remained in the RAF after the war, finally retiring on 4 April 1962. He died in 1993, aged 76.

Flight Lieutenant Henry Cuthbert 'Johnny' Marshall, MBE

Marshall enlisted in the RAF on 5 November 1938 as a flying officer and was promoted to the rank of acting flight lieutenant on 7 August 1939, then promoted to substantive flight lieutenant on 3 September 1940.

On 12 January 1941, whilst serving with No. 3 Photographic Reconnaissance Unit, he was on a photographic mission over Bremen when his Spitfire was shot down over France. With his aircraft on fire, and having sustained numerous shrapnel wounds, he was too low to bail out so had to crash land. Captured soon after landing, he managed to escape from captivity on 16 February, despite his injuries, but was recaptured on the 26th.

After taking part in the mass escape from Stalag Luft III, he was recaptured just two days later, on 26 March, and was one of the lucky ones who were returned to the camp.

Marshall remained in the RAF following his return to England after the war and on 27 September 1946 was made a Member of the Order of the British Empire (MBE), the citation of which included the following platitudes:

> Squadron Leader Marshall's courage and determination were evident throughout his captivity. Despite severe injuries sustained during a crash landing in France, he actively participated in escape attempts while interned in a German prisoner of war camp. His leadership and commitment set an inspiring example for fellow prisoners.

Flight Lieutenant Alistair Thompson McDonald

McDonald was born in Bishopmill, near Elgin, Scotland on 11 April 1907. A keen sportsman, he showed particular skills in both rugby and golf. Not long after his eighteenth birthday he enlisted in the Tank Corps of the Territorial Army, giving his occupation at the time as that of an apprentice land surveyor.

Finding himself in need of a new challenge, in 1928, he purchased himself a ticket on the P&O steamship the *Naldera,* and set sail for Malaya, where he started work on a tea plantation. He soon became restless again, however, and before long made his way back to the UK. Throughout the 1930s, he had a number of jobs, including working as a cinema manager in Southport.

McDonald enlisted in the RAF in 1940, by which time he was 33 years of age. To ensure he was accepted, however, he told the recruitment officer that he was 27. This is because those older than 32 would not be considered for aircrew training, and the general rule of thumb was that anybody at the upper end of the age spectrum would not be offered training as a pilot. Having successfully passed his pilot training, McDonald became a flight sergeant, before being given a temporary commission as a pilot officer in December 1941.

Initially flying Spitfires on reconnaissance flights for Coastal Command, whilst serving with the RAF's No. 1 Photographic Reconnaissance Unit (PRU), as part of D flight, McDonald became a POW on 13 March 1942. His aircraft had been fired upon by a German plane, forcing him to bail out before it crashed to the ground. He landed safely and was soon captured by German forces. Before being sent to Stalag Luft III, McDonald was sent to Luftwaffe headquarters in Amsterdam for interrogation. No torture or violence was involved, but detailed questioning did take place over the space of an eighteen-day period, after which time he was sent to Stalag Luft III. It was whilst being held as a POW there that he was informed he had been promoted to the rank of flight lieutenant.

His part in the detailed preparation and planning for the Great Escape involved the sending and receiving of coded letters to and from loved ones back home, which could ultimately be used in the escape. A system was put in place so that certain incoming parcels could be prevented from being examined by the camp's guards.

On the night of the mass breakout there had been a heavy snowfall, which greatly slowed the escapees down and thus made them easier to spot. McDonald was carrying false documents and forged papers when he was stopped and recaptured, but managed to get rid of his false documents by eating them before they were discovered by the Germans. He also managed to quickly sew RAF buttons into his greatcoat, so that if his captors saw them, it meant he would be recognised as an escaped POW, rather than shot as a spy.

After being returned to the camp, McDonald remained there until the forced march in January 1945. As the long line of exhausted and cold POWs reached the outskirts of Bremen, McDonald managed to escape, eventually encountering advancing British forces in early April.

After returning to the UK, McDonald was demobbed and settled back into civilian life in Edinburgh. He was killed in a plane crash in 1965 during a failed landing at Heathrow airport.

Lieutenant Alexander Desmond Neely

Born on 4 November 1917 in Chakradharpur, India, where his father was a railway builder, Neely returned to the UK in 1922, aged 5, following the death of his father. He joined the Royal Navy's Fleet Air Arm in 1935 and by the outbreak of the war was serving with No. 825 Squadron.

On 29 May 1940, Neely and his observer air gunner, Airman F.G. Rumsey, set off from RAF Detling in one of ten Fairey Swordfish Mk1 aircraft on a mission to attack German submarines spotted off the Belgian coast at Ostend. Neely and his colleagues should have been met at the coast by 30 RAF fighter aircraft, but, because of a misunderstanding in relation to time and location, the two groups never met up. Only three of the Swordfish aircraft made it back to Detling, with Neely's aircraft being one of the seven that were shot down over northern France.

Rather than ditch in the sea and risk hitting any of the small boats making their way across the English Channel, he managed to crash land in a farmer's field near Loos. Neely was slightly wounded after a bullet had pierced the fleshy part of the leg near to his right knee, but Rumsey was totally unscathed. The fact that Neely managed to land his damaged aircraft was not only a compliment to his flying abilities, but also a mark of his determination not to crash and kill any members of the British Expeditionary Force, who at the time were being evacuated from the beaches at Dunkirk.

After being arrested soon after landing, Neely and Rumsey faced a five-day march across Belgium, before arriving at the town of Bocholt, on the German border. From there they were placed in a fourth-class railway carriage and taken to the Oflag VII-C POW camp in Laufen, Bavaria. They remained there for six months, before being transferred to Stalag Luft I, and finally Stalag Luft III.

Neely's mother, Alice, was not told of her son's status as a POW until January 1941, which meant she had an agonising eight-month wait not knowing if her son was alive or dead.

Neely did not waste his time during his incarceration, choosing to learn how to speak both French and German. He was the twenty-eighth escapee to crawl through the tunnel on the night of 24/25 March 1944. Once out of the camp he caught a train to Berlin where on his arrival he spent four hours looking round the bomb ravaged city, before catching another train to Stettin. He then decided to try to get on board a ship heading for Sweden, but after five days with no luck, he decided to make his way to the Swiss border, which first meant catching a train to Munich. Sadly for Neely, his true identity was discovered by a Gestapo officer who was on board the train checking people's tickets and paperwork.

After arriving in Munich, Neely was taken to a local prison where he was interrogated for several hours, and where he remained for the following seven days before being sent back to Sagan. He spent the first three weeks in solitary confinement in a punishment camp a few miles from the main Stalag Luft III camp. He remained a POW until being made to take part in the enforced march at the end of January 1945, before being liberated in mid-April. On Wednesday, 6 June 1945, the first anniversary of the D-Day landings, he married Miss Janet Logan Maxwell Dawson of the Women's Royal Naval Service, at St Cuthbert's Church, Edinburgh.

Neely died in Devon on 16 October 2001, aged 83.

Flight Lieutenant Thomas R. Nelson

Born in March 1915, Nelson enlisted in the RAF and was commissioned as a pilot officer on 24 November 1937. Initially posted to No. 114

Squadron, shortly before the outbreak of war he was sent to Rhodesia as an instructor, during which time he was promoted to the rank of flying officer on 23 March 1940. He remained on training duties until 1942, when he returned to operational flying with No. 37 Squadron, who flew Wellington bombers in and around North Africa.

On the night of 18/19 September 1942, and after having previously completed twenty-two operational flights, Nelson took off from Abu Suweir airfield in Egypt at approximately 18:45. On his way to Tobruk, his port engine failed and caught fire. All the crew, apart from Nelson, who was piloting the aircraft, managed to bail out, whilst Nelson crash landed some 50 miles south of Sallum. He survived the impact and despite remaining at large until 7 October, was finally captured near El Alamein and taken to Stalag Luft III.

His contribution to the mass escape was his engineering expertise, which was put to good use with both the tunnel's ventilation and pully systems, enabling the escapees to be dragged through the tunnel faster. He was allocated as escapee number forty on the night of the escape and remained on the run for two nights before being recaptured on 17 March and returned to the camp.

He survived the war and later went on to become a commercial airline pilot with the Dutch national airline, KLM. He died in 1999, aged 84.

Flight Lieutenant Alfred Keith Ogilvie

Affectionately known as 'Skeets', Ogilvie was born in Ottawa, Canada on 14 September 1915. After his education came to an end, he decided his way forward in life was as a stockbroker.

Believing war to be imminent, Ogilvie wanted to play his part and so applied for the Royal Canadian Air Force. The immediate problem, however, was that they only accepted university graduates, and Ogilvie had not been to university. So instead, in August 1939 he applied to the British RAF for a short service commission. Less than two weeks later, his application was successful and he was soon on his way to England. Upon arrival he was sent to No. 9 Flying Training School, where Ogilvie left such an impression on his instructors, even with absolutely no operational experience, that they recommended he be sent to the Central Flying School at RAF Upton to undergo further training to become an instructor. However, Ogilvie had joined the RAF to be a fighter, not an instructor, and so wrote a letter to Air Marshal Sir Hugh Trenchard, pleading his case.

During the Battle of Britain, Ogilvie was credited with shooting down at least eight enemy aircraft. His luck ran out, however, on 4 July 1941 when he was shot down and he was sent to Stalag Luft III. Following the mass escape on 24/25 March 1944, he was recaptured after having been at large for a few days and returned to the camp.

Ogilvie was liberated by British forces in April 1945 and sent to the UK to recuperate before being sent home to Canada, where he became a member of the Royal Canadian Air Force until he retired in 1963. He died in 1998.

Flight Lieutenant Desmond Lancelot Plunkett

Born in India in 1915, where his father worked as an engineer, Plunkett had learned to fly before the war at Redhill Flying Club and went on to become a flying instructor for the RAF Volunteer Reserve.

He qualified as a bomber pilot in 1941 and was then posted to No. 218 Squadron at RAF Marham. At 23:30 on 20 June 1942, he took off in a Short Stirling, four engine heavy bomber aircraft on a mission to bomb nominated targets in Emden. Before making it to its destination, however, Plunkett's aircraft was shot down by a German night fighter at 01:50 in the early hours of 21 June, near Wognum, in the Netherlands. Five of the crew, including Plunkett, survived, whilst the remaining three were killed.

Plunkett's involvement in the preparation and planning of the escape from Stalag Luft III saw him producing maps that included escape routes through to countries such as Switzerland, France and Sweden. Plunkett and his dedicated team also produced permits and several other required documents for the camp's escapees.

Plunkett was to be the thirteenth escapee to make his way through the tunnel on the night of the mass breakout. His escape partner was Czech airman Bedřich Dvořák. The two men bought tickets and boarded a train at Sagan railway station, which took them to the town of Breslau. They made it all the way to the Czechoslovakia/Austrian border before their luck ran out and they were recaptured. Plunkett was held in a prison in Prague, before being sent to Stalag Luft I in January 1945, where he remained until the camp was liberated by Soviet forces on 2 May.

He stayed in the RAF until 1947, after which worked in civilian aviation until 1975, when he then took up the more sedate pastime of bee keeping. He died on 14 February 2002, aged 86.

Lieutenant Douglas Arthur Poynter

Poynter was born on 1 March 1920 in Ramsgate, Kent, where he lived with his parents John and Beatrice Poynter, and his three brothers. In the April 1939 England and Wales Register, the Poynter family are shown as living at 150 Grange Road, with Douglas Poynter being employed as a midshipman in the Royal Navy's Fleet Air Arm, but by the early months of 1940, he was serving as a pilot with the Fleet Air Arm's No. 825 Squadron.

In July 1940 he was one of the squadron's crews who embarked on board HMS *Furious* and then carried out night attacks on shipping at Trondheim and Tromsø on the coast of Norway. On 22 September, Poynter was part of a three-man crew flying in a Swordfish aircraft that had to carry out a forced landing northeast of Trondheim.

Poynter was captured and ended up in Stalag Luft III, where he took part in the mass breakout in March 1944, but was recaptured within a couple of days of having escaped. During his subsequent interrogation he was told that he would be shot, but probably because his uniform was dark blue rather than the RAF's light blue, the Gestapo sent him back to Stalag Luft III, where he remained until the enforced march at the end of January 1945. He survived the war and returned to his family in Ramsgate, later being selected as one of the witnesses to give evidence in the Nuremburg trials in 1946.

Poynter passed away in October 1999, aged 79.

Pilot Officer Paul G. Royle

Born on 17 January 1914 in Perth, Western Australia, after completing his full-time education Royle worked in the mining industry in Kalgoorlie.

In early 1938 he went to Perth where he sat before an RAF selection committee, which some weeks later resulted in him being offered a four-year short service commission in the RAF. Despite having never flown before, it turned out Royle and flying were a marriage made in heaven, and he and thirteen others were sent to the UK to undergo training. After an interview at the Air Ministry in London, Royle was sent to what was known as an Elementary Flying School at No. 2 School of Army Co-operation in Andover, Hampshire. Over the course of a year, he learned to fly several different aircraft, including Avro Ansons, Bristol Blenheims, and de Haviland Tiger Moths. On completion of his training, he was posted to No. 53 Squadron as a pilot officer.

On 17 May 1940 Royle was on a reconnaissance mission when he became involved in a dog fight with a number of Messerschmitt Bf 109 German fighter aircraft. Royle's plane was badly damaged in the exchange and he had no alternative but to crash land, whereupon he was captured by the Germans. Although first sent to Stalag Luft I, in June 1941 he was moved to Stalag Luft III and became one of the numerous 'penguins'.

On the evening of 24 March 1944, Royle was number fifty-seven in the queue of escapees waiting to make their way through 'Harry'. He was teamed up with the man immediately behind him in the tunnel, Flight Lieutenant Edgar Humphreys. The pair had already decided their intended destination was to be neutral Switzerland and that they were going to get there on foot. They managed to evade capture for two nights before being arrested near Görlitz by members of the German Home Guard. After being interrogated by the local Gestapo, Royle was returned to Stalag Luft III, whilst Humphreys became one of the fifty escapees to be murdered.

In January 1945 Royle took part in the enforced march west to Marlag und Milag Nord POW camp, where he and his colleagues were liberated by British forces on 2 May. On his return to Australia, he went back to his old job in the mining industry and died on 23 August 2015, aged 101.

Flight Lieutenant Michael Moray Shand, DFC

Born on 20 February 1915 in Wellington, New Zealand, Shand was working in the fruit industry in 1939 when he was accepted for a short service commission in the RNZAF. He began his training on 19 November at the Ground Training School in Weraroa, before moving on to No. 1 European Force Training School at Taiera, and finally to the No. 1 Flying Training School, where he received his wings.

Shand sailed for the UK on 7 June 1940 and arrived some six weeks later on 20 July. He was first sent to No. 1 Depot at Uxbridge to await his posting and eventually ended up flying Spitfires with No. 54 Squadron.

During the Battle of Britain, on 25 August 1940 Shand's Spitfire was attacked by a German Messerschmitt Bf 109 fighter and had to make a forced landing, coming down near Manston. He survived but was badly wounded and subsequently ended up being treated in several hospitals before finally being released towards the latter part of October.

It was more than a year before he returned to operational duties when he joined No. 485 (NZ) Squadron in October 1941, whose role involved convoy protection on vessels making their way through the North Sea, as well as bomber escort duties and sorties over occupied northern France. By September 1942, Shand had flown more than sixty such sorties, which on 16 September 1942 saw him awarded the DFC.

On 28 November 1942 Shand was one of several Spitfires who had set out on a low-level sweep across the Dutch coast, seeking out opportune targets rather than specific ones. Shand and his colleagues successfully attacked a tanker-barge making its way slowly along a canal. Having turned for home, Shand and another pilot spotted a train and decided to attack it. Whilst in the process of doing so, they were attacked by two Focke-Wulf Fw190s, which resulted in Shand being shot down and captured. After escaping, Shand and his fellow New Zealander, Squadron Leader Len Trent, planned to travel on foot to Czechoslovakia and then on into neutral Switzerland. Because of unforeseen delays, which included at least one tunnel collapse on the night of escape, it was almost 05:00 on 25 March before they reached the tunnel's exit.

Shand was the last to escape and was running across the open ground between the tunnel exit and the woods when a sentry spotted Trent emerging from the tunnel and arrested him before he could escape.

On seeing movement in the woods, the startled sentry opened fire. Thankfully, the shot missed Shand and he disappeared off into the trees. He managed to stay at large for nearly four days by only travelling at night but was finally caught by two railway workers whilst attempting to catch a train. He was handed over to the civilian police who took him to Görlitz prison, where he was interrogated.

After being returned to the camp, Shand continued his incarceration until it was evacuated in January 1945.

He returned to New Zealand on 23 September 1945 and took up farming on the country's North Island. He died on 20 December 2007, aged 92.

Flight Lieutenant Alfred Burke 'Tommy' Thompson

Born on 8 August 1915 in Ontario, Canada, into a prosperous middle-class family, Thompson's father, another Alfred, was a respected lawyer and politician who served as a Member of Parliament for ten years between 1925 and 1935. In 1933 Thompson junior enlisted as a part-time reservist in the Simcoe Foresters, an infantry unit in the Canadian Non-permanent Active Militia. After twenty months he received a commission as a 2nd lieutenant, which he eventually resigned in March 1937 so that he could take up a commission in the RAF.

Thompson arrived in England in 1936 as part of an RAF sponsorship and was sent to a civilian flying school in Hampshire. It was on the successful completion of this course that he relinquished his commission in the Canadian militia and took up a four-year short service commission in the RAF, at the rank of pilot officer. He began his initial officer's training course on 8 March 1937, and two months later began his intermediate flight training at RAF Sealand at No. 5 Flying Training School. With his six months of training successfully behind him, he was posted to No. 102 Squadron, a night bomber unit that flew Whitley Mk II heavy bomber aircraft.

At 23:55 on 8 September 1939, Thompson was the co-pilot of a Whitley bomber that took off on a mission to drop Allied propaganda leaflets throughout Germany's Ruhr Valley. During the flight the crew were forced to bail out after the aircraft experienced difficulties. There is some debate as to what actually happened, as the official version states the aircraft was forced to land, but as the crew took to their parachutes, this would appear not to have been the case.

Although all five of the crew survived and were captured, it was the aircraft's wireless operator Aircraftsman 1st Class Sam Burry, who was officially recorded by the Germans as being the first Allied POW of the Second World War. Thompson, meanwhile, became the first Canadian of the war to become a POW, which was ironic given that Canada did not declare war on Germany until 10 September, the day after Thompson's capture.

Having eventually ended up at Stalag Luft III, it would be fair to say that Thompson's time as a POW was an interesting one. On 21 December 1940, his four-year short service commission expired, meaning he had technically become a civilian. To rectify this anomaly, he was placed on the RAF Reserve and retained on the Active List. As he was the only Canadian POW, the Canadian Red Cross Society sent Thompson personalised food and clothes parcels, which he in turn was more than happy to share with his fellow POWs.

On the night of the mass escape from Stalag Luft III, Thompson was the sixty-eighth man to escape through the tunnel. He had only managed to make it a couple of hundred yards from the exit when the escape was discovered. Having teamed up with fellow Canadian escapee William Cameron, the pair travelled for about 2 miles, by which time it was starting to get light and so they decided to hide up amongst a clump of bushes. Once it was dark again, they brushed themselves down and started out on their journey once more. They had not travelled far when they came across two darkened figures ahead of them. Not knowing who they were, they quickly relaxed when they realised that they were two other fellow escapees. The four men stuck together and in the early hours of the following morning they came across a barn, and the allure of a warm place to shelter in was all the incentive they needed.

After spending all day in the barn, Thompson and the two other escapees left late on the evening of 26 March. Cameron remained behind as he was suffering badly with the cold and simply could not stop shaking. The three men only managed to travel about a mile from the barn before they were captured by a member of the German Home Guard and taken to Sagan prison. In the early hours of 28 March, Thompson and several other recaptured POWs were transferred to Görlitz prison where they were interrogated by the Gestapo. Over the course of the next few days, more POWs arrived. On the morning of 29 March, Thompson and three others were taken to the local train station and sent back to Stalag Luft III. The others were never seen alive again.

After the war Thompson became a lawyer in his hometown of Penetanguishene, where he also became the mayor. He died on 7 August 1985, aged 69.

Flight Lieutenant Ivo Tonder

Born on 16 April 1913 in Prague, before the outbreak of the Second World War Tonder was a pilot with Air Regiment I, which was part of the Czechoslovakian army. After his country was invaded and occupied by Germany, he was demobilised and worked as an aircraft designer. However, Tonder still wanted to fight for his country and decided to make his way to France and join the French air force. But no sooner had he made it to France than they were also attacked and occupied by German forces.

Tonder made his way across the English Channel to England and enlisted in the RAF. Once he had retrained in the use of British aircraft, he was posted to No. 312 (Czechoslovakian) Squadron at RAF Speke (now John Lennon Airport, Liverpool).

On 3 June 1942 he set off on a mission over occupied France but did not return after his aircraft was shot down by a Focke-Wulf Fw 190. Able to bail out before it crashed into the ground, he was captured and taken to the Dulag Luft POW camp in Oberursel, Germany, for interrogation, before being transferred to Stalag Luft III.

Tonder's role in the subsequent mass escape of March 1944 was as both a tailor and tunneller. Having made it through and out of the tunnel, his plan was to travel to neutral Switzerland, but he was captured by the Gestapo whilst travelling through Czechoslovakia. He then spent the following eight months imprisoned in a Prague cell in solitary confinement.

He eventually ended up as a POW at Colditz Castle under a death sentence, but he along with the other captives held there were liberated by American forces on 16 April 1945, before his execution could be carried out.

After the war Tonder was not seen as a hero by the new communist regime that had come into power in Czechoslovakia. Instead, he was demoted to the rank of private and demobilised with little opportunity to obtain any kind of work. On 31 May 1948 he attempted to escape to Germany but was captured by border police and given an eight-year prison sentence. Employing the same steely and determined attitude that had served him so well as a POW at Stalag Luft III, Tonder once again escaped from captivity and this time successfully made it to Germany and from there on to the UK, where he arrived with his wife and two children in 1950.

With the collapse of communism in Czechoslovakia in 1989, Tonder was promoted to the rank of colonel by the president of the newly formed Czech Republic, Vaclav Havel, in 1991. Just three weeks before his death on 4 May 1995, aged 82, he was made a major general.

Squadron Leader Leonard Henry Trent, VC, DFC

Born on 14 April 1915 in Nelson, New Zealand, between 1928 and 1934 Trent attended Nelson College, the oldest state secondary school in New Zealand, but he did not naturally excel academically. Instead, his interests were more taken with golf and flying.

Trent wanted to follow in his father's footsteps and become a dentist. Unable to afford this and having tried his hand at a couple of clerical positions, he needed no encouragement to answer an advertisement in a Wellington newspaper offering short-term commissions in the RAF. He successfully passed a selection interview and soon afterwards was accepted for flight training with the Royal New Zealand Air Force at Dunedin. He went on to complete further training at Christchurch, before sailing for England the following month. On 6 September 1938, the Air Ministry announced in the *London Gazette* that Trent and others had been granted a short-service commission as a pilot officer for five years, as of 23 August

1938. He was posted to No. 15 Squadron at RAF Abingdon in Berkshire, who were equipped with Fairey Battle light bomber aircraft. Soon after the outbreak of the war Trent and his squadron, who were part of No. 1 Group, Bomber Command's Advance Air Striking Force, were deployed to France and flew out of an air base at Vraux, their main purpose being that of photo-reconnaissance missions over occupied France. In December 1939, No. 15 Squadron returned to England to undergo conversion training to the Bristol Blenheim light bomber aircraft at RAF Wyton.

During the BEF's evacuation at Dunkirk in May 1940, Trent flew several sorties to try to stop German aircraft from attacking British and Allied soldiers on the beaches as they tried to escape. At the end of June 1940, he was given leave after not having had any kind of break since the war began. When he returned to duty it was as an instructor with No. 17 Operational Training Unit, and in August he was awarded the DFC for his actions in the Battle of France.

In December 1941, Trent was posted to the Operational Training Squadron at RAF Warboys and did not return to operational duties until March 1942, with No. 2 Group, which consisted of ten different squadrons and was based at RAF Wyton.

In August that year he was posted to the newly formed No. 487 (New Zealand) Squadron at RAF Methwold as a flight commander. The unit flew the unpopular twin-engine medium bomber aircraft, the Lockheed Ventura.

At 16:43 on 3 May 1943, twelve Venturas left on a daytime raid on a power station in Amsterdam. The crews were told to expect heavy German defences, both from the ground and in the air. It was Trent's twenty-fourth mission, and as they approached their target, they were met by a defensive force of more than seventy German fighter aircraft, which saw the demise of six of the Venturas, one having already turned for home having experienced an engine malfunction. Trent's aircraft was the only one of the Venturas to reach the target and drop its bombs. As he turned for home, his own plane was struck by German machine gun fire, which put it into a spin causing it to break up. Trent and his navigator, Flying Officer Vivian Phillips, were thrown from the aircraft at a height of approximately 7,000 feet, but the other two members of the crew were unable to get out before it crashed into the ground.

Phillips and Trent were both captured and sent to Stalag Luft III. Out of the forty-eight crew who had taken off from RAF Methwold, twenty-eight were killed, twelve were captured and only eight made it safely back home.

Trent's role in the preparation of the mass escape was as a 'penguin', helping to distribute the excavated soil from the tunnel around the camp. He was also the man caught by the German sentry as he broke the surface and tried to exit the tunnel.

In January 1945 Trent and the remaining POWs were force-marched out of the camp and headed west. The group were finally liberated by British forces on 2 May 1945.

Trent returned to England on 7 May and set about writing a report on the raid of 3 May 1943, which had ultimately led to his capture. Having considered the report and taking into account statements provided by others who took part in the raid, the commanding officer of No. 2 Group, Air Vice Marshal Basil Embry, recommended him for the Victoria Cross, which was announced in the *London Gazette* on 1 March 1946.

Trent remained in the RAF after the war before finally retiring on 23 June 1965, having served for thirty-seven years. He died on 19 May 1986 at the North Shore Hospital in Takapuna, New Zealand, aged 71.

Flight Lieutenant Raymond van Wymeersch

Born on 24 September 1920 at Asnières-sur-Seine, Wymeersch's father, Paul, was a station master on the French railway system and also a member of the French Resistance. Having been captured by the Gestapo, he was sent to Mauthausen concentration camp where he died on 13 March 1944.

Raymond van Wymeersch enlisted in the French Air Force in November 1939, with the added advantage of already being a qualified civilian pilot. He underwent his training to become a military aviator at Rochefort in May 1940. By the end of that course he was promoted to the rank of sergeant, before being sent to the town of Avord, in central France, to undergo further aviation training. After the German occupation of France in 1940, he escaped via the port of Bayonne on 21 June on board a Swedish ship. Having finally made his way to England, he enlisted in the Free French Air Force and was posted to No. 605 Squadron, who flew Hawker Hurricane aircraft, arriving there in November 1940.

He moved on to No. 174 Squadron in March 1942, with whom he took part in the Dieppe Raid on 19 August 1942. In thick fog his Hurricane collided with a German Focke-Wulf Fw 190 and in the subsequent crash landing, he broke both his legs but survived to become a POW. After spending a period of time in a German military hospital recovering from his injuries, he eventually ended up at Stalag Luft III.

Following his escape, he decided to head for Paris, where he hoped to make contact with members of the French Resistance, but was arrested in Metz before he arrived. He was taken back to Berlin, from where he escaped another two times from German captivity. By now the German authorities had started to find van Wymeersch's behaviour somewhat tiresome, so they sent him to Sachsenhausen concentration camp. Far from feeling despondent or beaten, however, van Wymeersch simply escaped again. He was recaptured once more, but this time he found the security a lot tighter than it had been before. At the end of April 1945, he was removed from the camp along with a number of other prisoners and moved towards the South Tyrol, to be held there as potential hostages by elements of the SS.

He was the only Frenchman to have taken part in the Great Escape and survive. He died in La Rochelle on 2 June 2000, aged 79.

Although the Great Escape of March 1944 is predominantly remembered because of the fifty men who were subsequently murdered by the Gestapo, and the twenty-three men who were recaptured after the escape and went on to survive the war, it is remarkable to think that just three of the seventy-six men who initially made their big break for freedom actually made it back to England whilst the war was still ongoing.

Those three men who did make it safely across the Channel were the Norwegian Per Bergsland, a member of No. 332 Squadron; fellow Norwegian Jens E. Müller of No. 331 Squadron; and Dutchman Abraham Lambertus 'Bram' van der Stok, from No. 41 Squadron.

Like many young men of their era, with a war waging across Europe and their own country occupied by German forces, Bergsland and Müller wanted to do their bit in the fight against Nazism and to free their country from its unwanted occupation. To this end they made their way to England and enlisted in the RAF. After they had successfully completed their flying training, Bergsland was posted to No. 332 (Norwegian) Squadron at RAF North Weald, while Müller was posted to No. 331 (Norwegian) Squadron, which was also based at RAF North Weald.

On 19 June 1942, Müller was on a mission in the skies just off the Belgian coast when, having run out of ammunition, he was shot down by a German aircraft. He parachuted out of his stricken airplane and landed in the cold waters of the English Channel. After spending nearly three days in a dinghy, he finally made it back to dry land where he was arrested by a German soldier and became a POW.

Having settled into life at Stalag Luft III, Müller's contribution to the mass escape was the design and construction of an air pump for the tunnel's ventilation system.

Meanwhile, on 19 August 1942, Bergsland had taken part in Operation Jubilee, the amphibious raid on Dieppe, as part of the Allied air support, during which he was shot down by a German aircraft. He was captured on landing and became a POW, eventually arriving at Stalag Luft III. Concerned about the welfare of his family back home in Norway, he gave his name as 'Peter Rockland' and passed himself off as an Englishman.

When it came to the mass breakout of 24/25 March 1944, Bergsland was allocated number forty-four on the list of escapees. The man immediately in front of him in the tunnel was fellow Norwegian, Jens Müller.

After making it back to England, Müller wrote a report for British military intelligence, outlining his and Bergsland's escape from Stalag Luft III, which included the following:

It took me three minutes to get through the tunnel. Above ground I crawled along holding the rope for several feet: it was tied to a tree. Sergeant Bergsland joined me; we arranged our clothes and walked to the Sagan railway station. Bergsland was wearing a civilian suit he had made for himself from a Royal Marine uniform, with an RAF overcoat slightly altered with brown leather sewn over the buttons. A black RAF tie, no hat. He carried a small suitcase which had been sent from Norway. In it were Norwegian toothpaste and soap, sandwiches, and 163 reichsmarks given to him by the escape committee.

We caught the 02:04 train to Frankfurt an der Oder. Our papers stated that we were Norwegian electricians from the *Arbeitslager* [labour camp] in Frankfurt working in the vicinity of Sagan. For the journey from Frankfurt to Stettin we had other papers ordering us to change our place of work from Frankfurt to Stettin, and to report to the Bürgermeister of Stettin.

The train arrived at Frankfurt at 06:00 and after a two-hour wait the two men caught a connecting train on to the Brandenburg village of Küstrin, which sits on the Oder River and the border with Poland. Once there, they waited for another two hours before catching a train to Stettin, where they arrived just after noon.

Prior to escaping from the camp, the two men had been given the details by the camp's escape committee of somewhere in Stettin where they could safely seek assistance. Having arrived in the town, they eventually made their way to the address they had been given. It turned out to be a brothel, which if nothing else would have undoubtedly brought a smile to their faces. They spoke with a Swedish sailor and decided to take a leap of faith and tell him who they really were. This was a brave decision as they knew nothing of the man they were talking to, or where his loyalties really lay. He could have betrayed them to the German authorities for a bounty, or indeed have been a German masquerading as a Swedish sailor.

The man told them that the ship he worked on was leaving that night for Sweden, and if they returned to the brothel later that evening, he would take them to it. The man was as good as his word and later that evening took them to the docks, but something went wrong and the ship sailed, just not with them on board. The men had no choice but to make their way safely out of the dock area and back to the centre of town, before finding a hotel where they could get a room and something to eat. As risky as it was, the pair decided to return to the brothel the following evening. After they had been waiting a short while, when two men came out of the building they decided to approach them. They asked if they were Swedish sailors, and when they said they were, the escapees once again took a chance and told them of their plight. They went with the sailors back to the docks for the second time and simply followed them onto their ship without even being asked to show their papers. Once on board, they had to simply hide and wait until the ship sailed for Sweden at 07:00 the following morning. Having arrived in Gothenburg, Sweden, Bergsland and Müller made contact with the city's British consulate; finally, they knew they were safe. The two men were sent on to Stockholm by train, where they then flew to Scotland before catching a train down to London, where they were interrogated by officers from British military intelligence.

Müller and Bergsland remained in the RAF but neither flew operationally again. Instead, they both saw out the remainder of the war as flying instructors in Canada.

As for Abraham 'Bram' van der Stok, he was completing his medical studies at Utrecht University in 1937 when he decided to enlist in the Netherlands Army Aviation Group reserves.

With the German invasion of the Netherlands in May 1940, after trying his hardest to hold back the German onslaught, van der Stok decided to make his way to England and continue the fight from there. After stowing away on board a Swiss merchant vessel, the *Saint Cerque*, in Rotterdam, he crossed the North Sea to Scotland. He was accepted by the RAF and after completing a brief familiarisation course to bring him up to date on the aircraft he would flying, in December 1941 he was posted to No. 41 Squadron at RAF Merston in Sussex, where he found himself in the cockpit of a Supermarine Spitfire.

On 12 April 1942, van der Stok left his home base on a mission to attack the railway marshalling yards at Hazebrouck, in occupied northern France. When his aircraft was hit by anti-aircraft fire, his aircraft was sufficiently damaged enough to cause him to bail out. He landed safely at Saint-Omer and was quickly arrested by waiting German forces, who had seen him and his parachute slowly making its way to the ground. After being interrogated, he was sent to the then newly opened Stalag Luft III POW camp.

His medical training was extremely useful in the camp's medical facility, but this did not prevent him from trying to escape. Before the mass breakout on the night of 24/25 March 1944, he had made three earlier attempts at trying to escape from Stalag Luft III, but all of them had been thwarted.

Van der Stok was the eighteenth escapee out of the tunnel and was one of only a few who, once outside the camp, decided to go it alone, with the belief that this provided the best opportunity of drawing the least amount of attention.

He described his moment of freedom in his memoir: 'Quickly, I climbed up to the surface and immediately found the rope. I felt no signal, so it was not safe yet. Then I felt three distinct tugs and slowly popped my head up. The nearest "Goonbox" was at least 200 feet away but, indeed, I was 20 feet from the edge of the woods.'

Once out of the camp and in possession of documentation in the name of 'Hendrik Beeldman', it would take him six weeks to step foot on British soil, albeit in Gibraltar. His journey was not all straight forward. On more than one occasion he was stopped by police who were keen to check his credentials, but fortunately, each time he was able to convince them that he was not an escaped POW. His route took him across five countries, four of which were occupied by Nazi Germany. His cause was helped somewhat by the Belgian and French Resistance, as well as the Dutch Underground, and the British consulate in Madrid. From there he was sent to the British territory of Gibraltar, where he arrived on 8 July 1944.

He left two days later and was flown back to RAF Whitchurch in Bristol, where he arrived the following day.

Having been interviewed by members of military intelligence, van der Stok made his way to the Air Ministry in London, desperate to return to flying. Eventually his wish was granted, and he was posted to No. 41 Squadron, who flew Spitfires in support of the Allied advance into Germany from bases on the continent, and to shoot down the Germans' dreaded V-1 rockets that were targeting the south coast of England.

The following year, van der Stok was placed in command of No. 322 (Dutch) Squadron RAF, which was a fighter squadron flying out of Schijndel in the Netherlands.

After the liberation of the Netherlands, van der Stok was able to return home to see his family, but it was not all good news. His two brothers, who had both worked for the Dutch Resistance, had been arrested by the Gestapo and sent to concentration camps, where they had later died. Meanwhile, his father had been arrested after his escape as the Germans did their best to discover the son's whereabouts. He was interrogated so severely by the Gestapo that he was left blind.

After the war, van der Stok returned to his medical studies and in 1950, having finally passed his exams, he qualified as a doctor and began working in Utrecht. The following year he immigrated to the United States with his wife and three children. He died on 8 February 1993 in Virginia Beach.

By the war's end, van der Stok was the Netherlands' most highly decorated pilot, having received the following awards:

Kruis van Verdienste (Netherlands) 3 September 1942
Vliegerkruis (Netherlands) 21 September 1942
Bronzen Kruis (Netherlands) 5 October 1944
Krzyz Walecznych (Poland) 9 May 1945
Bronzen Leeuw (Netherlands) 15 June 1946
Officer in de Orde van Leopold II (Belgium) 24 March 1947
Croix de Guerre 1940 (Belgium) 24 March 1947
MBE (Britain) 19 November 1947

Officer in de Orde van Oranje Nassau (Netherlands)
Oorlogsherinneringskruis (Netherlands)
Verzetsherdenkingskruis (Netherlands)
1939-1945 Star (Britain)
France and Germany Star (Britain)
War Medal (Britain)
Croix de Guerre (1939-1945) (France)

CHAPTER SEVENTEEN

Wilfred Bowes and Frank McKenna

❖

With the fighting over and the war finally at its end, the race was on for the British and Allied authorities to track down and find those responsible for the murder of the fifty men who had escaped from Stalag Luft III in March 1944, and who were subsequently murdered following their capture.

The authorities required the names and photographs of those responsible, but did not immediately know where these men were or even if they were alive. One thing was for certain: the men tasked with finding those responsible for the murders would leave no stone unturned in the pursuit of their aims. This was, after all, personal. They knew it was not going to be an easy task, but they were more than up for the challenge.

Those given the job of investigating the murders served with the Special Investigation Branch (SIB) of the Royal Air Force, making them the only branch-specific investigative unit entrusted to deal with a major war crime at the end of the Second World War. The team given the responsibility of investigating this difficult and emotive job consisted of five officers and fourteen non-commissioned officers (NCOs).

The man in overall charge of the mammoth task of tracking down those responsible for the murders was Wilfred Bowes. Born on 19 February 1904 in Heaton, West Hartlepool, Durham, Bowes had lied about his age and enlisted in the newly formed RAF in 1918, when he was still only 14, and served in Turkey as an aircraftsman

2nd class in the latter months of the First World War, remaining in the RAF when the fighting finally came to an end. It was not until sometime in the late 1920s, by which time he was a corporal, that he transferred to the Royal Air Force police. On 4 March 1932 he was promoted to the rank of sergeant and posted to RAF Halton, near Wendover in Buckinghamshire. He was further promoted to the rank of flight sergeant in 1935, and in January 1938 was awarded the Royal Air Force Long Service and Good Conduct Medal. Later the same year, on 1 December, he was promoted again, this time to that of warrant officer.

An entry in the *London Gazette* of 19 December 1941 shows he was appointed as a Deputy Assistant Provost Marshal. The following year, on 1 March 1942, the same publication records him as being promoted to the rank of temporary flight lieutenant: a rank in which he became fully substantive some two and a half years later, on 3 November 1944. In the summer of that year, he was placed in command of the RAF's SIB, whose headquarters were located at an address in central London. In the December 1944 he was joined by Squadron Leader Frank McKenna, who earlier in the war had seen active service with Bomber Command as a sergeant flight engineer, flying more than thirty operational missions. Before the war, McKenna had been a detective sergeant in the Blackpool police.

Although the decision to execute the fifty captured airmen who had taken part in the Great Escape originated from Adolf Hitler and was implemented by the German High Command, it was members of the feared Gestapo who carried out the actual murders. The RAF officers who were murdered were selected for execution by *SS-Gruppenführer* Arthur Nebe, who was based in Berlin.

The British government first learned of the murders following a visit paid to Stalag Luft III on 22 May 1944 by two members of the International Red Cross: Doctor Rossel and Monsieur Wyss. The senior British officer at the camp at the time was Group Captain Herbert Massey, who was repatriated to England soon after because of his ill health. He had a permanent limp, the direct result of having sustained wounds to the same leg in both wars. On his return he was able to confirm to the British government and military authorities what they had been told by the International Red Cross, albeit in much more detail. The Secretary of State for Foreign Affairs Anthony Eden updated Parliament on 23 June, promising that at the end of the war, those responsible for the murders would be found, arrested and brought to justice.

It was always going to be a difficult job for Bowes, McKenna and their team, to identify, and locate the individuals believed to be responsible for the murders. Some of them had already become victims of the war, whilst others had changed their identities and were hidden amongst the hundreds of thousands of German military POWs being held by Allied authorities.

It must be remembered that the men now being hunted by the Allies were members of Nazi Germany's Gestapo. It would be fair to say that the government and the Gestapo had planned for the eventuality of losing the war and what that would mean for those who served within their ranks should they be captured by Allied forces. With this in mind, each person involved would have been provided with forged identity papers and false identities, indicating they were just ordinary, low ranking military personnel from either the Kriegsmarine, Luftwaffe or Wehrmacht branches of the German military. This was another obstacle that Bowes, McKenna and their team had to overcome if they were ever to find those responsible for the murders.

In some respects, identifying and locating the suspects was the easier part of the operation, because once in custody, if these individuals stayed quiet or denied the allegations against them, or there was a lack of witnesses and insufficient evidence, then any subsequent court appearances and convictions were not forgone conclusions. To make matters worse, Bowes and McKenna did not begin their inquiries into the murders until some seventeen months after the events had taken place.

It was late in 1945 before Bowes, who by now a squadron leader, and his team moved to their new headquarters in Rinteln, in Allied-occupied Germany, making it a lot easier for them to carry out their enquiries. In the early stages of the investigation, Bowes and most of his men found themselves travelling to a number of countries across Europe, including Russia, in their efforts to track down the suspected murderers.

Bowes was unafraid of getting his hands dirty. He led by example and from the front, and when they had a suspect to arrest, he was more than happy to be the first one through the door. Many of the arrests could not be carried out by simply knocking on the front door of the accused. In some cases, the individuals had little to lose and so Bowes and his team would enter a building with no knowledge of what or who was waiting for them.

By the time their investigation had come to an end, the hard work carried out by Bowes, McKenna and their team had seen a number of suspects arrested and put on trial. A few managed to escape justice, either because they had been killed in fighting before the end of the war, had committed suicide once they had been detained, or had simply vanished into thin air, never to be seen again.

On 10 June 1948 it was announced in the *London Gazette* that Bowes, by then holding the RAF rank of wing commander, had been awarded an OBE (Military Division) for his work in the investigation of the Stalag Luft III murders.

Just five months later, the British government announced there would be no additional trials of any foreign nationals suspected of having committed war crimes against Allied military personnel. Bowes was so incensed by this news that he wrote to the provost marshal of the Royal Air Force to formally place on record his disagreement with the British government's decision. Between 1950 and 1954 there were at least two cases of German Gestapo officers suspected of being involved in the murders of the Stalag Luft III escapees who were acquitted of their offences.

Wilfred Bowes retired from the RAF on 12 June 1954, having reached the rank of wing commander.

Francis Peter McKenna had been born on 28 February 1906 in Accrington, Lancashire. His father, another Francis, was a police constable with the Blackpool police. Francis junior, along with his younger brother John, followed in his father's footsteps and became a police officer. Both brothers eventually became detective sergeants.

McKenna had an avid interest in flying, and by the outbreak of the war was already an accomplished civilian pilot. Wanting to do his bit for his country, he applied to join the RAF but was refused because his job as a police officer meant that he was in a reserved occupation. The rules on those in reserved occupations were eased in 1943, especially for those looking to enlist in the RAF, due in the main to the heavy losses of aircrews. McKenna wasted no time in enlisting and quickly became a sergeant flight engineer, going on to fly more than thirty missions with Bomber Command and eventually becoming a pilot officer on 24 November 1944. Less than a month later, McKenna transferred to the headquarters of the Special Investigation Branch and was allocated to Wilfred Bowes' team.

For McKenna, hunting down these individuals was a personal quest after he had become good friends with Flight Lieutenant Edgar Humphreys and Flying Officer Robert Stewart whilst stationed at RAF Squires Gate in Blackpool during his early days in the RAF. Both men had been POWs at Stalag Luft III and after taking part in the Great Escape, were two of the fifty Allied airmen executed by the Gestapo.

McKenna's skills and experience as a pre-war civilian detective sergeant would prove to be an invaluable asset to the team and after being appointed deputy assistant provost marshal in July 1945, he was sent out to Rinteln, in December 1945 to begin the investigation.

Like Bowes, McKenna was also awarded an OBE (Military Division) for his work in the investigation of the Stalag Luft III murders.

CHAPTER EIGHTEEN

Those Responsible for the Murders

By the time Wilfred Bowes and his team of four officers and fourteen NCOs had tracked down those involved in the murder of the fifty Allied airmen who had escaped from Stalag Luft III, they had identified a total of seventy-two men who were either guilty of murder, or conspiracy to commit murder, but only sixty-nine of these were ever found. Of these, just twenty-one were tried and executed, with some sentences being imposed because they included atrocities other than just those connected to Stalag Luft III. A further seventeen men were tried, found guilty and received prison sentences; five were arrested but never charged; three were charged but either acquitted or had their sentences quashed on appeal; one was arrested but not charged as he was used as a witness against some of his colleagues; eleven committed suicide, with ten either killed or presumed to have been killed, before the end of the war; and one who remained in the custody of the Russians in what became East Germany.

As head of the Luftwaffe, the man who ultimately had overall responsibility for German POW camps for Allied airmen was *Reichmarschall* Hermann Göring. It is interesting to note, then, that at the subsequent Nuremberg trials in March 1946, Göring went out of his way to deny that he knew anything of a decree issued by Hitler that captured, escaped Allied airmen should be shot. He also denied personally knowing about the actual escape and the subsequent murders until sometime later.

In relation to what are officially referred to as the 'Sagan Murders', an interesting aspect of the case is the amount of court time spent during the Nuremberg trials discussing which individuals and departments knew of Hitler's decree. The trials appeared to have spent a disproportionate amount of time on this aspect, rather more so than dealing with the individuals who were responsible for the actual murders of the airmen.

The Luftwaffe officer in charge of the security and welfare of captured Allied airmen was *General* Walther Grosch, along with his deputy *Oberst* Waelde.

Kriminalkommissar Dr Gunther Absalon arrived at Stalag Luft III the morning after the mass escape from the camp and began his investigation into how it could have happened. He took his time and was there for several weeks questioning guards and gathering any evidence he could find. It is not clear what happened to him after this, or whether he was involved in the murder conspiracy, but as one of the leading investigators into the escape, he is certainly worth mentioning.

Case No. 62 of the United Nations' War Crimes Commission was that of the trial of Max Wielen and seventeen others in what was known as the Stalag Luft III Case, which took place at the British Military Court in Hamburg, Germany, between 1 July and 3 September 1947. All the defendants faced the following three charges.

Charge I

Committing a war crime in that you, at different places in Germany and German occupied territory between 25 March 1944 and 13 April 1944, were concerned together and with SS-Gruppenführer Müller and SS-Gruppenführer Nebe and other persons known and unknown in the killing and violations of the laws and usages of war and of prisoners of war who had escaped from Stalag Luft III.

Charge II

Committing a war crime in that you, at different places in Germany and German occupied territory between 25 March 1944 and 13 April 1944, aided and abetted SS-Gruppenführer Müller and SS-Gruppenführer Nebe and each other, and other persons known and unknown in carrying out orders which were contrary to the laws and usages of war, namely orders to kill prisoners of war who had escaped from Stalag Luft III.

Charge III

Committing a war crime in that you between (place) and (place) on or about (date) when members of the (place) Gestapo, in violation of the laws and usages of war concerned in the killing of victims, in both of the (force), prisoners of war.

On 31 March 1944, *Kriminalobersekretär* (Chief Detective) Walter Lux and a number of Gestapo officers under his command attended Görlitz prison in Germany and removed the following ten Allied officers: flight lieutenants C.P. Hall, Henry J. Birkland, B. Evans, G.E. McGill, E.S. Humphreys, P.W. Langford, C.D. Swain, E. Valenta; and flying officers R.C. Stewart and A.D. Kolanowski. A total of thirty-one RAF officers who had escaped from Stalag Luft III were being held at Görlitz prison. It is unclear as to what the selection process was that determined who was to be shot. Not one of the men removed from the prison was ever seen alive again. It is known that their bodies were cremated, and their ashes returned to Stalag Luft III.

It is alleged that they were murdered by Lux and his men, although nobody was ever subsequently charged with their murders. This might have been because Lux is reported to have been killed fighting against advancing Russian forces in the Siege of Breslau in May 1945.

On 6 April it is believed that Lux also murdered Squadron Leader J.E.A. Williams, flight lieutenants W.J. Grisman and H.J. Milford, Flying Officer D.O. Street and Lieutenant C. McGarr. James Long, who was killed in the following days, is also believed to have been one of his victims. Lux is also believed to have killed Paweł Tobolski and Stanisław Król, who vanished in the same area as the others. In total it is estimated that Lux was personally responsible for killing at least twenty-seven of the escaped airmen.

The following is a list of those directly linked to the murders of the fifty murdered escaped airmen. What is unclear in some of the cases is which murder each of these individuals was responsible for, or involved in. Some of them carried out the acts themselves, whilst others were seen as conspirators who had taken part in the overall process.

Breslau Gestapo

Standartenführer Heinrich Otto Seetzen was a member of the Breslau Gestapo. Besides being connected to the murder of the escapees from Stalag Luft III, he was also involved in the mass murder of Jews in Belarus between April and August 1944, as the commander of *Einsatzgruppe B*.

He was not located until after the war was over, and only then after he was identified and 'given up' by former Gestapo colleagues with whom he had previously worked. He was arrested on 29 September 1945 in Hamburg, more than 300 miles from Sagan, whilst living under the name of Michael Gollwitzer. He died later the same day, before he could be interrogated, having committed suicide by biting down on a cyanide capsule he had hidden in one of his teeth. One can only assume that fearing he would face the hangman's noose, he took his own life. But as can be seen from others involved in the murders, that was not necessarily going to be the case.

Obergruppenführer Max Wielen was the local police chief at Breslau. In November 1943 Wielen and his men carried out a three-week inspection of Stalag Luft III, specifically looking for any tunnelling activities. At the end of his trial on 3 September 1947, he was found guilty and sentenced to life imprisonment for his involvement in the Stalag Luft III murders. His sentence was later reduced to fifteen years, but he was subsequently released on 24 October 1952 after having served only half of that time.

Two weeks after Wielen's release, the following question was asked about him by Earl Howe in the House of Lords:

My Lords, I beg to ask Her Majesty's Government whether a German war criminal by the name of Wielen has recently been released; what was his crime and original sentence; how much of it he served and what were the reasons for his release and whether the attention of Her Majesty's Government has been drawn to the speeches made at a gathering of ex-Nazis at Werden recently?

The Earl of Selkirk, Mr George Douglas-Hamilton, answering for the government, gave the following reply:

My Lords, Max Wielen, who is 69 and in bad health, was recently released from Werl Prison in the British Zone. He was tried on the charge of being concerned in the killing of Allied officers who had escaped from the prisoner of war camp, Stalag Luft III, and sentenced to life imprisonment. This sentence was subsequently reduced to one of fifteen years. He was released as an act of clemency after having served seven and a half years, which allowing for remission for good conduct, is the equivalent of an eleven-year sentence. Wielen was a regular police officer in charge of the district where the escapes took place. He was convicted of participation in the general conspiracy but not in any of the murders. All the other seventeen accused were, unlike Wielen, members of the Gestapo. They were found guilty on particular charges and fourteen of them were sentenced to death.

Earl Howe appeared satisfied with the answer but went on to push the point about other war criminals having also been released from British custody and enquired whether this was part of a government policy to try to appease certain sections of opinion in Germany.

The Earl of Selwick replied that each decision about whether a certain individual should be released from prison or not was dealt with on its individual merits.

The case of Gestapo Chief Dr Wilhelm Scharpwinkel, who had been the chief of the *Kriminalpolizei* in Breslau between 19 September 1942 and 19 June 1943, is a very interesting one. At the end of the war, he was discovered as a patient at the No. 6 military hospital in Breslau, under the name of *Leutnant* Haagamann, by the Soviets. How they discovered his true identity is unknown. When Bowes and his team eventually discovered Scharpwinkel in Moscow, the Soviets would only allow him to make a statement and would not hand him over to the British. It is not known with any degree of certainty what eventually became of him. The same murdered airmen he was believed responsible for are also shown against his associate, Lux. It is also believed that the pair were responsible for the murder of Flight Lieutenant Alastair D.M. Gunn, who was recaptured near Görlitz and last seen alive on 6 April 1944.

It was not until 1948 that the British investigation team finally caught up with the Gestapo field officer *SS-Sturmbannführer* Erwin Wieczorek, who was a former member of the Breslau Gestapo. He was involved in the murders of the recaptured escapees, flight lieutenants A. Kiewnarski, K. Pawluk and J.C. Wernham, and Pilot Officer S. Skanzikas.

Wieczorek's trial was held in the Curiohaus, Hamburg, and began on 28 August 1948. He was found guilty on 6 November 1948 and sentenced to death, an outcome which was then subsequently quashed on review.

At the trial the court heard how it was Scharpwinkel who had carried out the interrogations of the four recaptured airmen, after which he told Wieczorek that they were to be shot and that he was to select two fellow Gestapo officers to escort the men alongside him. The four airmen were taken in a convoy of cars, one of which Wieczorek travelled in, along with a colleague and one of the airmen. After having driven for about half an hour the convoy stopped by the side of the road and the four airmen were told they had the opportunity to take a toilet break. It was then that they were shot. Wieczorek said he was not involved in any of the shootings and that it was Scharpwinkel who was in charge and who was also present.

Out of all the Gestapo men present at the shootings of these four airmen, Wieczorek was the only one brought to trial for their murders.

Gestapo officer Richard Max Haensel/Hänsel was acquitted at the end of the same trial.

The Gestapo officer known only by the surname of Dankert was never traced and therefore did not stand trial for any of the murders.

Kreuzer was another Gestapo officer who simply disappeared after the end of the war. There is a suggestion that he was killed during the fighting in and around Berlin as Soviet forces closed in on the capital.

The following five members of the Breslau Gestapo, who were all implicated in the murders of at least one of the escapees, were all killed during the siege of Breslau, which took place between 13 February and 6 May 1945, when the city was surrounded by Soviet forces during the Lower Silesian Offensive Operation. They are only known by their surnames, Kiske, Knappe, Kuhnel, Pattke and Lang.

Hugo Romer, who was the former chief of the Brno Gestapo, is believed to have given orders for Squadron Leader Thomas Kirby-Green and Flying Officer Gordon Kidder to be murdered. His whereabouts and what happened to him in post-war Germany were never discovered.

Kriminalassistent Läuffer, who was a member of the Breslau Gestapo, is believed to have committed suicide, but there is no detailed information about when and where this took place. This means it is also possible that he was one of those killed during the Soviet siege of Breslau, although suicide is probably the more likely option, rather than risk capture, trial and execution.

Hans Ziegler was the head of the Gestapo in Moravia and arranged for the murders of Kirby-Green and Kidder. He was captured after the war and sent to England, where he ended up at the London Cage. It is alleged that Ziegler committed suicide on 3 February 1948, whilst being held there as a prisoner.

A man by the name of Prosse, who was a member of the Breslau Gestapo, died sometime in 1944 at a German military hospital, after having undergone what has been described as a routine stomach operation that went badly wrong.

Walter Hampel was a Gestapo officer who worked out of the Breslau office. He was not arrested until 1 September 1948, by which time the British government had already come up with a new war crimes policy, which in essence meant they would no longer prosecute Germany military officials who had allegedly committed war crimes.

Brno/Zlin Gestapo

Erich Hermann August Zacharias was a member of the Brno/Zlin Gestapo. He was arrested after the war in Wolfsburg, after he was given up by his estranged wife. He was then brought to England and initially held at the London Cage, where he was interrogated about his involvement in the murder of the fifty Allied airmen. The man in charge of the prison, Lieutenant Colonel Scotland, described Zacharias as being 'without doubt the most uncivilised, brutal, and morally indecent character in the entire story'. After his interrogation was complete, Zacharias was then sent to Kempton Park POW camp. He escaped but was recaptured on 13 May 1946. The fact that he chose to escape, a year after the war had ended, suggests that he knew, or had a very good idea, of the fate that awaited him.

The *Daily News* of Tuesday, 14 May 1946 included the following article on its front page.

Fugitive Nazi was caught at 14th hole

Sallow faced 28-year-old ex-Gestapo officer Erich Zacharias had only 18 hours' freedom yesterday after his escape from the prison camp on Kempton Park Racecourse, Middlesex.

He is back in captivity awaiting trial as a war criminal. The shadow of 50 RAF men murdered at Stalag Luft III hangs over him.

One of the most intensive manhunts for years followed the Nazi's midnight escape from the camp until his capture on the Manor golf course at Ashford, less than two miles from the camp last evening.

'Dangerous'

Zacharias, brought to England to answer war-crime charges, is described as one of the most determined Nazis ever brought to this country. The BBC warning of his escape described him as 'dangerous'.

Here is the three-act story of the Nazi fugitive's 18 hours of freedom:

The Escape. Zacharias, in solitary confinement at No. 9 Camp on Kempton Park Racecourse, which runs parallel with the main Sunbury to Kingston Road, broke down the reinforced door of his cell. Then with a crowbar, he smashed the barbed wire fence encircling the camp, climbed a tree, and dropped into the Staines Road. But at the fence he lost one of his shoes.

The Hunt. The Nazi had an eight-hour start. He escaped just after midnight. News of the escape was made eight hours later. The BBC gave out warning of it in the one o'clock news and then the hunt was on.

Alarm in Hotel

Armoured cars, police and troops with Sten guns in the ready took part. They concentrated on a square mile along both banks of the Thames near Sunbury.

The alarm was given in Sunbury by two men who, when they heard the one o'clock news warning at the Weir Hotel, exclaimed, 'Good Heavens! We have just seen that man.' And the hotel owner, Mr Charles Taylor, rang up the police.

The Capture. Police officers who had dashed to the golf course by car saw Zacharias walking across the course. He had been chased out of some shrubbery by the head greenkeeper, Mr Frank Williams, and ex-corporal in the Pioneer Corps.

The Nazi offered no resistance and was captured at the 14th hole. And his shoeless foot was wrapped in a sock.

Later the same day, a further article appeared about Zacharias in the *Leicester Evening Mail*:

Nazi Prisoner Gets 28 Days

Erich Zacharias, the dangerous Nazi prisoner who was recaptured on Ashford golf links after escaping from the prison camp on Kempton Park Racecourse, has been given 28 days detention as a punishment for his escape, the War Office stated today. He will be taken to Germany in due course.

Taking into account that Zacharias had been returned to the POW camp at Kempton Park Racecourse and was held there until he was returned to Germany, twenty-eight days in detention did not actually serve any purpose whatsoever.

On 1 July 1947, having been sent back to Germany, Zacharias was placed before a British military court where he faced charges of having murdered the recaptured Allied POWs Kidder and Kirby-Green on 29 March 1944.

An article in the *Aberdeen Press and Journal* of Saturday, 2 August 1947, described Zacharias' first day of trial.

SS Man: I Was Beaten into a Trance

SS former policeman, Erich Zacharias, giving evidence at Hamburg yesterday at the trial of eighteen SS and Gestapo men charged with the 'Stalag murders' of fifty Allied air officers, said that British interrogators 'beat him into a trance in a London prisoner-of-war cage.'

He added that he would have admitted killing twenty people had it been put to him.

Colonel Halse, the prosecutor, said he would call witnesses from the London 'cage' to answer the allegations of ill-treatment.

On 3 September 1947, Zacharias was found guilty of the crimes he had been charged with and sentenced to death. He was eventually executed by hanging at Hamelin prison on 26 February 1948.

Adolf Knippelberg was arrested in Czechoslovakia along with Friedrich Kiowsky, and Friedrich Schwartzer by Soviet forces. It is not clear whether the Soviet authorities knew Knippelberg's true identity, or if the British and Allied authorities wanted him in connection to the murder of the fifty Allied airmen. He was, however, released from a Soviet POW camp within six months of the end of the war and simply disappeared, never to be heard of again. As for Kiowsky and Schwartzer, they were both handed over to the Czechoslovakian authorities and executed by firing squad in 1947 for unrelated offences.

SS-Obersturmbannführer Wilhelm Nölle was not arrested until 10 June 1948. Charges against him were never pursued in relation to the murder of the recaptured escapees from Stalag Luft III. He died in Essen on 23 February 1991.

Danzig Gestapo

Chief of the Strasbourg Gestapo, *Mitarbeiter* Alfred Schimmel, who had been a solicitor before the war, and another unidentified Gestapo officer, took Lieutenant Anthony R.H. Hayter from Strasburg jail on 6 April 1944 and murdered him near Breslau. After the end his trial, which finished on 3 September 1947, Schimmel was found guilty and subsequently hanged at Hamelin prison on 27 February 1948.

Dr Günther Venediger was the chief of the Danzig Gestapo office. It was he who ordered several of the murders and who was ultimately responsible for the actions of the men under his command. He eventually came to trial in 1953 and was sentenced to two years' imprisonment, but after four years of appeals by his legal team, he did not begin his sentence until 17 December 1957.

Hauptmann Reinholt Bruchardt is believed to have been responsible for the deaths of flight lieutenants Henri Picard, Edward Brettell, Gilbert Walenn and Romualdas Marcinkus. He was not found until 1948, after which he was put on trial for the airmen's murders, found guilty and sentenced to death. This was later commuted to life imprisonment, but he was subsequently released in 1956 having served just eight years of his sentence.

Karlsruhe Gestapo

Oberregierungsrat Josef Gmeiner shot dead the recaptured escapee Flying Officer Dennis H. Cochran. Gmeiner, along with Heinrich Boschert, Walter Herberg, and Otto Preiss, who were all members of the Karlsruhe Gestapo, were all charged with Cochran's murder on or about 31 March 1944 in the vicinity of Natzweiler, in occupied France. All four men were found guilty and sentenced to death, although Boschert's sentence was later commuted to life imprisonment. The other three defendants, Gmeiner, Herberg and Preiss, were all hanged on 27 February 1948 at Hamelin prison.

Otto Gannicher, also a member of the Karlsruhe Gestapo, committed suicide whilst in custody on 26 April 1946, before he could stand trial. Meanwhile, his colleague, Magnus Wochner, was put on trial and found guilty. He was sentenced to ten years' imprisonment for war crimes committed whilst working at the Natzweiler-Struthof concentration camp.

Kiel Gestapo

Walter Jacobs, Oskar Schmidt, Wilhelm Struve, Artur Denkmann, Hans Kähler and Johannes Post, all members of the Kiel Gestapo, were charged with being involved in the murders of Flight Lieutenant A.G. Christensen, and pilot officers H. Espelid and N. Fuglesang, in Roter Hahn, Germany, on or about 29 March 1944. Jacobs and Schmidt were found guilty at the end of their trial and subsequently hanged at Hamelin prison on 27 February 1948, whilst Struve was sentenced to ten years' imprisonment.

In addition to these murders, Denkmann, Kähler and Post were also charged with being involved in the murder of Squadron Leader J. Catanach. For his part in the crime, Denkmann was sentenced to ten years' imprisonment, whilst both Kähler and Post were hanged at Hamelin prison on 27 February 1948.

After the war Post disappeared in the convenient vacuum that existed throughout post-war Europe. He was finally arrested after living under a false name at Minden in May 1947, after being reported to the local authorities by his mistress. Arrogant to the end, he freely admitted the murders of the four Allied airmen, Catanach, Christensen, Espelid and Fuglesang, claiming he did so under the orders and assistance of Danzig Gestapo Chief Dr Gunther Venediger.

Franz Schmidt, also of Kiel Gestapo, committed suicide whilst being held at Mindon prison on 27 October 1946, before he came to trial.

Munich Gestapo

Eduard Geith, Johan Schneider, and Emil Weil were charged with the murders of Lieutenant J.S. Gouws and Lieutenant Rupert J. Stevens in Schweitenkirchen, Germany, on or about 29 March 1944. All three men were executed by hanging at Hamelin prison on 27 February 1948.

Martin Schermer, also a member of the Munich Gestapo, committed suicide on 25 April 1945. He had received orders from the Reich Security Main Office in Berlin to kill airmen Stevens and Gouws, but having failed to carry out the orders, he decided to take his own life.

Reichenberg Gestapo

Obersturmbannführer Bernhard Baatz was the man in charge of the Reichenberg Gestapo, and along with his colleagues Robert Weiland and Robert Weissman, was involved in the murders of four of the recaptured escapees: flight lieutenants Leslie G. Bull and Reginald V. Kierath, Flying Officer Jerzy Mondschein and Squadron Leader John E. Williams. All three Gestapo men were arrested by Soviet forces at the end of the war and spent time in prison in Russia. After they were released, it is believed Weiland decided to remain living behind the Iron Curtain. Weissman, meanwhile, was arrested by the French, but it is unclear as to what became of him. As for Baatz, all trace of him was lost after his release until he was arrested on

26 June 1967 and charged with complicity in the mass murders of Polish workers and Jewish civilians whilst serving with the SD. He was held in Moabit prison in Berlin until the end of 1968, when it was decided that he would not be prosecuted.

Saabrüken Gestapo

Oberleutnant Dr Leopold Spann, Emil Schulz, and *Kriminalsekretär* Walter Breithaupt were responsible for the deaths of Squadron Leader Roger J. Bushell and Lieutenant Bernard W.M. Scheidhauer. Spann was killed in the Austrian city of Linz during an air raid on 25 April 1945. Despite providing a false identity when he was initially arrested, Schultz's true identity was subsequently discovered and he was charged with being involved in the deaths of Bushell and Scheidhauer. Found guilty at the end of his trial on 3 September 1947, he was hanged at Hamelin prison on 27 February 1948. Breithaupt was also found guilty at the same trial and was sentenced to life imprisonment but was released in 1956 after having served less than eight years.

Reading through the list of Gestapo officers who were subsequently located, arrested and put before the courts, or who committed suicide before they went to trial, it shows what a Herculean effort Wilfred Bowes, his deputy Frank McKenna, who personally arrested more than twenty of the Gestapo agents who were involved in the murders, and the rest of the team, put into finding the culprits.

Every one of the accused pleaded not guilty to the charges brought against them and used 'The Plea of Superior Orders' as part of their defence. Paragraph 47 of the German Military Penal Code states:

> If in the execution of an order relating to service matters, the penal law is violated, the Commanding Officer is solely responsible. Never the less, the subordinate obeying the order is subject to a penalty as an accomplice: (1) if he transgressed the order given, (2) if he knew that the order of the Commanding Officer concerned an action, the purpose of which was to commit a general or a military crime or misdemeanour.

This allowed the defence to argue that sub-paragraph (2) required positive knowledge of the illegality of the order on the part of the accused, and that in this case each of the accused had no such positive knowledge, even though they may have had doubts as to the legality of the orders they were given.

This highlighted a particular issue in the case, as the defence lawyers attempted to use German military law in the defence of their clients, whilst the members of the British Military Court were using existing international law to formulate their decision-making process.

The Judge Advocate in the case looked to accepted international law of the time to counter the defences' claims, saying, 'The accused could not escape liability, if in obedience to a command they committed acts which both violated unchallenged rules of warfare and outraged the general sentiment of humanity.'

He went on to say, 'I think there can be no doubt apart from any other matter, that none of the accused in this case would be outside those concluding words if they really knew that they were taking part in the killing of recaptured prisoners of war, who had done nothing else but escape.'

CHAPTER NINETEEN

Paul Brickhill

A man who deserves a mention in the story of Stalag Luft III and the Great Escape, even though he was not one of those who actually escaped from the camp, is Paul Chester Jerome Brickhill, who, in 1950, published a book about the escape and made the story – which may have otherwise remained unknown for years to come – known across the globe.

Born on 20 December 1916 in Melbourne, Australia, in 1927 the entire family moved to Sydney, where Brickhill attended the prestigious North Sydney Boys High School. When he was 15, he was forced to curtail his education and look for work after his father was made redundant.

Brickhill found himself a couple of jobs, but because of his pronounced stutter, neither lasted that long. With the help of a friend, he acquired a job working for *The Sun* daily newspaper in Sydney, where with the help of his steely and dogged determination, he eventually made his way up to the position of sub-editor. Initially, Brickhill saw the war as something taking place thousands of miles away that had no personal effect on him. It was only after Germany had swept through France and the rest of the low countries, and Britain had survived by the skin of her teeth at Dunkirk, that Brickhill started to think about the war from a more global perspective.

On 6 January 1941, Brickhill enlisted in the Royal Australian Air Force. His training to become a pilot began in Australia, but learning the skills required to be a fighter pilot took place in both

Canada and the United Kingdom. Having successfully completed his training he was posted to No. 92 Squadron, which was stationed in Egypt to help with Allied operations in North Africa.

Whilst flying over Tunisia on 17 March 1943, the Spitfire Brickhill was flying was shot down. After landing in a minefield, he was located and detained by Italian soldiers, before one of them stepped on a mine and was killed. After being first held in Tunisia, he was then transferred to Italy before being sent to a Dulag Luft at Oberursel in central Germany, from where he was finally sent to Stalag Luft III, arriving on 4 April 1943.

He took an active part in the escape's organisation and preparation, initially as a lookout within the camp ensuring that work on the escape was never compromised by an over inquisitive camp guard. Next, he was involved in the digging of 'Tom', but it quickly became apparent he was unsuited to the role after he developed claustrophobia. The potential risk of him having a panic attack in the tunnel, and the potentially catastrophic events this might lead to, sadly meant he would not be able to take part in the escape itself. Brickhill was a sensible individual and knew his participation would not be fair on the other escapees.

Like every other POW at Stalag Luft III, when the full extent of what had happened to fifty of their fellow POWs came to light, Brickhill was appalled, not only because of their cold-blooded murders, but because he was shocked and horrified that such events could take place, even in a time of war. Brickhill decided that he would document everything he knew about life in the camp, including those held captive, the German guards, and, more importantly, the mass escape of March 1944, and what happened to the escapees. However, he had to be extremely careful because prisoners were only allowed to write letters home to loved ones: the keeping of diaries or recording anything to do with events within the camp was strictly forbidden. If discovered, such notes would be confiscated and destroyed, and the men in question punished.

Brickhill did not write in a book or diary, but instead wrote his thoughts on any scraps of paper he could get his hands on. Once written, the notes had to be securely hidden to make sure they were not discovered. One thing Brickhill was certain about was that the sacrifice the fifty escapees had made would not go unknown once the war was over. He and fellow Stalag Luft III POW Conrad Norton decided to canvass the rest of their camp mates about other escapes they had been involved in, with the intention of compiling them all into a book to be published after the war. This came to fruition in 1946 when their book *Escape to Danger* was published, even though at the time, Brickhill was still a member of the RAF.

After leaving the RAF, Brickhill returned to his pre-war job as a journalist in Australia, and in early 1949 was approached by a London-based publisher to write a book about the escape from Stalag Luft III in March 1944. *The Great Escape*, published in 1950, finally brought to the attention of the wider civilian population the dedication to duty and the bravery, not to mention the murders, of the Allied airmen who took part in the largest mass breakout of British and Allied POWs of the whole Second World War.

Around about the same time as *The Great Escape* was published, Brickhill was approached by the RAF to write a book about the history of No. 617 Squadron, which, of course, included their wartime involvement in what history has chosen to call the Dambusters. Brickhill's book of the same title was published in 1951 and three years later, the biography of Second World War fighter ace Douglas Bader, *Reach for the Sky*, was published. Written by Brickhill, it was subsequently adapted as a screenplay and released as a film in 1956.

Paul Brickhill died on 23 April 1991 in Sydney, aged 74.

Epilogue

※

The Great Escape was a remarkable display of human courage, ingenuity and the relentless desire to do one's duty for one's country. It stands as a testament to the indomitable spirit of the Allied POWs incarcerated at Stalag Luft III, which at the time had been promoted by Nazi Germany as one of its toughest camps to escape from.

As the seventy-six brave men made their daring bid for freedom, it has to be remembered that the escape was the culmination of nearly a year's planning and laborious effort, involving the digging and construction of three separate tunnels, as well as the making and forging of numerous documents and the crafting of RAF uniforms into passable civilian clothing. Those who managed to escape represented a diverse group of nationalities united by their desire to stay at large, overcome the hurdles they knew they would encounter along the way, and with luck and good fortune on their side, find their way back to England so that they could rejoin the fight against the evil tyranny that was Nazi Germany.

If nothing else, the mass escape from Stalag Luft III in March 1944 certainly resulted in large numbers of German forces being involved in searching for the escaped airmen, which alone would have been seen by the escapees as part of their duty in the fight against Nazism.

In war, ideals can easily become blurred and what was once perceived by most right-minded thinking people as being abhorrent, can quickly become the new norm, where men, who before the war had been polite, friendly, and family-focussed, suddenly became cold-blooded killers, who were able to shoot unarmed POWs in the back of the head.

It could be said that the legacy of the men who took part in what history has chosen to call the Great Escape is not one of tragedy, but one of inspiration. Maybe it is a bit of both. Either way, what happened all those years ago is still spoken about to this very day. Maybe it is because people are still inspired by the bravery and ingenuity of the human spirit that was displayed by the men of Stalag Luft III.

The question always asked in the aftermath of events such as the Great Escape is 'was it all worth it?' The murder of fifty of those who had escaped and then been recaptured meant it was unquestionably an extremely high price to pay, but for the men who paid that price, would they have turned down the opportunity to take part in the escape if they had known beforehand what awaited them? This author believes it is doubtful.

Ultimately, the Great Escape symbolises the enduring basic human desire for freedom and the unwavering resolve to challenge evil tyranny and injustice, even in the face of uncertainty and overwhelming odds. It stands as a poignant episode in the events of the Second World War, and highlights both the best and worst of human nature.

Sources

www.ancestry.co.uk

www.britishnewspaperarchive.com

www.prisonersofwarmuseum.com

www.grammarphobia.com

www.bbc.co.uk

www.comstation.com

www.luftwaffedata.co.uk

www.ibccdigitalarchive.lincoln.ac.uk

www.aircrewremembered.com

www.rafcommands.com

www.warsailors.com

www.fifaranking.net

www.lostaircraft.com

www.goefoundation.org

www.historien.nl

www.aviation-safety.net

www.losses.internationalbcc.co.uk

www.wemlocal.org.uk

www.veterans.gc.ca

www.boztek.com.au

www.canada.ca

www.phdn.org

www.pressreader.com

Brickhill, Paul. *The Great Escape.* Faber and Faber Limited (1950)

Burton, Graham. *Escape From The Swastika.* Marshal Cavendish (1975)

Vance, Jonathan F. *The True Story of the Great Escape.* Greenhill Books (2019)

Walton M.J., and Eberhardt, M.C. *From Commandant to Captive.* Lulu Publishing Services (2015)

Author Biography

Stephen is a happily retired police officer having served with Essex Police as a constable for thirty years between 1983 and 2013. He is married to Tanya, who is also his best friend.

Both his sons, Luke and Ross, were members of the armed forces, collectively serving five tours of Afghanistan between 2008 and 2013. Both were injured on their first tour. This led to Stephen's first book *Two Sons in a Warzone – Afghanistan: The True Story of a Father's Conflict*, which was published in October 2010.

Both of Stephen's grandfathers served in and survived the First World War, one with the Royal Irish Rifles, the other in the Mercantile Navy, whilst his father was a member of the Royal Army Ordinance Corp during and after the Second World War.

Stephen corroborated with one of his writing partners, Ken Porter, on a previous book published in August 2012, *German POW Camp 266 – Langdon Hills*. They have also collaborated on four books in the 'Towns & Cities in the Great War' series by Pen and Sword.

Stephen has co-written three crime thrillers which were published between 2010 and 2012, and centre round a fictional detective named Terry Danvers.

When he is not writing, Stephen and Tanya enjoy the simplicity of going out for a morning coffee, lunch time meals or walking their four German shepherd dogs early each morning, whilst most sensible people are still fast asleep in their beds.

Other works published by Pen & Sword include:

The Surrender of Singapore: Three Years of Hell 1942-45 (2017)

Against All Odds: Walter Tull, The Black Lieutenant (2018)

Animals in the Great War (2018) (co-written with Tanya Wynn)

A History of the Royal Hospital Chelsea – 1682-2017: The Warriors' Repose (co-written with Tanya Wynn) (2019)

Disaster before D-Day: Unravelling the Tragedy of Slapton Sands (2019)

Mystery of Missing Flight F-BELV (2020)

City of London at War: 1938 - 45 (2020)

Holocaust: The Nazis' Wartime Jewish Atrocities (2020)

Churchill's Flawed Decisions: Errors in Office of the Greatest Britain (2020)

The Lancastria Tragedy: Sinking and Cover-up, 1940 (2020)

The Rise & Fall of Imperial Japan (2020)

The Shetland 'Bus': Transporting Secret Agents Across The North Sea (2021)

Dunkirk and the Aftermath (2021)

St Nazaire Raid, 1942 (2022)

The Blackout Ripper: A Serial Killer in London, 1942 (2022)

HMS Turbulent (2023)

Dieppe – 1942 (2023)

The Battle of Itter Castle, 1945 (2024)

Operation North Pole (2024)

Index

Absalon, Dr Gunther, 193
Anderson, George Dormer, 44-6, 48-50
Armstrong, Flight Lieutenant Albert Armstrong, 146-7

Baatz, Obersturmbannführer Bernhard, 204
Bethell, Flight Lieutenant Richard Anthony, 101, 147-8
Birkland, Flight Lieutenant Henry J., 83-4
Boschert, Heinrich, 93, 203
Bowes, Wilfred, 77, 187-91, 192
Braune, Oberst Werner, 22, 76
Brettell DFC, Flight Lieutenant Edward Gordon, 84-6
Breithaupt, Walter, 205
Brickhill, Paul Chester Jerome, 207-209
Broderick, Flight Lieutenant Leslie C.J., 148-50
Bruchardt, Hauptmann Reinholt, 202
Bryett, Pilot Officer Alan, 36-9
Buckley, Jimmy, 64, 153
Bull, Flight Lieutenant Lester G., 86-7

Bushell, Roger Joyce, 61-6, 71, 80, 81, 87-8, 133, 205

Cameron, Flight Lieutenant William J., 150
Casey, Flight Lieutenant Michael James, 88-90
Catanach DFC, Squadron Leader James, 90-1
Compounds at Stalag Luft III:
    Centre, 2, 8, 11, 13, 19, 20
    East, 2, 13, 19, 20, 53
    North, 2, 20, 65, 66, 115
    South, 2, 8, 10, 20
    West, 2, 8
Christensen, Flight Lieutenant Arnold George, 90, 91-2
Churchill, Flight Lieutenant Richard S.A., 150-1
Cochran, Flying Officer Dennis Herbert, 92-4, 203
Codner, Lieutenant Michael, 52-8
Cooler, 7
Cross, Squadron Leader Ian Kingston Pembroke, 94-5
Cundall, Pilot Officer Howard Goolding, 78-9

Day, Wing Commander Harry
    Melville Arbuthnot, 64, 80,
    151-4
Deanes, Flight Sergeant James, 19
Denkmann, Artur, 203
Dodge, Major John Bigelow
    Dodge, 154-6
Dowse, Flight Lieutenant Sydney
    Hastings, 115, 157-9
Dvořák, Flight Lieutenant Bedřich
    'Freddy, 159-60, 170

Eden, Anthony, 40-3, 189
Espelid, Sergeant Halldor, 95-7, 99,
    203
Evans, Flight Lieutenant Brian
    Herbert, 97-8, 194

Fanshawe, Peter 'Hornblower', 80
Ferret, 7
Floody, Flying Officer Wally, 80, 81
Foodacco, 4
Fuglesang, Second Lieutenant Nils
    Jørgen, 91, 98-9, 203

Gannicher, Otto, 203
Geith, Eduard, 204
Geneva Convention, 6, 7, 24,
    74, 77
Gefangenen Gazette, 12
Gmeiner, Oberrgierrungsrat Josef,
    93, 203
Goon, 7
Gouws, Lieutenant Johannes
    Stephanus, 99-100, 135, 204
Green, Flight Lieutenant Bernard,
    160-1

Grisman, Flight Lieutenant William
    Jack, 100-101, 194
Gunn, Flight Lieutenant Alastair
    Donald Mackintosh, 101-102

Hake, Warrant Officer Albert
    Horace, 102-104, 131
Hall, Flight Lieutenant Charles
    Piers Egerton, 104, 194
Hampel, Walter, 198
Harsh, Flight Lieutenant George
    80, 82
Hayter, Flight Lieutenant Anthony
    Ross Henzell, 104-105, 202
Herberg, Walter, 93, 203
Homme de Confiance see Man of
    Confidence
Humphreys, Flight Lieutenant
    Edgar Spottiswoode, 106-107,
    172, 191, 194
Hut 104, 28-9, 39, 68,70
Hut 122, 38, 67, 70
Hut 123, 67, 70

Jacobs, Walter, 203
James, Pilot Officer Bertram
    Arthur 'Jimmy', 121, 134-5,
    161-3

Kähler, Sturmbannführer Hans,
    91, 203
Kenyon, Flight Lieutenant Ley,
    11, 25-7, 32
Kidder, Flight Lieutenant Gordon
    Arthur, 107-109, 151, 198
Kierath, Flight Lieutenant Reginald
    Victor 'Rusty', 109-10, 204

Kiewnarski, Major Antoni
    Wladyslaw, 110-11, 129, 197
Kiowsky, Friedrich, 109, 202
Kirby-Green, Squadron Leader
    Thomas Gresham, 108, 111-12,
    198
Knippelberg, Adolf, 202
Kolanowski, Flying Officer
    Włodzimierz Adam, 112-14,
    194
Kriegies, 2
Król, Flying Officer Stanisław
    Zygmunt 'Danny', 114-15,
    158-9, 194

Lagergeld, 5, 7
Langford, Flight Lieutenant Patrick
    Wilson, 116-17, 194
Langlois, Flight Lieutenant Roy
    Brouard, 163-5
Leigh, Flight Lieutenant Thomas
    Barker, 117-18
Long, Flight Lieutenant James
    Leslie Robert 'Cookie',
    118-20
Lux, Walter, 136, 194

Mackay, Alan, 11
Man of Confidence, 13, 18-22
Marcinkus, Flight Lieutenant
    Romualdas, 120-2, 202
Marshall, Flight Lieutenant Henry
    Cuthbert 'Johnny', 165
Massey, Group Captain Herbert
    Martin, 12, 19, 27, 80, 188
Maw, Squadron Leader Denys, 29

McBride, Squadron Leader Robert
    Frederick, 28-9
McDonald, Flight Lieutenant
    Alastair Thomas, 165-7
McGarr, Second Lieutenant
    Clement Aldwyn Neville,
    122-3, 195
McGill, Flight Lieutenant George
    Edward, 123-4, 194
McKenna, Frank, 77, 188-91
Milford, Flight Lieutenant Harold
    John, 124-5, 194
Mondschein, Flying Officer Jerzy
    Tomasz, 125-7, 204
Moul, Flying Officer Jack, 29
Müller, Jens E., 181, 183

Nebe, SS-Gruppenführer Arthur,
    115, 153, 188, 194
Neely, Lieutenant Alexander
    Desmond, 167-8
Nelson, Flight Lieutenant Thomas
    R, 168-9
Nölle, Obersturmbannführer
    Wilhelm, 202

Ogilvie, Flight Lieutenant Alfred
    Keith, 169-70

Pawluk, Flying Officer Kazirierz
    'Kaz', 111, 127-8, 197
Penguin, 7
Philpot, Flight Lieutenant Oliver,
    52-4, 58-60
Picard, Flying Lieutenant Henri
    Albert, 128-30, 202

Plunkett, Flight Lieutenant
   Desmond Lancelot, 81, 160,
   170-1
Pohe, Flying Officer Porokoru
   Patapu 'John', 103, 130-1
Post, Sturmbannführer Johannes,
   91, 203
Poynter, Lieutenant Douglas
   Arthur, 171
Preiss, Otto, 93, 203

Red Cross, The, 4-5, 13-24, 51
Rees, Wing Commander Ken, 29
Romer, Hugo, 198
Royle, Pilot Officer Paul G., 106,
   171-2

Saxelby, Squadron Leader Clive
   King, 29
Scangriff, 11-12
Schneider, Johann, 100, 204
Scharpwinkel, Dr Wilhelm, 84, 89,
   95, 136, 196-7
Scheidhauer, Sous Lieutenant
   Bernard William Martial,
   131-3, 205
Schermer, Martin, 204
Schimmel, Mitarbeiter
   Alfred, 202
Schmidt, Franz, 204
Schneider, Johan, 204
Schulz, Emil, 205
Schwartzer, Friedrich, 202
Scotland, Lieutenant Colonel
   Alexander P., 77, 199
Seetzen, Heinrich Otto, 195

Shand, Flight Lieutenant Michael
   Moray, 28, 103, 172-4
Simoleit, Major Gustav, 75-6
Shand, Flight Lieutenant Michael
   Moray, 28
Skanzikas, Pilot officer Soitiris
   'Skan', 134-5, 197
Spann, Oberleutnant Dr Leopold,
   133, 205
Stevens, Lieutenant Rupert John,
   135, 204
Stewart, Flying Officer Robert
   Campbell, 136, 191
Stooge, 7
Stower, Flying Officer John Gifford,
   136-8
Street, Flight Lieutenant Denys
   Oliver, 138-9, 149, 194
Stroller, 8
Struve, Wilhelm, 203
Swain, Flight Lieutenant Cyril
   Douglas, 139

The Circuit, 10-11
The Daily Recco, 11, 48
The Kriegie Times, 9
The Shaft, 10
Thompson, Flight Lieutenant
   Alfred Burke 'Tommy', 174-6
Tobolski, Flying Officer Pavel W
   'Peter', 139-40, 194
Tonder, Flight Lieutenant Ivo, 138,
   139, 176-7
Travis, Johnny, 81
Trent, Squadron Leader Leonard
   Henry, 173, 177-9

Trojan Horse Escape, 51-60, 135
Tunnels:
  Dick, 67, 70, 71
  Harry, 67, 68, 69, 70, 71
  Tom, 67, 70

Valenta, Flight Lieutenant Arnošt,
  140-1
Van Wymeersch, Flight Lieutenant
  Raymond, 179-84
Venediger, Dr Günther, 202, 204
Von Lindeiner-Wildau, Oberst
  Friedrich Wilhelm, 13, 22, 30,
  73-7

Walenn, Flight Lieutenant
  Gilbert William 'Tim', 81,
  141-2, 202
Weasel, 8
Weil, Emil, 204
Weiland, Robert, 204
Weissman, Robert, 204
Wernham, Flight Lieutenant James
  Crystall, 142-3, 156, 197

Wieczorek, Sturmbannführer
  Erwin, 197
Wielen, Max, 193, 195-6
Wiley, Flight Lieutenant George
  William, 143
Williams, Flight Lieutenant Eric,
  52-8, 60
Williams Squadron Leader John
  Edwin Ashley 'Willy', 144,
  194, 204
Williams, Flight Lieutenant John
  Francis, 144-5
Wilson, Group Captain Douglas, 24
Winston, Flight Lieutenant Mark S.,
  11
Wochner, Magnus, 203
Wyss, Monsieur Paul, 22, 24, 188

YMCA, 3

Zacharias, Erich Hermann August,
  109, 199-202
Ziegler, Hans, 198
Zillessen, Marcel, 33-5